Advancing Business Concepts In a JAD Workshop Setting

Selected titles from the YOURDON PRESS COMPUTING SERIES
Ed Yourdon, *Advisor*

Advancing Business Concepts In a JAD Workshop Setting

Business Reengineering and Process Redesign

Anthony Crawford

YOURDON PRESS

P T R Prentice Hall Building

Englewood Cliffs, New Jersey 07632

Library of Congress Cataloging-In-Publication Data

Crawford, Anthony.
    Advancing business concepts in a JAD workshop setting / Anthony
    Crawford.
        p. cm.—(Yourdon Press computing series)
    ISBN 0-13-146226-1
    1. Work groups. 2. Decision-making, Group. 3. Forums (Discussion
and debate) 4. Planning. 5. System design—Methodology.
    I. Series.
    HD66.C72 1994
    658.4'036—dc20   93-29395
                                                                 CIP

Editorial/production supervision: *Mary P. Rottino*
Cover design: *Karen Marsilio*
Buyer: *Alexis Heydt*
Acquisitions editor: *Paul Becker*
Photo credits: *background photo - Columbia Artists Management*
                foreground photo - The Stock Market © Gabe Palmer

©1994 by P T R Prentice-Hall
Prentice-Hall, Inc.
A Paramount Communications Company
Englewood Cliffs, New Jersey 07632

Advancing Business Concepts in a JAD Workshop Setting (TM) has been rewritten from Systems Excellence by Design ® 1987 JAD Implementation Guide © 1988. The concepts and techniques described herein have the following trademarks for Process Improvement Institute - PII (TM) and users of ABCWorkbook (TM) and Process Improvement Group(s) - PIG (TM) licensed by Anthony Crawford and Associates. Process Improvement Expectations (PIE) TM, Process Improvement Model (PIM) TM, and Book Building Process TM are trademarks of Anthony Crawford and Associates.
Joint Application Design (JAD) ® is a registered trademark of IBM.

The publisher offers discounts on this book when ordered in bulk quantities.
For more information, contact:
        Corporate Sales Department
        P T R Prentice Hall
        113 Sylvan Avenue
        Englewood Cliffs, NJ 07632
        Phone: 201-592-2863
        FAX: 201-592-2249

Printed in the United States of America
10 9 8 7 6 5 4 3 2 1

ISBN 0-13-146226-1

Prentice-Hall International (UK) Limited, *London*
Prentice-Hall of Australia Pty. Limited, *Sydney*
Prentice-Hall Canada Inc., *Toronto*
Prentice-Hall Hispanoamericana, S.A., *Mexico*
Prentice-Hall of India Private Limited, *New Delhi*
Prentice-Hall of Japan, Inc., *Tokyo*
Simon & Schuster Asia Pte. Ltd., *Singapore*
Editoria Prentice-Hall do Brasil, Ltda., *Rio de Janeiro*

CAREFULLY CRAFTED WORDS

In the fifteen years I have been involved in developing business analysis structures and implementing over five hundred workshops, I have learned to express interactive workshop concepts toned by experience. When people look to reasons for successful systems they realize quality has as much to do with carefully crafted words to describe business design as orderly symbols define technological design. Carefully crafted words are not too easy to arrange, but once they exist, people tend to know what to do and take charge to reshape business and develop effective systems.

AND IN DEDICATION

My wife has been involved in all of this. Jill has operated the business, kept the financial records and arranged all the logistics to visit all our clients when we are supposed to. Everybody appreciates her. Jill has worked on many assignments to document the results of many debates. She has typed and reviewed this book through its many changes. And we have managed to socialize. We have two wonderful children and live happily in a little nest just north of the United States of America. Our home office is 15 feet from the back door. It has been the gateway to work on many exciting assignments and to meet many interesting people. All the flights to and frow are described as domestic—with no boarders. We feel the same way when we reach out to our many friends the world over.

Table of Contents

Introduction

Background

Section One

Classic JAD

Section Two

Chapter 1

Chapter 2

Section Three

Chapter 3

Section Four

Chapter 4

Chapter 5

Section Five

Chapter 6

Chapter 7

Chapter 8

Section Six

Chapter 9

Section Seven

Chapter 10

Section Eight

Chapter 11

Chapter 12

Section Nine

Chapter 13

Chapter 14

Chapter 15

Section Ten

Chapter 16

Chapter 17

Recap

Experience

Appreciation

Index

Anthony Crawford in praise of happy guesses, an empirical approach for quality messages in business engineering and procedure design

em-pir-i-cism n. Scientific method of proceeding by inductive reasoning from observation to the formulation of a general principle, which is then checked by experiment.

em-pir-i-cal adj. Making use of, or based on, experience, trial and error, or experiment, rather than theory or systemized knowledge.

ap-proach v. To come close or closer or go near or nearer; seek a way of dealing with.

ap-proach n. A method of beginning; efforts to establish personal or business relations.

qual-i-ty pl. **qual-i-ties** n. Grade, degree of excellence, worth, characteristic, attribute, etc.

mes-sage n. Written or spoken communication from one person to another; an inspired revelation; ethical or spiritual teaching; an official communication.

busi-ness n. Regular employment, profession, occupation; one's personal affair, concern or duty; something requiring attention.

engineer v. Carry out engineering work; manage, using tact, craft or ingenuity; achieve a result, *engineer* an election victory.

pro-ce-dure n. An act or manner of proceeding; a prescribed way of doing something; a particular course of action.

de-sign v. To invent or bring into being; to prepare plans, a sketch, or model of something to be made. **re-de-sign** v. Reiterate design.

de-sign n. Instructions for making something leaving the details to be worked out; a *plan* conceived in the mind.

plan n. A design for construction, layout, system etc.; a formulated *scheme* setting out stages of *procedure*; proposed or intended course of action.

INTRODUCTION

in-tro-duc-tion n. Something that introduces a subject, an outline of the ABCs; an explanatory or commenting section of a book, preceding the text proper.

ABCs n. The alphabet, the first principles of a subject.

In Praise of Happy Guesses

Joint Application Design (JAD) is a proven workshop approach to system design which has gained wide acceptance as an alternative to analyst and user interviews. Group discussion led by a session leader, involving business people and technology professionals in a structured workshop forms the basis of the JAD technique. A session leader plays a key role in the process. In a meeting with business professionals and system developers the session leader provides a discussion environment to bridge the knowledge gap separating specialities. A sound understanding of structured design concepts and application of workshop techniques is essential to the success of the workshop and overall quality of a design product.

In this how-to book, the JAD concept is explained so that business people and system developers can understand how to benefit from a team approach to business system design and technology application development. The concept is demonstrated using proven structures and guidelines to create the basis for mutual trust and cooperation in a workshop setting.

The analysis structure for the workshop approach is geared for logical and thorough descriptions of business. The workshop provides an unparalleled setting for business professionals to explain their views of business plans and objectives, define work task procedures, and specify, evaluate and document business system requirements under the guidance and control of a session leader. As such it can be adapted to many situations and utilized on several occasions during a systems development lifecycle. Many development methodologies can be enhanced using the JAD process whenever there is need for effective communication between people with different specialist skills and background knowledge.

JAD is designed as a communications technique using analytical structures which promote interactive discussions between people in need of exchanging information and learning from each other. The concepts described in this book can be used by putting a pen to paper with or without technological support. Moreover, a session leader can lead the team without being a business expert or a systems specialist. In this environment, success is measured in terms of intellectual advancement. The hallmark of success is being better informed and making the right decisions in order to advance business concepts and leverage emerging technologies. Follow the productivity guidelines here for quality analysis and design improvements and JAD practitioners will experience a sense of accomplishment, creativity, and team pride in the result.

The structures described in this book are logically related in page headings and descriptions identified by the letters *ABC*. Forms provide a road map for composing high level statements of direction for business vision which leads to detailed business and technical design specifications for systems development. While the structures are described for information technology applications, they work equally well for different technologies and non-technological systems. Several examples are provided to demonstrate results.

The JAD structure is geared towards practical analysis of business situations. It works using forms and design exhibits, proposals or perhaps prototypes, to test ideas until valid solutions emerge. The analysis structure and supporting exhibits are created prior to the meeting in staff work done by people willing to provide knowledge and insight about a subject.

You might have heard someone say that business people do not know what they want in the context of system requirements. I have found that for as many times people don't know what they want, they do know what they don't want. From either point of view, this approach, using a prototype, can be successful in finding out what they think about it, discovering if they really need it, and understanding if it can be implemented.

If an idea cannot be documented from a well-informed source, an educated guess will do. If an educated guess is not available, a happy guess will do just as well. All that is required for the workshop is a good example of intent which can be corrected and refined through constructive criticism and contributions from skilled and knowledgeable participants. Teamwork is easier, and in a group participants do not feel uncomfortable using approximately right or wrong answers to examine and solve problems.

The principle of guessing answers is well known and applied by many school children in all grades. At least I got away with some of it in my school days. The technique is also applied by seasoned professionals in many business disciplines, at various levels of expertise, and by honorable session leaders. There is no shame in guessing an answer to complete a puzzle. There is a chance you can be right the first time; if not, the answer will emerge as you think more about it. There is a mathematical formula, no doubt computerized, based on suggested answers and gradual refinement until the correct answer emerges. With high pressure in the business world to be right, this approach is a welcome change.

During my acclimatization to North America, I learned to use upside-down light switches, recognized that cars point forward in another lane and that you stop for traffic lights before you reach them. In some confusion, I refreshed my spelling habits and reviewed my use of the English language. I learned how to "fill out" instead of "fill in" the typical forms needed to get through a busy day. In time, I picked up the expression "I guess." Despite my IBM background, I now tend to favor it over saying "I think" for its flexibility and relief from rigid demands for accuracy. This approach may not sound too sophisticated, but it works and is easy to use. I hope you experience satisfaction as I do combining knowledge and intuition for more successful solutions.

While some might disagree with empirical methods, I have met many people who support and share the views in this book. Upon reflection, it seems improbable that research in my office, my days spent pacing the floor to rehearse JAD presentation materials, and holding conversations in an empty room to practice the concepts would become a benchmark to hasten the industry into team meetings using a variety of analysis methods. There are so many interpretations of JAD structures that I am sometimes credited for many I would not dream of using and berated for those I regularly use and prefer to be known by. Those who have been taught in technical subjects or have read about JAD from technological perspectives may not even recognize this work. To me this is classic JAD, as I always think about it and live by it in my profession. In workshop reviews, I have thought of some experiences as "classic" in the way the meeting progressed and in the results. If you apply these techniques and feel as good after your experience, you can call your workshop classic, a measure of acceptance by many standards of excellence.

In this book, I have collected my thoughts from my teaching notes, publications of many years, and the experience from hundreds of workshops. This guide is organized in much the same way as my class materials. It is the kind of information I would have liked before I put my career on the line to pioneer JAD. The introduction explains business engineering and the workshop approach as a process for people involved in quality design analyses for business procedures with or without technology. This leads to JAD explained as a concept to be applied by a skilled session leader. I have illustrated JAD as a communication technique to work in concert with development activities using "books" as key reference sources in structured workshops to reduce the number of interviews. After these explanations, the guide describes the analysis structures and steps involved as if you were implementing JAD yourself in a context of "this is how I would do it if I were you."

Over the years as I have taught JAD from the perspectives in this book, people have often explained it in return using terms and interests they already understand. Some people like the JAD idea to promote special interests and have become enthusiastic spokespersons for "JAD-like" structures for different methods.

Published experience describes a JAD workshop to be either a nontechnical or a technical environment. In this range people might know JAD to be merely a group hug, or more generously a brainstorming session or focus group. Others think of JAD as a time for a group hands-on experience with system development tools or involvement in project management methodologies. Enthusiastic technology suppliers promote a strong message for something "JAD", or "JAD-like" in their products. At times, popular language and subject referees of the day make it difficult to answer point of view. In these circumstances recommendations for non-technical JAD are not welcome. To many, these points seem competitive or defensive, and to some undoubtedly naive and due for advice if not open for sound criticism. Sometimes the range and strength to guide the opposition reach trial proportions. It took me by surprise and on several occasions I questioned my own convictions and nerve to continue to emphasize business views for systems analysis.

Some of my publications were returned marked, "Not relevant to systems development," "Not strategic," and another "Don't understand this—try the sports editor." Pioneering is not easy and coaching others with personal goals produces mixed results. This type of coaching creates individuals competing for personal business. It is not a player's game with a supportive coach for members to compete as a team. Eventually I had to retreat to the relative calm of personal assignments with JAD déjà vu for the experience to demonstrate these concepts and the knowledge to write the story and hopefully answer the critics.

Arguments for better methods will prevail and the jury will still be out on claims for the best approach. Your criterion for a better method could be that understanding the expression of analysis would not be mistaken for thinking you actually understand the subject matter. Ultimately the easiest language to define policies and practical procedures is the working language of people in business. For many, using business language to analyze business logic and define business procedure for system plans and technology applications is recognized as a requirement for good systems development. In an attempt to empathize with modern terminology, this account of JAD experience responds to recent interests in business engineering, process redesign, system re-engineering, rapid systems development, and popular software acquisition.

In all these workshops several significant events have coincided with meetings and raised many interesting conversations. Immediate conversational interests surface in personal situations people find themselves compelled to mention. Talking about the weather and local politics is something hard to avoid. Aside from business conversation you need to socialize. Ongoing themes have included trying to convince others that dragging Canadians through years of constitutional debate is really a cunning plan to bore people to death to avoid anarchy. I have gained a lot of pleasure in talking about the trials and tribulations of the Toronto Blue Jays battling for a win in a World Series defined in the boundaries of the North American continent. For humor I collect *Herman*®, *Peanuts*®, *Tumbleweeds*® and *Calvin and Hobbes*® and volumes of *Asterix and Obelix*®. For newsworthy conversation I listen to the CBC for *As it Happens*, *Ideas*, and *Quirks and Quarks*, NPR for *All Things Considered*, and the BBC World News Service on shortwave.

In developing JAD, and in consulting, I have learned from many people through shared experience. I have recorded these notes as a progress report. In my chosen profession I have little time available to be as well read as other writers unless you count magazines like *The Economist*, *Discover*, *Omni*, and *Popular Science* as good reading. Without an academic environment and backing for theoretical research to other written work, I have included references in acknowledgment to those involved in providing encouragement and assistance. Along the way I have been told many jokes, given numerous anecdotes, Murphy's, and a few great posters and even hats and T-shirts. It is only fair that I mention these without taking credit. I cannot remember everyone, but I know I have benefited and enjoyed the experience. I hope you enjoy these concepts and benefit from JAD as much as I have appreciated the opportunities to assist people in many exciting and interesting assignments.

WORDS ARE NOT WHAT THEY USED TO BE

For good diction, words are selected and arranged to express an idea, but the right words may not be best for clear meaning. A rich language leaves written words open to interpretation; local dialects have cultural and political nuances. To complicate comprehension further, spoken words also have inclination in tone and expression from which meaning and intent must be discovered to document a correct statement for acceptable understanding. A dictionary will help in choice of definitions and a thesaurus assists in language. Even so, what you think you heard is not necessarily what they thought they said, and you cannot be sure of understanding. Furthermore, a few words have become plastic in time from the fickle application of fashionable meaning, so that what you think should be clear may not be. An old-fashioned sense from a word can be appropriate, and in using traditional language you should not worry about showing your age. Reaching consensus need not be dreary—even in euphemistic dialogues you will find interesting conversation as you indulge in common terminolgy and discover quotable quotes. Most of the language you need will be in a thesaurus, and invariably you will be able to relate to regular conversation and conventional wisdom for understanding. To share ideas, people sometimes explain situations in terms of Murphy's Law (defined here from Webster's Dictionary). Examples of these and workshop experiences are described in several illustrated JADs.

> **Mur-phy's law** *A satiric principle based on the theory that if anything can go wrong it will; nothing is as easy as it looks; everything takes longer than you think it will.*

BUSINESS ENGINEERING WITH DESIGN IN MIND

busi-ness v. Regular employment, profession, occupation; one's personal affair, concern, duty; something requiring attention.

en-gine n. Device used to transform one form of energy to another, especially to kinetic energy; origin—a tool; heat engine, internal combustion engine, locomotive; war machine.

en-gi-neer n. An expert in the design and construction of engines, mechanical engineer; or of electrical equipment, electrical engineer; or expert in the organization of civil works (roads, bridges etc.), civil engineer; person qualified in any branch of engineering; fitter, mechanic or other skilled worker in charge of engines; engine driver, locomotive driver; person in charge of ship engines; one of corps trained for road making, bridge building etc. *Someone behind the scenes achieving success.*

en-gi-neer v. Carry out engineering work; engineer an election victory; *manage, using tact, craft or ingenuity, to achieve a result.*

de-sign v. To invent or bring into being; to prepare plans or a sketch or model of something to be made. **re-de-sign** v. Reiterate design.

de-sign n. Instructions for making something leaving the details to be worked out; a *plan* conceived in the *mind*.

mind n. Seat of consciousness as an element of reality, thought, feeling and will, intellect, opinion.

mind v. To have charge of, be careful of, look out for, pay attention to, concern oneself with; occupying one's thoughts especially as a source of worry; continue to remember.

JAD—Business Engineering with Design in Mind

ILLUSTRATED JAD

At the start of my computer industry career, I was named Systems Engineer. With this title my mission was to design and develop computer systems which would change procedures and hopefully improve business productivity. Now, I regularly look for definitions in words and find engineering is "the science of applying knowledge of the properties of matter and natural sources of energy to the practical problems of industry." Calling me an engineer for what I did did not seem quite right but it related to my college studies; indeed we learned a saying, "Yesterday I didn't know what an engineer was, and now I are one."

ENGINEERING IMAGES

Engineering terms are often used to connote special or symbolic meanings for products and services. Real engineers have concerns that others misuse the title. Still, some promote genuine engineering content while others have a loosely coupled relationship. Others want to express an idea or different image. Examples include "landscape engineer" for a creative gardener, "sanitary engineer" for a busy janitor, "combat engineer" for the modern day soldier, even "social engineer" for a caring politician.

    The computer industry also enjoys the practice. Apart from using an engineering label for professional work, such labels may be used to imply improvements and flexibility in the application of concepts. As a technological concept, information management is described as better when data is engineered. People talk about it in terms of "information engineering" with the objective to improve computer systems design. Lately engineering titles are ascribed to business analyses in terms of "business engineering" and "re-engineered processes." For some, the word combinations are confusing. They feel that they have missed something when normal problem solving activities are described as engineering. Others simply think of it as fashionable use of words or marketing language without substance. In any event the connotations sound powerful; it impresses people to pay attention, to invest in it, or just to do something more.

ENGINEERING PERSPECTIVE

Most engineering perspectives are promoted as the application of good procedures and practices for design and development testing in order to plan the manufacture of a quality product. While engineering principles are laudable, they may not be directly transferred to the creation of a business plan for a system. It is not the same as testing a completely engineered model of an airplane, bridge or car for real-size construction. Generally, available computer hardware is configured and adapted using coded instructions to manage information in certain ways to solve problems. In this, there may be little difference in the outward appearance of a system prototype and desired

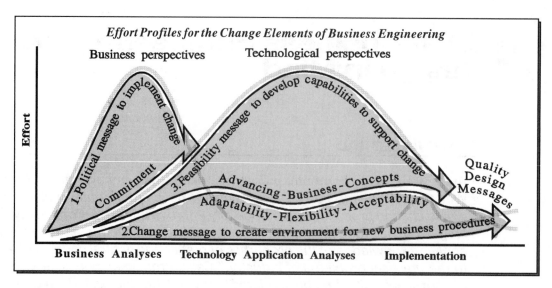

Effort Profiles for the Change Elements of Business Engineering

result. Indeed, modern prototypes may produce code with methods for system construction and delivery. In managing the process, this chart illustrates the effort profiles for the elements of business engineering where quality designs result from business and technology analyses for systems implementation.

BUSINESS ENGINEERING MESSAGES

The effort profile shown combines business and technological perspectives in a collaborative process explained later in the use of interactive workshops. Future system users debate business issues and decide on needs for change. From a business engineering point of view, the first effort profile produces a political message of endorsement and commitment for results. Second and third effort profiles provide design messages of business and technical concurrence. The business message to create new environments and procedures originates from future system users and continues through to implementation. The technology message concerns feasibility to develop the necessary support capabilities. To advance business concepts, people think of adapting to change and demand corresponding flexibility in a system for acceptable solutions. In reaching a change target, the process creates a rhythm of denial, modification, and acceptance shown and illustrated below.

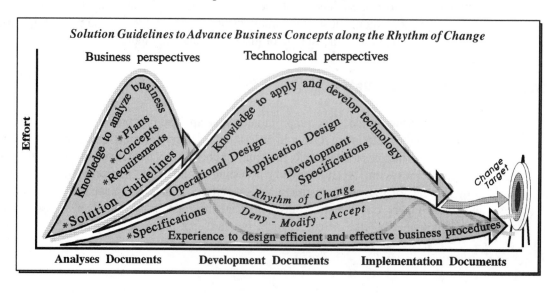

Solution Guidelines to Advance Business Concepts along the Rhythm of Change

ILLUSTRATED JAD

In one situation at a steel company, I was invited to lead a workshop to redesign a work order maintenance system. The environment was paper intensive, subject to errors, and factory maintenance work was frequently delayed because of the difficulty a paper intensive system brings to scheduling resources and materials. The center of the manual operation was a maintenance request which was written out on multi-part forms sent to various departments involved. The form had been used for twenty years by the shop foreman to receive a request to start the work and see it through to completion.

In the workshop we used illustrative icons to show the request form starting out and travelling to several involved departments. As we designed a data entry screen to capture the initial request, we placed an icon to illustrate a display screen and keyboard next to the form. The foreman realized he could key all the information from the form into a database, also illustrated by an icon. I did not remove the icon of the form at this time but asked where it went next. He pointed to another team member and explained the routine of sorting the papers to prioritize the work requests. His colleague said he would prefer not to use the paper now that he could sort a backlog of requests on a computer. The foreman resisted the idea and told his colleague he would still have to use the paper form. His authority over the man resulted in my placing another icon form at the next work area. In another related process he did not have the authority to insist on the document being used. However, he insisted on a carbon copy returning to his office I had to place yet another icon of the same form in another department. Five copies in all! We had illustrated the current process with a modern computer thrown in. Periodically I referred to our stated objective to eliminate unnecessary paperwork to question the design.

The project leader and systems analyst were getting frustrated with the result. In the first day we had the potential for a system design to gain several benefits once the form could be removed. In the second day, at about lunchtime, the foreman mentioned, "maybe we don't need the form in our department after all." I started to take the icon away from the board and watched his expression pale at the thought of losing his beloved work order document. Even though others did not want it, I put it back to see his face return rosy. At the end of the day he gave us permission to remove the form and the team gave out a cheer.

On the start of the final day he wanted the form back. He complained he really could not trust the system without his form. Our assurance that he could print the form on demand did not comfort the man. As I put the form illustrations back on the board I reminded the team about the objectives. By lunchtime he agreed to let us document "print on demand" as a business specification note and he walked up to board and removed all the form icons himself.

The result was an excellent systems design and twenty years of tradition changed in three days. An application of Business Engineering ready for implementation.

MEANINGFUL CHANGE IN CAREFULLY CRAFTED WORDS

Meaningful communication documented in carefully crafted words brings about meaningful change. The political advantage of people in favor of change is worth every system user's weight in gold. In systems development, understanding what change means and what to expect is almost priceless. When you allow people to participate in change design you establish acceptance and commitment for results. Change targets become clear and realistic and more attainable in manageable timeframes. Involvement for results is appreciated by the business community which encourages participation in the effort profiles.

It may seem odd that recognizing and attending to apparently additional effort saves time in the long run. Previous attempts for similar benefits have traditionally drawn system owners and future system users into technological conversation in the development effort profile and later in the operational design for a developed technology. The range of discussion need not dwell on technology. Indeed, the less technological detail in the first politically oriented and second procedurally oriented design, the better. Stronger political messages for direction and commitment for change emerge. Nonetheless, the details must be discussed to relate business logic as defined policies and procedures with technological decisions for a suitable design and application of technology.

ADVANCING BUSINESS CONCEPTS AS SOLUTION GUIDELINES

While the effort profiles produce quality design messages, solutions generally unite business and technological perspectives to advance business concepts. Political endorsement messages merge with business plans and concepts. Commitment for results messages mix with stated requirements for efficient operations and procedures. Finally, business concurrence messages mingle with operational procedure specifications designed to carry out target changes effectively.

Plans, concepts, requirements, and specification documents emerge as progressive solution guidelines and provide the design information needed to implement a system. Collectively, and in business engineering terms, these documents model an operational business before system construction. In this, people have more confidence in design decisions incorporated into the third effort profile documents as technology application design and application development specifications.

STEPPING TO THE RHYTHM OF CHANGE

Quality business design messages have different characteristics than those involved in quality systems development. Success depends on the knowledge and skills people bring to each business engineering effort profile. Everybody must be willing to work on the details to do whatever is necessary to achieve results. There is enough complexity to go around, and while the issues are debated, everyone becomes involved in the rhythm of change. For any change decision, people go through greater and lesser amounts of situation analysis as they deny ideas and modify thinking so that a change becomes acceptable, or as they raise counterpoints to discuss alternative solutions. Many issues only require a few minutes' reflection to discuss alternatives and settle design questions. Considerable progress can be achieved in a few hours of team effort in a workshop setting. Several complex issues might take days or weeks or months in post-workshop reflection and follow-up as individuals and groups understand and come to terms with decisions for new and required realities. It is an emotional roller coaster pulsating to conversational topics and feelings of the moment.

SENSE OF MOVEMENT TO CHANGE

Perspectives of change draw many into conversation and business engineering messages involve different people at different times to provide required analysis. In any assignment one or more workshops might be needed to achieve desired results. While JAD analysis structures are geared for results, an appropriate workshop technique should also respond to the dynamics of a working situation. The following examples characterize a prevailing sense of movement towards change in trace lines for different politics, cultural influences and implementation strategies.

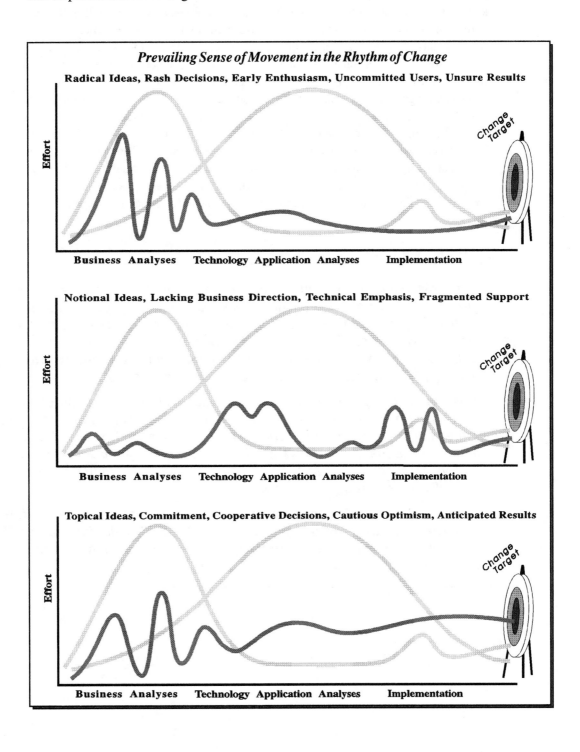

BUSINESS ENGINEERING HEALTH CHECK

With effort profiles shown as background, the above charts illustrate possible waves of change in sentiments and attitudes toward ideas while people position themselves to make their views known. The resulting trace will take almost any course but generally it follows the rule, "For any action there is an equal and opposite criticism."

Any change process needs continuous attention to guide and develop it towards a target result. While the rhythm of change shifts and reacts to local politics and culture, managers of change should observe and respond to characteristic traits to be more successful—recognize the human factors rather than view a process as a matter of technological excellence. It is not easy to flatline the rhythm even for a short while. Indeed, difficulties will be assured when you ignore people, exclude points of view, or simply challenge feelings with technology perspectives.

Reasonable discussion and involvement for results is a more successful formula. In each effort profile, a business engineering health check will indicate what needs to be done to keep people in the right frame of mind for results. Like a doctor, a JAD session leader looks for symptoms of concern and asks questions about how things are going. Questions need not be personal, but healthy signs of commitment and adaptability, or lack of it, should be noted when you ask, "Do you feel we are on the right track?" When you need more detail and you would hope to recognize signals of flexibility and acceptability, you ask simply, "Do you think it will work?"

For many, a Classic JAD workshop setting is the time and place to ask questions to reach agreement and document the detailed messages you need for good business engineering results.

ILLUSTRATED JAD

Notwithstanding engineering labels, business people want to deal with progressive and manageable change. They want to respond to business needs and develop effective and practical system solutions for identified and urgent problems of the day. To me, the word in the noun form remains in the domain of traditional engineers. Lately I have become more comfortable with engineering in the context of results achievement described in the verb form.

This use of an engineering label perhaps signals that the data processing industry is coming to terms with the realization that systems development is more than promoting terrific technological solutions ready to search out problems or make change for the sake of it. In the past it might have been sufficient to have a technological disposition, but many now understand that very different skills are required to be successful.

Today a Business Engineer must also be a composer of language to describe and understand plans, an architect to design supporting business infrastructures, and a diplomat to work with everybody involved in effecting change. Quite a job!

⌘ CLASSIC JAD OVERVIEW

clas-sic adj. Received into the accepted canons of excellence; authoritative; having familiar historical or literary association; having simple tailored lines which never go out of fashion.

JAD (TLA-Three Letter Acronym) Origin IBM. **Joint Application Design (JAD)** Teamwork involving business and technical people to identify business objectives and define design requirements and operational specifications for the application of nontechnical and technological solutions to business problems.
Also known as, but not to be confused with; **Joint Application Development (JAD)** Teamwork involving business and technical people to define system requirements and technological design for development and implementation of technology.

over-view n. *Introduction.*, A general *survey.*

sur-vey v. To measure the extent of a subject with the view to *document* an accurate and detailed report.

JAD—A Process for Results

WORKSHOP INVOLVEMENT FOR SUCCESS

The Joint Application Design concept is designed to be an interactive communication technique for experienced business people to participate in business planning and design in a workshop setting. It is a process to be implemented when there's a need to explore ideas and exchange knowl-

JAD a Process for Results

edge to solve problems. The technique is for people with business plans and system solutions in mind. In the preceding diagram, the center column illustrates key activities to involve future system users and system developers in a structured workshop approach for thorough analysis and informative design documents. JAD promotes teamwork to advance business concepts and prepare business plans in which people have greater confidence and ultimately more successful applications of technology.

THE JAD PROCESS

The JAD process is best implemented by an experienced session leader with the skills and knowledge to use structured analysis concepts. The process starts with an activity to define the overall purpose of what has to be accomplished. This step is shown in the center column as *Management Guidelines* and documents key business goals and scope as terms of reference. In this activity the JAD *Workshop Approach* is decided using prescribed *Analysis Guidelines* to accumulate development information as a business plan and systems design. The Management and Analysis Guidelines lead to *Team Selection* and preparation for a meeting. This includes a *Workshop Orientation* for the session leader and selected participants who assist in *Workshop Preparation*. The process is complete in the administration of a *Workshop Agenda* orchestrated to involve participants in debating issues, defining analysis information, and documenting design decisions as an action plan to develop a system.

Plans and designs for business concepts and technology applications can be documented in one or more workshops. Design results are shown as book cover outputs for system owners and system developers involved. Economical and operationally feasible design may not include technological solutions, and team decisions about how to implement business design emerge as *Solution Guidelines* for a system plan with or without technology. Business requirement decisions and solution information is documented as procedure design specifications in which a system is defined as an operational or technological environment, or both, and the specifications of each are used to develop and implement the design.

In this sense, design documents for a technology application, shown in the lower right column, can be for any technology, a combination of several types, or none at all with only a change to business routine. Innovative technology becomes available at a pace greater today than earlier times, and new computer equipment is frequently involved in new systems design. Evolutionary technology may not be reason enough to change–indeed, many problematic situations emerge because of change. Business issues have more to do with reduced risk and managed change. Other important concerns deal with the correct choice and appropriate application of technology. The process allows prioritization of debate for the important issues and consideration of the implications and consequences of change before investment in technologies and application development for business automation.

The approach can be used for various levels of detail, starting with business vision and concepts analysis through business requirements analysis and business automation. Design analysis considers a plan for feasibility and practical use as an operational design concerning business practices and people activities.

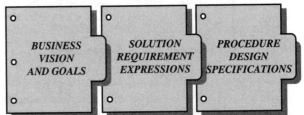

Plans... Concepts... Requirements... Design...

The JAD process is managed and administered by a skilled session leader who can work in a variety of business situations and alongside people with different skills and personalities. Personal charm and charisma will not be enough to do the job, and presentation skills by themselves will not be sufficient to provide the team leadership needed to manage a workshop process. Participants will be more successful when they understand JAD structured analysis concepts and practice debating techniques. And a session leader will have better results implementing essential procedures to get the right people with the right attitude and right materials, all in the same place at the right time. To understand the reasons for procedure, you need to start with a background and basics for JAD.

⊔₊⊔ ANALYSIS CONCEPT

a-nal-y-sis n. The process of analyzing (*synthesis*); a *document* setting out the results of this process (*Greek - analusis - a dissolving*).

syn-the-sis n. (logic) Method of demonstration consisting of reasoning from self-sufficient propositions, laws, or principles to arrive by a series of deductions at what one seeks to establish; an exposition assembling the various parts into a whole.

doc-u-ment v. To support or supply with documents.

doc-u-ment n. An official paper; certificate; anything (*e.g., a workbook*) that gives information or supplies evidence.

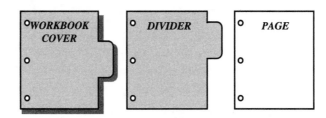

work-book n. A pupil's exercise book with printed problems, etc., and space for answers; a book of instructions for procedure and operation; a book in which is recorded work accomplished or planned.

con-cept n. Thought or opinion, general notion or idea, especially one formed by generalization from particular examples.

CHAPTER ONE

⊟ JAD—For All Reasons

SYSTEM EXCELLENCE BY DESIGN

In 1980, when IBM Canada announced JAD experience, a great deal of interest and hopeful anticipation arose among system developers. The promise of easier methods for business involvement in systems design and improved quality from user-stated requirements was a timely and newsworthy item for the data processing industry.

These were changing times–managers in industry and commerce were becoming more aware of quality and productivity issues. Many companies were reorganizing and setting up new operating and financial structures for business. Indeed, the data processing industry itself was changing with emerging technologies and new development tools. All in all, the demand to enhance existing systems, the need for new systems, and the drive to install new technologies created an urgent need for more business information and new operational systems. Today, business environments are still evolving and the need for rapid and quality responses to business needs are even greater.

Computerized business systems involve people working with technology customized for special needs and applied to prescribed operational procedures. Computer technologies are delivered as hardware attachments with software environments for customization. In this, software is designed and coded to utilize specific hardware features and configured to support various operational interactions required for business purposes. The effectiveness of a system will depend on how well the system is designed and how well technology is adapted to special needs. The issue of design excellence will be different for system users and technology developers.

QUALITY AND SYSTEMS DEVELOPMENT

Business people measure quality by the ability of a system to support business operations, and how well it assists routine procedure, keeps records for management reports, and responds to changing business situations. System developers measure success in terms of effectively and creatively adapting available technology to solve problems. To measure the quality of a delivered system people must consider the system operations for business and information management to determine how well it works. Deficiencies must be identified and their origins explained. Once the source of imperfection is discovered, the potential exists to avoid future development faults and improve system quality. Generally, the data processing industry responds to the quality issue through methods and guidelines for project management, improved technical design, and more efficient coding environments. Traditionally, the business community delegates the responsibility for system excellence to the developer.

Even with better methods and technological assistance to build a system, a better system will not emerge if a future system user is not involved to define expectations and requirements clearly and provide development direction for the result. On average, and regardless of project size or development methods used, a greater percentage of software defects originate from poor design. Faulty code can represent 25 to 35 percent errors, poor design can represent 60 to 65 percent errors, and the remainder can be found in other sources, including faulty system manuals and operator guides.

SOURCES OF DEFECT

A proportionally higher percentage of design errors can be explained by the character of the problem. Coded defects differ from design defects in that code only fails due to factors within the code whereas business design also fails due to factors not known or misunderstood at the time of development. Indeed, some design information may not be realized until after systems delivery. For this reason it is relatively easy to implement a technological approach to identify quantifiable and internal factors used to resolve faulty code. In contrast, it is more difficult to implement and use an approach which identifies and resolves faulty design characterized by both quantifiable and subjective factors which are harder to define.

Several technological approaches for development automation demonstrate the potential to eliminate the dreaded program bug. Several technology vendors have even predicted the programmerless environment as the ultimate systems development solution. Getting rid of the programmer does not eliminate the problem. In any event, an estimated two trillion lines of COBOL code alone exist in an installed and growing base, so to many, the programmer is a scarce and sought-after commodity.

Typical, programming effort represents only 10 to 20 percent of system implementation effort and development budget. While application coding assistance contributes to an overall improvement, information management and programming, versus business design analysis, has benefited most from technological advances. Productivity tools and development methods might be planned to start after planning and business analysis, explained by the statement, "once you have the business design requirements from the user".

TARGETED IMPROVEMENT

As the above perspectives show, targeting design quality for a proportional improvement provides the greatest leverage to the overall result. In more recent years, design technologies have become available to test the factors which make up good technological design. When anyone thinks of designing a computer application for a business, he or she has to think of systems design in the context of people and machine interactions and machine to source information interfaces. These require both business and technological analyses for a complete design to include an operational environment and data organization. Of the two, data organization is more definite and easier to validate than operating procedures which for flexibility are personal and subjective. Information analysis is important in the scheme of applying technology because of the need to organize data to support the record keeping aspects of business. For these reasons, design methods might only evaluate and determine information criteria for technological application design. These methods promote the view that data analysis is sufficient in itself to create a business system. The theory being that defining the relationships and changing states of data explains the functions and reveals the business process design. This approach is traditionally called data gathering. More recently, people describe this type of requirements analysis to be data-driven or information-architecture-driven.

On the other hand, the very character of a business system and the personality of an organization is mirrored in the operations used. Business people take pride in character and promote their own uniqueness in the way they go about their work and the methods they use to provide service. For these reasons, it is easier to hold conversation with future system users about business concepts and functions and the operations involved than to discuss an information organization for automation. People prefer to tell you how they want to organize themselves and the way they would then use business information. In using this approach to conversation, you tend to hear more about the business. You can increase your understanding about system interactions and the information used and obtain the guidelines for a better solution and more acceptable and successful design. This approach to requirements analysis is called business-driven.

ILLUSTRATED JAD

The difference between the two approaches is similar to the difference between knowing the ingredients needed to make a good cookie and knowing how to mix and bake it to perfection. My children like the delicious melt-in-the-mouth gingerbread men made by their mother and her mother. As far as I can tell, they both use the same ingredients and the same recipe. However, the cookies are different, at least as far as the children are concerned. I have no opinion on the matter but they eat one and love the other. If you try to pin down the difference, Granny says she adds a little magic. Whatever it is, the distinction between acceptable and desirable results for the consumer is more than just knowing how the parts add up to make the product.

Knowing about and understanding the factors which make up good business is fundamental to system design quality. Much of this knowledge depends on people communicating with people, an issue which is different from improved development methods and technology. To understand JAD, it is important to make a distinction between good communications for exchanging knowledge and quality methods for developing systems as separate but related issues. For this reason, while the jury may still be out on which approach is better for building systems, your first choice for JAD will be to use a technique which promotes easier conversation and more effective communication for understanding.

Communication difficulties translate directly into misunderstanding for technology application design and development. From a business perspective, lack of understanding about business situations and system requirements always results in less than optimum design. Business processes can be overlooked and system features might be unresponsive to the business environment or incomplete for regular operations. From technological perspectives, lack of understanding about computer potential can result in disappointment based on unrealistically high expectations for system excellence.

For these reasons, Joint Application Design (JAD) is a communication concept which provides the business professional a business-driven approach for business analysis and design, and the system developer the information needed for subsequent technological analysis and application design and development. JAD is an open forum for debate using communication and presentation techniques to guide and demonstrate the results from team evaluation of business requirements and design. The word design is used to describe the business view, the people view, and the technological view to apply a computer technology. Excellence is described subjectively and in the eye of the beholder. After the development work is done and the technology installed, this is always the system user.

> ### *Quality Is in the Eye of the Beholder*
>
> - *All the effort put into delivering a quality software product will mean nothing to the user if the system does not meet business objectives in terms of user expectations.*
> - *The measurement of system quality is therefore subjective and relatively independent of technological excellence. It is more a measure of accurate communication and documented exchange of information between the people who will use the system and the people who will build it.*

JAD COMMUNICATION MODEL

Simply put, JAD is a time-saving workshop approach designed for people to convert opinions and abstract thought into agreement and decisions for action.

The following model illustrates how different specialties are separated by a knowledge gap, and how the JAD process bridges the gap using opinions from present experience and predicted future experience to create an understanding and agreement for decisions and actions to implement change.

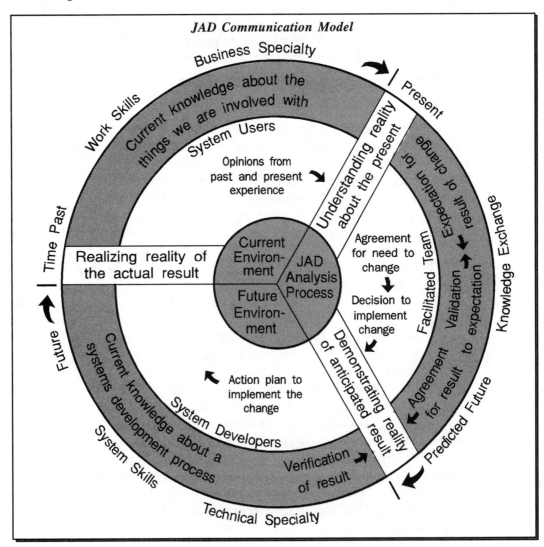

CONTEMPLATING CHANGE

The JAD communication model is represented in time where knowledge about a current environment starts the cycle and knowledge about the development and delivery of a future environment completes the cycle. JAD is shown as a segment of time in which analysis structures are used to contemplate the present and the potential for change with a future involvement of a new or enhanced system.

Thoughts and various opinions about present situations are documented and illustrated to create an understanding in a preamble about the current environment so as to reach an agreement and expectation for a need to change. The JAD process continues to facilitate decisions for the actions needed to establish a new environment. The technique is more powerful when the consequence of design decisions can be demonstrated as an actual or predicted outcome using a systems development process to verify that change results can be implemented and to validate the consequence of change to expectations. In this way it is possible to qualify decisions and reach agreement for an action plan to develop a system.

The model illustrates three zones of reality separated by time and experience. The present time zone illustrates understanding for what happens now. In the predicted future zone, potential change is demonstrated in terms of design delivered to an actual future zone where people experience the change in the effects of a developed system. The cycle starts again when actual results become a future time past, creating new experience and new opinions. Using the above analogy of involvement, it is clear that the quality of the result depends on well-informed input from those knowledgeable about a current environment and those skilled in implementing business and technological agents of change.

SUBJECT MATCHED ANALYSES

The structure used to obtain agreement for change and facilitate decision making for action can vary according to the factors which influence the analysis process. These include the current system and user experience, the development process and developer experience, and the politics and attitudes for people involvement. Each situation will require a customized structure for analysis. The overall success of the approach will depend on matching the structure to the subject material within the bounds of the knowledge gap. Unlike Lewis Carroll's *Alice in Wonderland*, the session leader must be very much aware of the point of origin and the path to a target destination.

ILLUSTRATED JAD

The importance of structured analysis for implementing change became apparent to me when I struggled with a decision for a career change. My current situation was easy to describe and my alternatives were to stay with the same company, join another company in another location, or start my own company from home base.

Several weeks of thinking about my situation led only to indecision and a sense of frustration. Eventually I realized that I had to use a technique to illustrate what I had already, what I was satisfied with, what I needed to change, and if change was really needed. The technique best suited for this turned out to be a simple list of objectives and a pros and cons list for each alternative.

We used the lists in private and family discussions and obtained opinions and advice from several sources. In this way the model of our present and future became apparent in a list of key words. The decisions we made from the model were better informed and jointly reached by the implementers and beneficiaries of change. Over the years the changes have been realized with hardly any need to redirect our plan.

In the context of systems development, the JAD concept allows business people and system developers to work together to make business planning and requirements analysis decisions for design specifications which can be implemented in a quality system. A key role is played by the workshop session leader who uses a tabulated process to guide the team through the analysis process and facilitates an exchange of knowledge to reach understanding and agreement. Unlike traditional approaches known as data gathering for system requirements and specifications, JAD welcomes the participation of future system users in system design activities and promotes a sense of purpose and responsibility for those involved.

WELCOMING THE FUTURE SYSTEM USER

The concept is described as a communication technique which is related to a development methodology in the following illustration. The block diagram shows the lines of communication associated with design analyses, system development processes, and system delivery using a loop mechanism to ensure quality and continuity of process. This includes validation to expectations for design analysis and verification of each system output developed to the requirements and design specifications from business analyses.

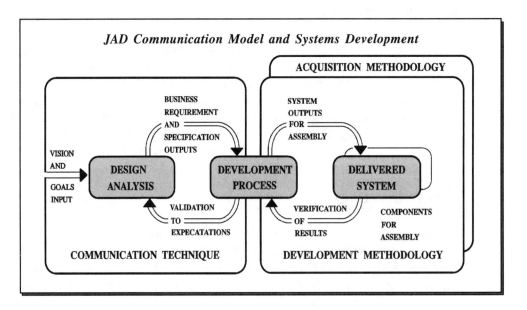

DESIGN AND DEVELOPMENT

The model illustrates the input to a design analysis process as intellectual property in terms of vision, and goals for the final product of development with analysis outputs as requirements information in an acceptable form to input to technology development or acquisition processes. A development process usually includes several related steps to create various system outputs for assembly. A delivered system output is defined as the result of a completed development step which can be assembled with other development results to make a finished product. The model is independent of size and time and applicable to small and large projects using different strategies for complete or staged system development.

Levels of detail between design and development vary and the process is repeated in a loop for progressive steps to the final assembly of a delivered system. The model is analogous to any technology development and is not used exclusively for computer application analysis. Here, the model is referred to as a business analysis technique and explained for the intricacies of computer application development.

When considering systems development, the information used for business design analyses is studied in the context of business plans and system specifications. Business people should provide their own designs to be successful. Their language originates from business backgrounds and is usually expressed in management and procedural terminology. The languages used and the level of details vary from descriptions of business perspectives and business objectives to explanations about special business operations involving procedures, mathematical formulas, and analysis reporting methods. For system developers, additional information is needed in the context of technological design and operating environment. The language used and the level of details vary from information logic in terms of data organization and characteristics to processing logic for system interactions and data manipulations. In this case the language originates from technological backgrounds and includes technical jargon.

LEVELS OF PRECISION

Apart from the stated differences between business and technical perspectives, a major difference is characterized by precision. Business language is often expressed in abstract terms in the context of alternatives and flexible responses to varying situations. Technological language is more definite in terms and context for rigorous and specific consequences. People are a product of their surroundings and the environment where people work is often reflected personally by how they function. Business people want flexibility rather than precision to cope with daily routine. These differences can make communication and understanding difficult to comprehend and often results in alienation and polarization between the people describing system needs and the people building systems. This truth is self evident in many systems. For this reason, computers might be said to be impersonal, or perhaps restrictive and frustrating, for people operating them in the normal, wide, and varying range of skills and human behavior.

Typical information technology applications are designed to set boundaries on procedures and limit work errors. Such systems regulate the scheme of things with authoritative and expert control. Implementing system disciplines for an ordered process may be unsettling to the random order of business. From a user's point of view, difficult systems are perceived to originate from difficult people lacking in business knowledge. Systems are developed from current understanding and available resources. Even with the best intentions for a good design, results are not always positive. Any frustrations felt cause much the same response towards the system as those occurring in people relationships when awkward situations arise. Reactions include petulance about the tone of an error message to reluctance, or even fear, in using system functions involved in critical business processes. To solve a problem the situation complexities must be discussed, and business design described in detail. And when all is said and done, it is important to find out how comfortable the people feel about working with the solution.

THE JAD CONCEPT

JAD is designed to enhance systems development by adding precision to business plans and design requirements and specifications. It is teamwork involving group dynamics and communication techniques to analyze business. The process is designed to exchange knowledge in a workshop setting under the guidance of a session leader to discuss subject materials and to facilitate the documentation of design decisions. Conversation and understanding is supported using selected exhibits which are prepared for team discussion and used to stimulate a debate about various analysis topics. The technique includes a structured agenda to sequence and pace discussion, and a logical relationship to provide a means to focus analysis. This results in greater levels of detail and more complete business plans, new procedures and technical design specifications for systems development.

The analysis structure is fundamental to the JAD concept for purposeful and thoughtful debate, exchanging ideas, reaching compromise, and obtaining documented consensus for action plans. As such it can be used in any situation where it takes more than one person to supply all necessary information. The structure allows several contributions from conversation, and supports and involves each team member on an equal basis. The quality of the structure and the ability of the session leader to administer and implement the workshop is key to success.

THE JAD ENVIRONMENT

The JAD process includes preliminary research on business topics and the preparation of summary presentation materials for a team to evaluate in a workshop setting. The workshop venue is geared for people needs and creature comforts in a conference atmosphere which is conducive to analysis and creative thinking. Success depends on a number of factors.

JAD Success Factors

- A skilled session leader who can create a team environment for the workshop sponsor and deliver usable documentation to the system developer consistent with planned development processes.

- A qualified team of specialists, including informed decision makers from business communities experienced in business practices and procedures and skilled technicians with application design and technology implementation responsibilities.

- A customized agenda for the session leader to orchestrate the players and promote team evaluation of goals and objectives.

- A customized analysis structure to focus analysis and explore and test ideas and solution alternatives on problem solving activities for business design.

- A presentation technique to translate and convert abstract discussion into organized documents and illustrations demonstrate design results with representative of consensus for action.

- Conference facilities with comfortable surroundings for people to work in groups using multimedia presentation materials.

- Tools to assist a session leader in managing a series of preparation tasks, customizing a workshop structure, preparing various workshop materials, and organizing dynamic results into readable documents for a team to use in a meeting.

Enhancing the communication among people so that they can recognize several points of view and bring earlier understanding and resolution to complex issues has a number of benefits. Chief among these are removing the barriers which would otherwise stall people from starting and making the progress needed to save time and reduce costs. The effective use of JAD can be seen to change the effort profile normally associated with systems development.

CHAPTER TWO

👥 JAD–Changes Tradition

TRADITIONAL DEVELOPMENT EFFORT PROFILES

JAD brings a significant change to systems development effort and design quality. The following charts illustrate changing effort profiles for typical development activities. Documents are created over time shown in the horizontal reference and effort increases vertically.

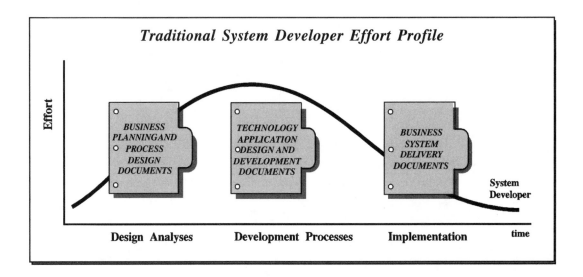

Traditional System Developer Effort Profile

Effort

BUSINESS PLANNING AND PROCESS DESIGN DOCUMENTS

TECHNOLOGY APPLICATION DESIGN AND DEVELOPMENT DOCUMENTS

BUSINESS SYSTEM DELIVERY DOCUMENTS

System Developer

Design Analyses   Development Processes   Implementation   time

Traditional systems development is managed by a systems analyst with the responsibility and title of project leader. The effort required to implement a computer system is shown above in a characteristic curve for development effort over a period of time. Involvement effort rises slowly at first as the analyst discovers business needs and what the user wants in design requirement interviews, peaks in the development process, and then tails off as the design product is tested for completion and delivery.

ILLUSTRATED JAD

In my early experience as a systems programmer, I worked with a project leader and staff in a sales department of a fisheries and food processing company in England. Our meetings to discuss requirements with system users were occasional and sequential as incremental development work was completed. Most of the meetings were unplanned and included a few casual out-

ings for a pub lunch, to discuss the latest design ideas and answer unresolved questions. Development would then continue from various notes taken on beer mats and envelopes. Good traditional stuff in the good old days.

FUTURE SYSTEM USER INVOLVEMENT

The necessary time to interview future system users during a meeting is often taken for granted and not included in a development budget. The combined effort is shown in the next profile.

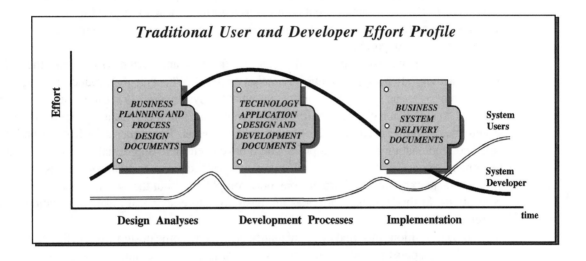

The traditional system user effort for interviews follows a gradual and slight increase up to the first peak during design analyses. At this event an agreement to proceed is needed and effort increases as the future system users review the design requirements document to understand and weigh the benefits. This is one of several "go" or "no go" decision points.

Decision points are needed to allow the systems developer to proceed to completion. Usually the first decision point occurs when business people are asked to validate system requirements and specifications for the system they want. Often the question is posed in terminology representative of technology application construction. Technical documents, which typically include a data flow diagram and other specialist references, may not be easily understood in business circles, thus reaching agreement can be difficult. A decision point can be traumatic. Lack of understanding can result in disagreement or defaulted agreement–"it's OK by me." However decisions are made and whoever is absolved of responsibility, the result can be project cancellation, more design work, or permission to continue. Once the design is approved and the interviews cease, the user effort line is shown to level out until the next peak in the development process when the system is ready for testing.

Another determination occurs during systems testing. Depending on system quality, a decision to install the system has to be made. The impact of operational change due to a new system may not be fully understood in a business community. The decision to accept a system can be difficult; even after considerable investment, a project can be subject to cancellation or redevelopment. The degree of difficulty to decide is proportional to the amount of resource already expended on development.

Typically, after system installation, the user effort profile shows an increase. At this time the future system user becomes the actual system user and has to learn and document how to use the system. In addition, users realize what they really wanted and how the system would have turned out had they had the chance to explain it properly. Generally, users get most of what they need least, and follow the principle to tell the designer only what is really needed after the plans are complete. This leads to a new process called system maintenance.

JAD CHANGES TRADITION

The most significant distribution of work in the above traditional user and developer effort profile is shown for the future system user after implementation. This is the time people express the result in terms of compliments or complaints. Unfortunately, complaints are more frequent, and system developers start to use management controls to determine how to respond to numerous change requests. The maintenance effort after installation has been known to represent 40 to 70 percent of a typical systems support budget.

Regardless of the reasons behind a system deficiency, and what has to be done, the reality of the user activity after implementation is design analysis. Whatever the product quality, the user literally redesigns the system by pointing out what the system does to spoil life at work and what it should do now that it can be seen for what it really does. Maintenance is a process to respond to system change requests and manage system enhancements. The requests for features and the detailed communication now taking place would have been more appropriate at the start of the development process. The difference is that now the evidence of an available system is the basis for comparison to expectations. Furthermore, new complaints about the system emerge against fresh perceptions. In this, criticism provides the basis for expressing real business situations and requirements for automation.

JAD repositions this kind of maintenance effort to become design work at the start of development using a paper model and exhibits for comparative analyses and a structure to manage and convert criticism into usable documents. Such a model is based on expressed opinion with valid assumptions created from a combination of known references, foresight, predictions, and guesses. When solving a problem, it is helpful to know the answer already, and a proposed design can be used to show prepared solutions to an extent possible before the workshop. Such design can be real to demonstrate what is already known as fact, or proposed to demonstrate strategic design alternatives which might yet work. The accuracy of a model does not matter as long as it is plausible and promotes discussion towards more valid and agreeable solutions with consensus for implementation plans.

FLEXIBLE JAD

The idea of using a proposed design to simulate a final result in order to invite critical analysis similar to that found in systems maintenance brings another break from tradition. It also allows future system users to specify the details of a systems external design. In the range of JAD, it is possible to discuss issues about business concepts and functions, including business procedures and system interactions. Ultimately the level of detail allows the use of sample screens and reports in a proposed design scenario for system analysis. In this case, future system users can confirm requirements for information dialogues as well as define the procedural specifications compatible with redesigned business operations.

Typically, business representatives are interviewed in a series of meetings, and the results are documented as requirements. Responsibility for converting requirements into business process design has rarely been in the hands of the future system user. It is rarely done before systems development. It is more usually left to a systems analyst with the job and the time to interpret and create the result. Systems analysts are presumed to have, or have the ability to acquire, enough business knowledge to understand system design best and explain how the users should operate new procedures and interact with technology. In other words, and hopefully, intuitive business procedures involving an easy-to-use computer.

DESIGN EMPHASIS

More often than not a system analyst is unable to think in the same terms as the user. Not having the benefit of operational experience, a technology developer cannot design a system with business first and foremost in mind. Indeed, system developers are usually mindful of implementing technology and may only design user interactions so that system technologies actually work. And, for reasons that technology only works in certain ways, future system users may not be consulted and end up with little choice but to accept a design and then accommodate the constraints of a new system in revisions to business operations and procedures. While a technological design might be excellent, business design may not be so and thus may have to be modified. Resulting change to business routine may be of little consequence or may have subtle or more direct impact. Design change requests are often turned down under the premise that technology applications cannot be redesigned, or that it would be very costly to make revisions for more demanding business requirements now explained. Rather like a car owner told by a mechanic not to interfere with what has to be done to fix a problem, the user can end up with a feeling of frustration or remorse for a result which would have been different had he or she been involved.

ILLUSTRATED JAD

In a situation at a grain company, I was involved in a review meeting for a newly developed inventory accounting system to be used at several grain elevators in farm country. The design included a data entry screen to capture truck weights on arrival and departure. Accuracy was an important issue to the farmers, and the operators wanted an easy method to weigh the grain, meet the driver, and talk about the information needed for the transaction. The proposed design included several procedures which could work for one truck at a time, but would severely limit the operations needed when the traffic volume increased to typical levels. In the discussion that followed about changing the system for a more practical approach, the analyst became defensive and would not hear of redesign. The meeting degenerated into a stand-off. It ended in frustration for one in the team who said, "If you think it's good, then we think it's good," and as he left the room, "I've got to see to these truckers out here."

Lessons were learned from this encounter and to the relief of many, we proposed different technology which was easier to implement and provided a better operating system with greater flexibility for a business user dialogue to work through data capture. The system was redesigned to include an automatic weigh scale reader and easier system interactions to streamline the business operations involved.

PRODUCTIVITY AND QUALITY IMPROVEMENTS

The overall effect of using JAD is beneficial for productivity and quality in a results-oriented environment which promotes teamwork from beginning to end. Work can be targeted to the most appropriate and skilled resources to avoid duplication of effort. Better design analyses discover more situations and opportunities for automation and recognize potential design flaws which would otherwise only be found later and dealt with as maintenance.

The beneficial effect of using JAD is that system user and developer effort can be redistributed to compress the development life cycle profile over time. Corrective maintenance activity is brought into design effort as requirements and specifications analyses thought of as revisions to ideas. The life cycle duration is shorter, and any incremental increase in effort is easily offset by significant improvements in design usability and fewer requirements to change the result. Unstructured approaches have been used in the past, and by comparison, JAD completes design analysis 30 to 40 percent sooner with an overall saving of 20 to 30 percent in the life cycle elapsed time. Similar savings in required resources needed to complete the development process can be expected. JAD will reduce design effort due to teamwork for design analysis, increase development effort due to more and better design information, and reduce maintenance due to better usability.

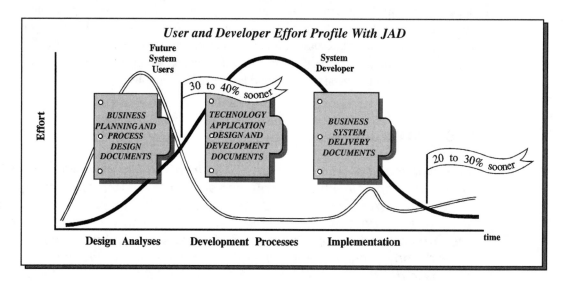

In this approach, future system users play a key role in design analysis prior to development. The JAD structure is used for effective communication in systems analyses between business and technical specialties. This starts at the beginning of the life cycle with one or more workshops, and the results are integrated throughout development and implementation activities. In implementation, JAD design structures can be reused to review delivered system capabilities with design specifications.

TEAM BENEFITS

The team approach provides a better environment for business people to influence technology decisions which results in more creative technological solutions. The overall system design will be better matched with the business environment and more responsive and acceptable in the business community. JAD is not magic and will not replace normal development work. Rather, it repositions work effort and accelerates otherwise slow activities for better results in productivity and quality.

While the productivity and quality improvements are remarkable enough, a significant saving is available through cost avoidance. It is generally accepted that life cycle costs increase rapidly, if not exponentially, from analysis through implementation. The cost of redesigning a developed product is an order of magnitude more costly than designing it right in the first place. The sooner, and the more you are involved in team design, the more desirable the system will be and the greater the benefit. From this perspective JAD is a very attractive alternative to redevelopment.

DEVELOPMENT TIME LINES

Properly implemented, JAD provides an unparalleled environment for business representatives to explain business situations, define requirements, and specify design. When analysis structures and workshop agendas involving different people are used, more frequent meetings can be considered for more effective planning and design. In this people enhance their understanding for systems development or package software acquisition processes. For whatever reason you implement JAD, you bring people together and join forces to tackle problems and decide future actions.

Implementing workshops and achieving effective design discussion depends on a number of factors to do with combining structured analysis techniques with development effort. To do this, you might consider the JAD process in the context of using documents at various stages of completion in a linear time line as one activity is completed after another. Alternatively, you can compare this to completing activities in parallel.

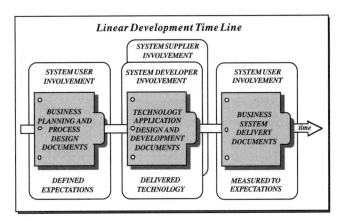

PARALLEL DEVELOPMENT TIME LINES

The above time line includes documents from an information exchange in which people first consider requirements and take systems delivery to a later measure of results to expectations.

Within linear systems development certain parallel activities occur. A session leader would differentiate business and technical design documents and build them from several conversation loops. In this, people who need to participate can communicate frequently and more effectively to manage activities and expectations.

To understand JAD in the context of systems development, you need to consider cyclical involvement in which future system users and system developers work cooperatively to synchronize business plans and design with technology application design and development to establish expectations before system delivery.

⊢⊣ ANALYZING CHANGE

an-a-lyze v. To study a problem in detail by breaking it down into various parts; to describe a sentence in terms of its *grammatical* components.

gram-mar n. The science of dealing with the systematic rules of language, its forms, inflections, and *syntax*, and art of using them correctly; the system of forms and syntactical usages characteristic of any language; the basic principles of art or science.

syn-tax n. The arrangement of words in a sentence showing their constructional relationship.

change n. Alteration; the exchange of one thing for another; a new occupation or fresh outlook; the passing from one form, phase, place, or state to another.

CHAPTER THREE

JAD–A Process to Advance Business Concepts

PROGRESSIVE DEVELOPMENT

Business change is brought about through progressive development activities. These can be shown by relating documents to design analyses, development, and system deliverables in the JAD Communication Model and Development Effort Time Line charts. Over a period, development steps accumulate information to result in work outputs at various stages of completion. Such progressions are needed to prepare a technology for a business application. For typical development methodologies, individual steps are defined and labelled for specific work outputs which amount to technological deliverables. Work outputs from methodical steps depend on the technology to be installed, the tools used for development, testing methods, and project management guidelines.

Using the distinction of JAD as a communication technique for debate with a documentation approach to support development methodologies, JAD outputs will be the documented results of conversation in concert with a systems development process. Identifying documentation to development inputs and outputs allows you to represent a development life cycle as a series of books to do with progressive system development. This may be too simplistic for some, but it allows a temporary step away from the methodical details usually considered to manage a systems development process and the technical details usually associated with development tools. Furthermore, it allows consideration of JAD as a communication tool which can work with system methodologies whether technological tools are used for systems development or not. All that is needed is to integrate the information needed for project management and development tools into the workshop conversation and document the results of debate in the context of particular needs.

ILLUSTRATED JAD

Viewing business or technical activities in the development life cycle as a series of documents is a valid approach when you consider a few similarities. Business and technical information and system code are recorded in languages in which dictionaries, statements, expressions, and verbs and nouns are meaningful in the syntactical sense. Lines of information are grouped in paragraphs and files are contained in libraries in the management sense. Similar automation for source input and edits can be found in office systems and system development tools. Moreover, the information will be written and read by people one way or another.

DOCUMENT LIFE CYCLE MODEL

The following life cycle model illustrates generic development processes from the perspective of documentation and the JAD Communication Model. Various documents at different levels of detail are identified using book cover titles with headings for Business Planning and Design in the range of Business Analysis Structures and Application Development in a range of Technology Development Analysis Structures. The cycle is returned in Testing and Implementation documents.

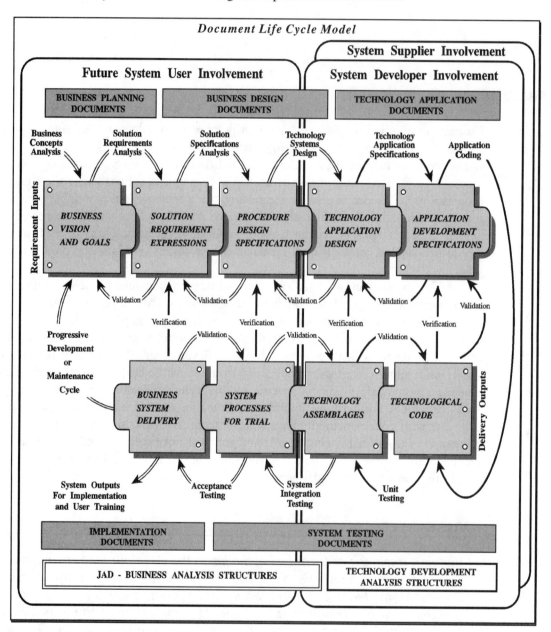

DOCUMENT LIFE CYCLE MODEL

The above cycle illustrates both business and technical analysis structures in related documents. Book covers containing business plans and system design specifications are shown in the range of Business Analysis Structures to involve system users. Book covers containing technology application design are shown in the range of Technology Development Analysis Structures which involves system developers or suppliers. Testing and implementation documents involve all parties.

LIFE CYCLE DOCUMENTATION

While JAD Business Analysis Structures are designed to assist business people in discussing business issues, at some point both business and technical representatives should work together to make design decisions. Technology Development Analysis Structures convey little sense and little interest, if any, to business representatives, unless perhaps they create their own technology application. For this reason, the range of JAD is shown in the double lines to include the Business Analysis Structures with future system users involved in business planning and design and system testing documents prior to implementation. The range which relies on solution guidelines and information outputs from JAD is shown in solid line paths in which system developers are involved in Technology Development Analysis Structures for application development and system testing documents.

In the above Document Life Cycle Model, individual book covers are shown with one document overlapping another to make a complete loop under various headings and book titles in content and context with system life cycle development steps. Each book cover illustrates a document associated with a key development activity. Generally, left-most books contain designs for a business environment and the right-most contain technology application designs for hardware implementation and software development. Each book is related to another with increasing detail from the top left and clockwise through a cycle of development steps. Uppermost books represent requirement inputs from business and technical design analyses. Lowermost books represent delivery outputs associated with technology development testing and implementation. Progressively, the documents relate a greater content of system functionality until a system is completely workable at the end of the life cycle in the lower left-most book. Due to the range of book titles, contents might overlap in the headings used for different types of documents. Business analysis books might only contain business planning or system specification information or both. And technology analysis books might only contain system specifications or application development information or both.

LIFE CYCLE METHODOLOGY

Systems development processes are shown in a loop linking several steps around documents shown as overlapping books. The JAD communication model is illustrated in the development process as a validation loop connecting the documents associated with and reflecting a previous development step. In this model the steps are labelled Business Concept Analysis, Solution Requirements Analysis and Specifications Analysis, Technology Systems Design, Technology Application Specifications and Application Coding, Unit Testing, System and Integration Testing, Acceptance Testing and Implementation. While these labels are typical of many methodologies, different labels can be superimposed for similar sequence representing your own methodology. As with the JAD Communication Model, the cycle represented in the sequential books is independent of scope and time. JAD processes are positioned to support development design activities. Overall, development time might be a matter of weeks or months while the time involved in JAD meetings is a matter of a few days.

Actual development time after JAD for design depends on the magnitude of a project and methods used to create system outputs for implementation shown in the lowermost books. In some situations business problems can be solved in a single systems design; in others, a systems development plan might be staged with several implementations of smaller and manageable technological solutions. The model can start at any requirement input document and end at a related delivery output document. The cycle might be used entirely and repeated for small incremental system deliveries. Paired requirement and delivery documents might be skipped or all of them used in a systems maintenance cycle.

VALIDATION THROUGH DEBATE

In the JAD Communication Model and System Development illustrations described earlier, the validation loop shown can be exercised at any level of detail. It can be extended to any previous document shown in the above document life cycle. Sequential book covers are shown paired up in a clockwise validation loop which is labelled and associated with a development step. Business Analysis Structures (JAD) are shown in a double lined loop to emphasize analysis in which business design validation is provided mostly through conversation and thoughtful debate. Technology Application Development Structures are shown in a solid lined loop in which technical design validation is provided through technological testing using development tools to verify results.

Typical workshop discussion includes topics within the range of information needed for the next development step. However, other issues pertinent to future or different steps can be included in a workshop agenda whenever necessary. In this way validation can be immediate and based on current or near term knowledge from team members. Alternatively, it can also be predictive advice based on experience and assumptions to be later verified in future development results. In the Document Life Cycle Model, validation loops are shown between and across development steps. Verification, otherwise known as testing, is shown as an upward joining line from each delivery output document as a result of a development process started out by related design requirement input documents. In this way design can be validated to expectations expressed in a previous book and development outputs verified to design information used to create the result. For JAD to be successful, each document should include sufficient design information for a corresponding level of validation and verification information for an equivalent development life cycle process.

DOCUMENTS IN STEP WITH DEVELOPMENT

In the life cycle of books, documents migrate business analysis guidelines and analysis information through solution guidelines and solution information. The loop is complete in the return to business information when developed technology is explained in operational terms for the systems user. The cycle starts with a Business Vision and Goals book containing high level information about business or technology concepts. Document details increase in business content and progressively add technical content through Solution Requirement Expressions and Procedure Design Specifications until Technology Application Design and Application Development Specifications become entirely technical for hardware and software construction. A major transition from business to technical content occurs between Procedure Design Specification and Technology Application Design books. These typically describe physical and logical systems design. After coding, technical information then migrates through Technical Assemblages and System Processes for Trial books, into business context again in a Delivered Business System book otherwise known as User Documentation, or Operator Guides.

In this model, design and development documents are collected under Business Planning, Business Design and Technology Application headings. Delivered system documents are shown with System Testing and Implementation headings. Each book cover is characterized by a development step and the detail individualized to a development methodology for system technology. In the context of the above cycle the books may contain overlapping information. A Business Planning document may contain technical design considerations relevant to an implementation architecture or development feasibility. Sometimes, Business Design contains a reference to management policy and regulatory guidelines to substantiate design. Overlapping information is often needed to provide summaries and cross references to provide detail summaries for general reading.

MEANING IN THE EYE OF THE BEHOLDER

The books may or may not be mutually exclusive. It depends on the complexity of subject matter. Overlapping information may be required for general reading or due as input for a development methodology. Generally, the greater a separation between levels of detail for requirement input design documents in the top row, the greater the difference in language and information content. However, certain documents can mix information levels to provide validation in terms of business logic, verification in terms of advice, or concurrence for known outcomes of technology development.

To include appropriate levels of information, a workshop is usually supported by one or more skilled individuals with specialist knowledge to document language in meaning and content for the scheme of technology development and implementation. Although meaning is in the eye of the beholder, specialist information can be shared at a summary level between people from different professions and experience. This is achieved using the JAD technique to ponder on presentation materials devised to discuss business and technical issues and reach consensus for general design.

DOCUMENTATION LOOPS

The JAD concept is designed for team involvement in business analysis using an appropriate structure to review, edit, and make additions to the books. Documents are considered to move forward through a

revision loop. Following the JAD Communication Model, an expression of ideas and opinions starts the cycle. As they become available, references from existing documents are sorted and prepared as source material for the workshop in staff work needed to decide the content and discussion topics. Selected samples and proposed scenarios are provided as inputs to prime the workshop process.

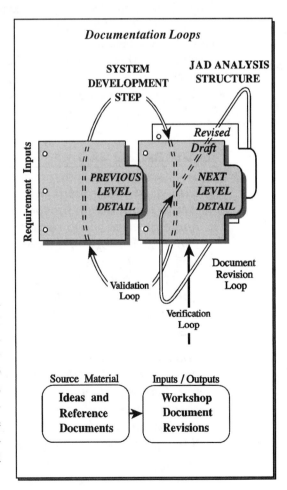

The JAD analysis structure is designed to discover and debate business and technical issues for resolution and document consensus to a prescribed level of detail for a systems development process. Input documents are regenerated as new outputs with changes and additions from debate. Development advice and technical information is added to the output document as it becomes available from a verification loop provided as advice during the meeting or as subsequent research and analysis. Both reference and workshop documents can be revised when the validation loop exposes an omission or limitation in previous documents. For example, during a JAD workshop in the Solution Specification step, the team may define the need for control information not thought of or simply not documented from previous analyses.

QUALITY DOCUMENTATION

Design materials from JAD need not be considered final or absolutely correct. As design results emerge from iterative conversation, new perceptions foretell new opportunities which in turn establish different expectations expressed as new and additional requirements. Furthermore, in the overall scheme of development, technical influences should be expected to cause retroactive design changes as the look and feel of a delivered product is shaped for testing and implementation.

While the opportunity for business automation is often used to redefine or eliminate function, this is not always so. New procedure design will probably uncover new responsibilities for previously unknown and unrequired business functions. Furthermore, when business automation is defined, needs for additional business functions arise, usually to support technology operations. When this occurs, to provide more realistic and complete design information, source materials and documents in the previous level and next level detail should be reviewed and updated. Typically, requirement input documents are changed about 30 to 40 percent in revisions and additions to clarify proposed ideas. In the sense that new knowledge is gained through each development step, and validation is an expected part of the process, retroactive revisions can occur to about 10 to 20 percent of previous JAD detail or other provided documents and materials. Revisions are inevitable as life cycle loops continue into application development where inconsistencies are discovered and corrected or design alternatives tested. The whole process should be managed to contain the scope to reasonable and practical levels for staged change and automation.

An iterative process of revising materials in a documentation loop for a development step supports a greater amount of more valuable information. Additional detail is essential to the propagation of quality throughout the information exchange and subsequent development steps. The design information becomes more accurate throughout the life cycle and fewer changes are needed once the business is more completely defined as procedure design specifications from user involvement. This benefit is in marked contrast to managing information exchange and design changes for more traditional decision points in the typical life cycle. Using this approach, managing change is easier and has less impact on the overall design as development continues.

ILLUSTRATED JAD

During an assignment with an oil company, we used a two-day planning workshop to define functional requirements for an inventory management and customer billing system. This was followed by several design specification workshops and a review meeting over a three-month period. In the review, a business manager from corporate finance announced a misunderstanding concerning invoice data and an interpretation of legislative requirements for reporting information on the invoice. This resulted in a change to the invoice layout and data content of summary and detail information.

The changes were not trivial, but the project leader easily found the affected pages and discussed the revisions in the presence of the team. This included the business planning documents and related system specification documents. Several references were affected in various detail. All this was done in a few minutes because the participants were aware of the detail and knew the importance of adding new understanding to the books. This timely recognition and corrective action signified the importance of teamwork and involvement in structured documentation.

In a different situation during a project for a Canadian telephone company, we produced a plan for six workshops to define requirements and system specifications for a sales and customer service system. This involved sales cycle activities including customer call reports, telephone site planning, proposal and quotation, order processing, installation, and customer service reporting. The meetings, held over a period of three months, involved managers and representatives from several business units as well as the system developers.

The system developers had selected a development environment prototyping tool. In the first meeting the technician explained the development plan and special requirements for information to be used by the productivity tools for programming. We used the guidelines for discussion and documentation and in this way provided the business and technical design to the developers to start to code programs.

Our plan included development activities between workshops and we found that the CASE development tool did not perform quite to the expectations described in the marketing brochure. The analyst realized that unforeseen development constraints would influence the design, and in particular the screen formats for user interactions. We developed a plan to adapt the workshop content to utilize the prototyping tool as it really worked. This was presented at the second workshop as a problem which could be addressed by a small change in workshop activity and special attention to certain technical information needs. We changed the guidelines for participation and documented the newly learned constraint as an assumption and continued relatively unharmed by the setback.

By setting expectations for what could be done, the team environment evolved into a buddy system for responding to business needs while managing the scope for the development plan. The project team went on to develop the system with excellent results in terms of system quality and timely implementation.

JAD—STRUCTURES FOR CONVERSATION

The structure used for discussion is the key to the JAD process. It must be adapted for each specific situation. It may not be necessary to use a workshop process for each development step. This workshop approach is commonly used to involve a group of people in conversation with each other to reach agreement jointly about design issues. However, not all development steps benefit from a structured workshop. For system developers, professional activity such as programming is typically an individual responsibility in a cubicle on a computer workstation. Although programmers might be moved to soliloquy, a code walk-through is probably more appropriate for good code than a JAD workshop.

More to do with design than development, workshop structures should nevertheless be responsive to technology developers as consumers of information for development processes. Analysis structures also have to take into account information from previous steps. The fundamental purpose of structure is to trigger appropriate discussion and to organize thinking to reach consensus and turn abstract conversation into usable documents. In addition, the structure has to manage workshop activities and cater to a wide range of skill levels, personalities, politics, and hidden agendas. Each workshop is personal and each situation different. A JAD structure must be customized each time it is used. Notwithstanding, development steps have similarities and relationships which can be used as a basis to customize workshop content and prepare analysis material. A basic agenda and analysis structure is recommended and adapted by the session leader in concert with an overall development plan.

INDEPENDENT JAD

System developers promote plans and methodological guidelines for successful technology implementation. It should be possible to match methodological development documents with those described in the Document Life Cycle Model. However, the document life cycle might cover a broader scope in that conversational results and business decisions from debate can be recorded before methodical demands for design information. Traditional development methodologies start at a time when technological perspectives are needed. A JAD document life cycle usually starts much earlier when business perspectives are extremely important. It also continues where typical methodologies end in that design discussion documents provide system delivery and operator training notes.

While JAD can be used with a development methodology, it can work equally well without one. Indeed, as a communication technique it might well be used in one or more workshops to define solution guidelines before choosing a technology when a development methodology is more likely to start. To some, a development methodology might be regarded as a cookbook approach for people new to computers to adapt technology to business needs. It may provide instructions to follow once the requirements are available, or it may recommend data gathering interviews. It might be quite sophisticated and provide guidelines for the information needed and might even describe using JAD techniques for analyses. Development methodologies may or may not recommend interactive structured analysis techniques. It becomes a matter of judgment to decide when to use a workshop.

PROGRESSIVE SOLUTIONS

All of the books in the life cycle documents may not be needed. For an assignment already started, workshop documentation might begin with a Solution Requirement Expressions book and use all the remaining book covers throughout development. For an assignment having no need for a technology solution, a JAD Document Life Cycle might start and end with a Solution Concepts book detailing business vision and goals. Other involvement may start and end only using requirement statements documented in a Solution Requirement Expressions book. For software selection without extensive systems development, a system supplier can be selected from a list of requirement statements documented in a Solution Requirement Expressions book, followed with a Procedure Design Specifications book for system customization and testing. In this case, you may never need a detailed Technology Application Design book. For system acceptance testing, you might only need a workshop structure using an Implementation Document book for analysis after development without previous JAD involvement.

Considering JAD as a time saving workshop approach to convert opinions and abstract thought to agreement and action decisions, it should be convenient to arrange workshop meetings to development activities. Plan why to meet, what to discuss, which decisions are needed, and how to use workshop information for an informative business design and successful applications of technology. While design information is needed, people can only contribute certain amounts of information with a precision regarded as progressive solution guidelines from which design continues.

PROGRESSIVE SOLUTION GUIDELINES

pro-gres-sive adj. Moving forward or onward; increasing or advancing in stages or in series; of or favoring modern education ideas which stress informal teaching methods and the encouragement of self expression.

so-lu-tion n. The answer to a problem; the act, method, or process by which such an answer is obtained; (*computer*) the act by which *technology* is *applied* to business problem solving processes.

guide-line n. A lightly drawn line used as a *guide*; an outline policy statement. n. (pl) Instructions for a procedure.

guide n. One who shows the way to strangers.

guide v. To go before or with in order to show the way; to direct the course of; steer; to control, direct, or influence.

tech-nol-o-gy n. (pl) The science of technical processes in a wide, though related, field of knowledge. Industrial technology embraces the chemical, mechanical, and physical sciences as *applied* to industrial processes.

ap-pli-ca-tion n. (*computer*) The system or problem to which a computer is applied, being either a computational type, wherein arithmetic computations predominate, or a data processing type, wherein data handling operations predominate.

CHAPTER FOUR

🖳 JAD—Solution Guidelines for 🖳 Business Systems

PROGRESSIVE DETAIL FROM CONVERSATIONAL ANALYSIS

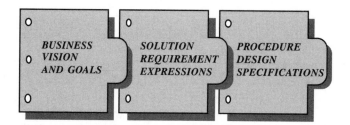

The JAD approach is based on business analysis techniques which involve team discussions while workbook materials and design information document are developed to increasing levels of detail. People are invited to participate in a workshop for their knowledge and ability to express ideas and authority to make decisions for change. Participants are only expected to exchange knowledge from personal experience and make decisions for change in the scope of authority they have over themselves and over others. For this reason, appropriate personnel attend different workshops for team discussion on a range of issues to do with responsibility.

Team conversations about issues which concern them track the usual course for decision making shown in the JAD communication model. In this, team agreement for the need to change and the solution guidelines to implement that change is documented with the expectations for results described. Workshop conversation provides perspectives from which design information is realized as documented guidelines for acceptable change. In providing detail, design information may not be overly abundant; indeed, people are generally more willing and able to describe expectations and give approval for change and less forthcoming with the knowledge actually needed for design. Fortunately, in a group of people solution guidelines can be developed to greater levels of detail than through individual contact. As a session leader, you must judge for yourself the precision needed and how detailed a conversation should be for group dynamics. In this sense, design information will be as detailed as possible, and as sufficient as solution guidelines need to be to achieve satisfactory results.

ILLUSTRATED JAD

Recently I was invited to work with a well-established map publishing company near Chicago and given directions to get there. To make a plan, we discussed where I would start from and where and when I should turn up for a meeting. Even though they were quite capable of providing a detailed map, it was sufficient to let me get from New York to Chicago and then to Skokie to find the hotel. In the next part of the plan, a street outline was enough to get me to the office. More detail was available even to pinpoint it on a satellite photograph. I love to look at maps and would have been interested, but given information, I have been known to become preoccupied over detail and distracted to destinations other than the ones I am supposed to reach.

PROGRESSIVE SOLUTION GUIDELINES

In the following diagram, JAD workbooks are shown to provide progressive solution guidelines with business and technical knowledge exchanged in discussion documents. As business people analyze various issues, they think of solution guidelines in terms of how to design and organize a business environment. System developers think of the same information in terms of how to design and implement a technology application. Whichever way people think of it, at some point in discussion enough insight will be gained to document business issues and identify appropriate technology plans.

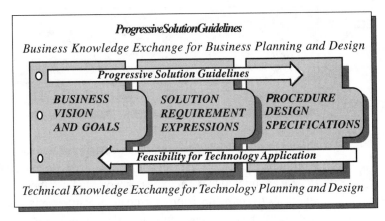

From a knowledge perspective, a team works together on various ideas to provide solution guidelines. While business people feel comfortable providing analysis information, they usually rely on others to provide technical perspectives for concurrence. At certain times, as people contribute to workshop conversation, natural limits in communication are reached when knowledge is exhausted or boundaries for the need to know, and for some people, the need to tell are crossed. At these limits, information will be less forthcoming, and it will be difficult to hold interest and maintain a useful dialogue. For people to discuss change and exchange information without difficulty, the right agenda must be planned and the right analysis technique must be used with the right people at the right time.

BUSINESS PLANNING AND PROCEDURE DESIGN ANALYSES

The Document Life Cycle Model described in the previous chapter shows business analysis structures distinctly for future system users and technology development structures as separate involvement for system developers. For business people, analysis is best conducted using one of two approaches to organize debate and structure analysis documentation in a format they prefer to understand.

Business analysis techniques are used to start and develop progressive solution guidelines at the beginning of the JAD Document Life Cycle. To be complete, ideas and decisions in these books should be supported by an understanding about technology in terms of feasible design. For this reason, appropriate technology development analysis topics are included with business topics.

> ### *Analysis Techniques for Business Engineering and Process Redesign*
>
> **QUESTION FORMS BASED TECHNIQUE FOR BUSINESS PLANNING**
> For Business Planning documents, a question forms based analysis technique is appropriate to discuss change to business vision and define new goals and objectives and document Solution Guidelines for business functions.
>
> **ACTIVITY BASED TECHNIQUE FOR BUSINESS PROCEDURE DESIGN**
> For Business Design documents, an activity based analysis technique is appropriate to define business function details and procedural require-ments for operational interactions and business procedure design specifications.

TECHNOLOGY DEVELOPMENT ANALYSES

After business planning and procedure design documents, business technology application information is considered as specialist information used by highly trained technicians responsible for creating and testing technological design. The Document Life Cycle model illustrates the principles of structure, validation, and verification for all development steps, including related requirement input and delivery output documents used for application development. Specialized analytical and design techniques for application development are used by technicians as the basis for technical design and software coding. Several examples include entity relationship models, data dictionary, data flow diagrams, normalized data, pseudo code, and high level programming languages.

Most system analysts and computer programmers take several weeks to learn the tools of their trade. It may take months or years for a person to become proficient in an analysis approach or computer language. Such subject matters are often complex and follow rigorous disciplines which are not intuitive to untrained people. It is a mistake to think business people adapt to such thinking during a meeting. The novelty of working with unfamiliar analysis materials soon wears thin. Technological development techniques are not recommended for business representatives, although they can be used in a meeting when all participants are willing to use technology-oriented materials.

Some people think of JAD as an approach in which technology development points of view are used to make business decisions. The fact that JAD is a tool for business people to use business discussions to result in decisions for technology applications can be overlooked. While a technical point of view might be helpful to confirm business procedure design decisions or validate requirements to expectations, it will not easily or clearly define business situations or fully explore business logic. Indeed, sorting out the issues alone can be confusing–adding technical analysis can easily sidetrack an issue and distort business perspectives. Furthermore, business managers will not thank you for time spent working on an entity relationship model, a data flow diagram, normalizing data, or writing pseudo code when trying to resolve a public relations problem, respond to environmental legislation, or decide how to promote and handle new products in a competitive market.

PLAN YOUR JAD AND JAD YOUR PLAN

The JAD structure for business analysis must be prepared so that it can be used easily and intuitively applied in conversation by all team members. While you might work in familiar surroundings you will have to adapt to different situations. As session leader, you will surely work with different levels of people and have to respond to varying situations and individual points of view. In a consultant role, you might meet with directors and senior managers of a public or private company. You might discuss plans and visions with assistant deputy ministers from a government department, steel workers from a metal foundry, or engineers from an oil company. You could exchange views with managers and clerical assistants from an insurance company or a bank. In any event you will meet different people with unique responsibilities and distinct backgrounds. Whoever they might be, you need to be flexible and provide workshop agendas and analysis structures adapted for personal and special needs. In session leader terms, you plan your JAD and JAD your plan. Based on what you hear for analysis guidelines, you recommend an approach to deal with discussion topics and validate your agenda with a project leader and selected team members. With a well prepared plan, participants should be able to use your process and contribute to it after a short orientation to workshop materials. The approach should require little explanation and few should find it difficult to use prepared materials for structured analysis from which business solutions become apparent and emerge from teamwork.

BUSINESS ANALYSIS TO START AND END A DOCUMENT LIFECYCLE

In the Documentation Life Cycle model, the scope of JAD is shown to include business analyses for business plans and procedure design specifications for business solution guidelines at the start of the life cycle. JAD can also be used for system acceptance testing at the end of the life cycle. In between, during systems development business people are not usually involved in detailed technical analyses associated with software development. For these reasons JAD need not be confused with other methods used to develop computer technologies. The approach is not necessarily a replacement for an application development methodology or activities in which established automated processes are well understood and supported by paid technicians. However, analysis techniques can be used to resolve technical issues in a workshop setting for system developers.

ILLUSTRATED JAD

The difference between business design and technical design must be demonstrated in certain workshops. Not all analysis need include technological issues for business decisions. Indeed, it may be confusing to do so and lead to inappropriate results.

In a workshop for a Canadian telephone company, business managers wanted to create a marketing advantage by implementing a global order processing system for their international accounts. The goal was to provide a customer service and order desk at any location and extend financial incentives to customers based on business volume. The meeting started with a presentation on the current order processing environment which included numerous different systems around the world. In the debate about how to interface orders and marketing information to a central administrator, the team realized the enormity of system logistics involved for the incentives program to work. The problems seemed insurmountable and without a technological solution. It was suggested the idea be dropped.

During the lunch break we discussed the issue with the business project manager and decided to restart the debate from the basic concept of doing business and not the current systems involved. This time it became clear that or-

der delivery could be the point at which a customer could benefit from the program. A similar approach to their own warranty program emerged as a viable alternative. The team recommended a system using a paper form to capture market information and an administrator for a customer rebate. The meeting closed with direction for further analysis and design for a standard customer return form to be packaged with product delivery documents from the many shipping locations.

Later, the actual solution turned out to be a different but equally effective form designed to be administered in the customer billing department with other documents. The computer technology turned out to be a relatively simple data base application on a PC workstation placed in the department where people handled invoice documents sent out to customers.

CHAPTER FIVE

JAD–A Technique for Business Planning and Procedure Design

JAD ANALYSIS TECHNIQUE

The analysis technique for debating workshop material is based on delivering representative models to provide Solution Guidelines in increasing detail with the final outcome being the demonstration of an operational system. Each level of documented detail is organized for discussion in characteristic lists by which sequential features are arranged for topic management and relational features for topic analysis. Sequence is identified by the alphabet letters ABC and the relational aspect shown in topic titles and descriptions and detailed definitions. One of two analytical techniques can be applied, depending on the kind of analysis information and the detail needed for follow up actions. The chart below illustrates how business analysis is documented at different levels of detail. Change is considered first at a high level for business managers who initially define **Process Improvement Expectations** as vision and goals, then at a more detailed level **Process Improvement Models** for functional managers and system users who describe business requirements and procedure design specifications. For analysis, change is discussed at a strategic level for business executives and a more detailed tactical level for functional managers and professionals shown.

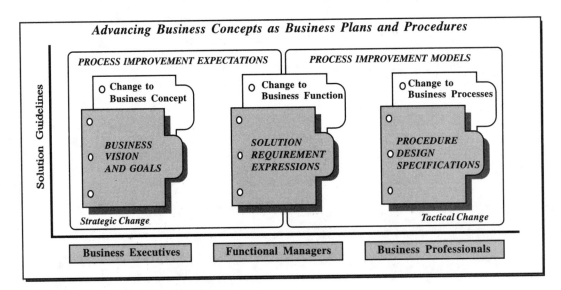

CHANGE EXPLAINED IN DOCUMENTS

The JAD analysis and documentation approach supports business analyses at different levels from chief executives to working professionals involved in business routine. For business planning, the causes and effects of change and how to implement strategic goals to support and respond to new business situations are considered. To understand and explain change, workshop debate is focused to define business direction as business executives and managers become involved in conversation about solutions. Once change is defined at a high level, analysis can continue to increasing levels of detail through business planning for functional managers and process redesign and procedure specifications for business professionals. Several levels of people might be involved to the extent needed to communicate vision and design concerns and commit support to the change result.

BUSINESS APPROACH TO SYSTEMS ANALYSIS

In the previously mentioned Document Life Cycle, left-most books define business design for an information technology application and the right-most books define hardware and software design for construction. To be effective for business representatives, workshop discussion should focus on business design for an information technology application rather than on the actual design for hardware and software. Since the quality of a system depends on good information for many aspects of design, this should not exclude detailed technology development information from workshop consideration. For this reason, JAD business involvement is highlighted under the Business Planning and Design headings using a double lined loop for development steps. In these loops, conversational decisions are fundamental for complete analysis and business considerations are essential to validate the requirements language used to document business design. Further into life cycle books, under the Technology Application heading, a solid line traces application development steps in which technical development results are fundamental to complete analysis and technological considerations are essential to validate the requirements language used to document technology application design.

Generally, to record business design decisions, business planning and design analyses benefit from documentation assistance as text processing. To record technical design, technology development analysis benefits from automated organization in design schematics and systematic testing logic for information processing. Application development design information and construction processes are usually validated and verified using special technologies made to automate certain requirement input details. A combination of the two recording environments might be used in a workshop when business and technical design analyses and development activities benefit from being merged.

FORMS BASED AND ACTIVITY BASED ANALYSES

Using either the Forms Based Analysis or the Activity Based Analysis technique is a matter of judgment and depends on the life cycle step and the level of detail required from a workshop. Question form structures are more likely to be used for relatively high level plans and requirement expressions and activity analysis structures for procedure design specifications. Technology Development Analysis Structures are used for explicit application detail. Generally, question form structures are used to start design analysis with closed questions such as, "What products and services do you provide?" Business activity structures use more open discussion. In business planning, this might be, "What do you track to manage the order process?" and for procedure analysis, "What do you do when a customer calls in an order?" To organize data and design screen dialogues technology, design structures are more concerned with "How many items can you put on a customer order?"

In this sense the JAD approach includes what and how analyses. *What* has to do with the concept of achieving a business result. *How* has to do with work processes involved in business functions and automation. Business processes are inevitably redefined or replaced due to supporting automation and the requirements for automation are likely to be redefined yet again as automation potential is realized and the need for system interactions explained. Evaluating what is needed for people to interplay with technology helps explain how a technology should work and promotes the character of business into the design. For a new business environment analyzing *what* and *how* perspectives for requirements and automation together as procedure specifications allows the system interactions defined to actually provide the technology design specifications. Finally, and from a business point of view, the accuracy of design is measured in the similarity between descriptions of new business procedures and the instructions to work the system from an operator's guide.

BUSINESS POLICIES AND PROCEDURE DESIGN FOR TECHNOLOGY APPLICATIONS

From a skills perspective, business representatives and technical representatives might appear as two solitudes. Business people know how they do business but do not know how to automate business information. Technology representatives know how to automate information but do not know how, and often question why, to work through business routine. The following schematic illustrates the relationship between business policies and procedures design and technology application design. Business and technical perspectives are shown as life cycle documents in areas where an appropriate Forms Based or Activity Based analysis structure can be used for different detail.

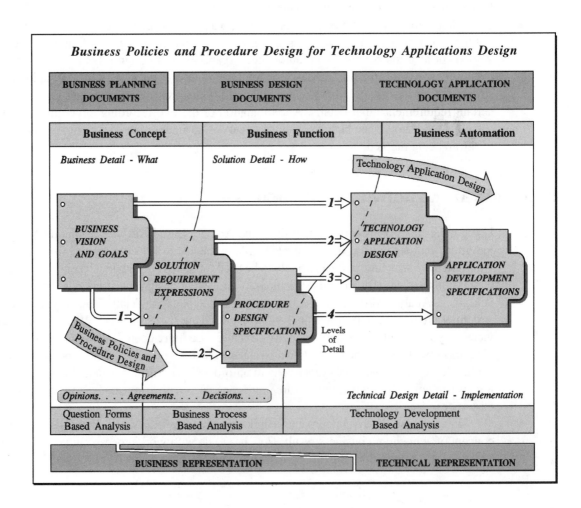

DOCUMENTATION DETAIL AND ANALYSIS TECHNIQUE

The types of documentation and information contents are shown in the headings in a transition from high level business views to detailed design documents shown from left to right and top down. Business Planning Documents are usually used to define business concepts. Business Design Documents can define business concepts but are frequently used to define business functions. Technology Application Design documents can define business functions but are more typically used to define technological information to assemble hardware and develop technological code.

In the above illustration, different documentation levels relate opinions, agreements and decisions in each zone for three specific analysis techniques. High level detail describes the *what* aspect of a business concept and more detailed documents describe the *how* aspect of systems implementation. Question Forms Based Analysis is always used for Business Vision and Goals and sometimes used for Solution Requirement Expressions when defining business concepts. Business Activity Based Analysis is sometimes used for Solution Requirement Expressions, always used for Procedure Design Specification, and in some instances used for Technology Application Design when defining business functions. Technology Development Based Analysis is always used for Technology Application Design and Development Specifications, and in some cases used for Procedure Design Specifications to define business automation. In a single workshop, depending on the information needed for a development methodology, you might have to combine two of the above techniques to create the right environment for team discussion and workshop documentation process.

The footnotes relate analysis techniques to content and representative participation. A business representative may only attend one or a few JAD meetings and will probably need a brief orientation to workshop structure for involvement and useful contribution. Generally, technical representation is provided by a project leader and one or more system analysts depending on the size of the project. These people have a better understanding of the development steps in which the JAD process could be used and are more likely to attend each workshop for continuity in development activities.

The life cycle documents contain both business design content and technical design content. Business design information increases in detail under the Business Concept and Business Function headings as business planning and design documents. A text processing environment operated by a secretary will usually provide the skills needed to create meaningful documentation about business concepts and functions. Technical design information is provided from each level of business analysis to application development books under the Business Automation heading. Operational design information concerning system interactions is provided from the Procedure Design Specifications book to both the Technology Application Design and Application Development Specification books. A development technology and a skilled systems analyst with specialist knowledge is usually needed to create meaningful information for technological design under the Business Automation heading.

CUMULATIVE LEVELS OF DETAIL

The above diagram shows two levels of business design information providing four cumulative levels of technical design information. First level business plans provide Vision and Goals, Solution Guidelines, and Solution Requirements Expressions from the analysis of business concepts and functions. Solution Guidelines from this level provide the preliminary inputs to outline a technology application. Second level Procedure Design Specifications provide details about business operations and system interactions. The first level of technical design describes a technological environment available from documented Business Vision and Goals. The second level outlines a more detailed architecture for technology including the data descriptions available from Solution

Requirement Expressions. The third level provides additional design for system interactions as Procedure Design Specifications. Documented discussion at this level also provides a fourth level of technical information in the form of screen and report designs. The first three levels of technical information are used by system analysts to define technological design. The details in Technology Application Design, plus the fourth level of technical information about operational interactions, are used by programmers to define Application Development Specifications to code the system.

Referring to previous diagrams, the time line for systems development with JAD illustrates analysis, development, and implementation information as progressive documents. The progressive nature of systems development is usually managed using guidelines from development methodologies. This involves set procedures and methods to acquire the above four cumulative levels of technical detail. Traditional development methodologies work through each of these levels as a data gathering exercise. With JAD you have the opportunity and flexibility to consider the business and data in one workshop. For Business Concepts, data levels one and two can be combined in Forms Based Analysis to result in business vision and goals and requirement expressions. For Business Functions, data levels two and three can be combined in an Activity Based Analysis workshop and results in more detailed requirement expressions. For Business Automation, data levels three and four are combined to result in system specifications including screen and report scenarios to define physical design and clarify logical design. How one or more levels are combined becomes a matter of choice, depending on the need to know the business, the size and complexity of the project, the stage of previous design analyses, and methods used to automate systems development.

Based on the above four levels of technology development information needed to de-

---

JAD Analysis Structure Hierarchy

Business Planning Documents — Question Forms Based Analysis

Business Plan Concept — Vision and Goals
Structured analysis of business environment and concept opportunities
Defines business objectives and scope
Documents business design overview and general solution guidelines
Key implementation activities and responsibilities

Business Plan Solution — Design Requirements
Structured analysis of business problems and opportunities
Identification of issues and change requirements
Defines business environment and technology solution information
Documents business involvement and information processing requirements

(Business Design Level 1 / Technology Design Level 1 & Level 2)

Business Design Documents — Business Activity Based Analysis

Business Design Solution — Process Requirements
Structured analysis of business activity model
Emphasis on business operations and business automation
Definition of business processes and solution details
Documents business design and technology application requirements

Business Design Solution — Procedure Specifications
Structured analysis of business activity model
Emphasis on business procedures and business automation
Defines operational interactions and screen and report dialogue
Documents technology application design specifications

(Business Design Level 2 / Technology Design Level 3 & Level 4)

fine business change, the previous chart generalizes workshop processes as Forms Based or Activity Based Analysis structures under the headings for business planning and design documents.

WHAT YOU THINK YOU HEARD IS NOT WHAT THEY THOUGHT THEY SAID

In the Document Life Cycle Model, validation is shown as a double lined loop connecting books through development steps. Validation is applied to confirm the accuracy of stated Solution Requirements Expressions and Procedure Design Specifications by referring back to the expectations for change in a business or technological environment. In a workshop, to validate business perspectives key words and syntax can be used to reach consensus in meaning and purpose. Technical validation is possible in conversation by referring to the developer for technical concurrence at each level of understanding through progressive business analyses. Technical *validation* is not as precise as technical *verification*, which is ultimately the process of testing developed automation to technical design documents. Even without immediate verification, system developers can, in discussion, provide technical validation in the form of advice from personal skills and the experience of knowing a development process. When technical validation is unclear, design notes and assumptions can be documented pending a future verification from completed development.

Ultimately the technology development information needed for the overall integrity and robustness of the system will not be complete until all the business functions within the scope of design are fully defined in the second level Procedure Design Specification document. Due to the iterative nature of analysis at one level of detail followed by reflective thinking and analysis at another, it is not possible to document all design information in one meeting. Moreover, it may not be possible to complete all analysis in one workshop. Depending on the scope and complexity, only one requirements analysis workshop might be needed, or a business planning workshop followed by a few workshops for requirements and specifications might be required.

For a more productive workshop, predict business and technological solution results and demonstrate the feasibility of implementing team decisions to the extent possible. This, might include using a development technology in the meeting to complement technical advice. To be effective, any assisting technology development tool must provide an appropriate level of verification information to make comparisons to business understanding and technical design validation. The first choice for technological assistance will be for the one which adds precision to the professional advice you would expect as technical concurrence in the course of debating workshop material.

When you as session leader include advice or demonstrate results, you will have greater assurance that what you think you heard is what they thought they said and is in fact what they want, and you can deliver. Different perspectives and variety of expression require workshop disciplines for comprehension.

WORKSHOP PERSPECTIVES

In the following illustration, business perspectives and technical disciplines are positioned for the systems development effort profile, including JAD. Quality workshop results and documentation depend both on thorough business analysis and good technological analysis. The two points of view are shown in a connecting loop for consensus about business requirements with a feedback loop to provide concurrence about technical design and cost feasibility. In this illustration a business discussion precedes a technical discussion. This may or may not always be the case but each viewpoint should be given equal opportunity in debate to reach agreement for progressive solution guidelines.

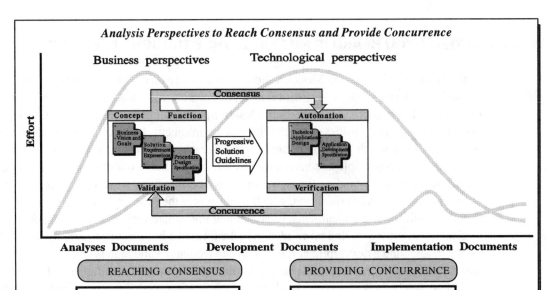

Analyses Documents   Development Documents   Implementation Documents

REACHING CONSENSUS	PROVIDING CONCURRENCE
Primary language to reach consensus about business concepts and functions	**Secondary language to provide concurrence for a technology application**

Future Perspective	Entity Relationships
Management Policy	Data Flow Diagrams
Business Direction	Development Protocols
Business Goals	Data Dictionary
Success Factors	CRUD Diagrams
Risk Assessment	Data Attributes
Business Model	Data Architecture
Business Benefits	Normalized Data
Business Assumptions	Third Normal Form
Organizational Units	Function Decomposition
Activity Model	Function Point
Business Role	Development Guidelines
Business Tasks	Development Cost Guidelines
Work Flow	System Architecture
Document Flow	Network Protocols
Product Flow	Context Diagrams
Processing Rules	Pseudo Code
Screens and Reports	ASCII Code
Business Interfaces	Object Oriented Code
Audit Guidelines	Fourth Generation Languages
Legislation	Fifth Generation Languages
Regulations	Report Writer Languages
Professional Guidelines	Query Languages
Community Guidelines	
Industry Standards	

Business interpretations for concept and function validation	**Technology development interpretations for automation verification**

CONVERSATION FOR RESULTS

Depending on individual interests, participants emphasize a business focus or a technological focus to influence discussions according to the discipline they normally work with and are measured by. It is important to use a workshop structure which supports conversation and debate without biasing a result to favor a particular discipline. For this reason, appropriate workshop analysis guidelines should be defined for discussion and documentation according to the approach for debate. With this understanding, it is possible to customize a structure to promote equal opportunities for people to debate the issues and narrow the knowledge gap which normally separates the specialties. In the above chart, typical specialty topics are listed under headings for business and technical interpretations.

The list of specialty information illustrates a few of the different and seemingly diverse methods for understanding business and technological concepts. Depending on education levels and experience, any one or more of the above topics might be discussed and emphasized in different ways and at different times during the development life cycle. Any combination might be used to explain a point of view during a workshop. Even using similar methods, people can make the same point and sound quite different. It is unlikely, and fortunately not necessary, for the session leader or any one person to become skilled in or comprehend several methods of expressing different points of view. During a workshop one team member may use one method of making a point and another participant use a different approach. Indeed, the team is selected for having different qualifications and background so that they can share and exchange knowledge to be successful. Your role in leading conversation is to ensure a common level of understanding using analysis guidelines and a customized structure to combine and illustrate several points of view for team decisions and documentation.

USING A FAMILIAR LANGUAGE

When you prepare a structure for a workshop certain characteristics must be taken into account. People are best able to talk about the things they know about using familiar references and methods of expression. Business conversation about system requirements tends to be abstract while technical conversation about systems design tends to be more concrete. Generally, people want to express opinions about an issue rather than take a stand or make a decision about a problem. As conversational statements are recorded decisions emerge in terms of what is needed and what must be done. For these reasons, a workshop structure is tailored to address various topics in an open forum for different methods of conversation with fair and unbiased approaches to reach consensus.

Some publications promote the view that analysis topics outside a technology development structure are useless for systems development and should be disregarded because only certain information is needed for a technology design. Indeed, people can make quite convincing arguments in favor of ignoring certain conversation which appears to generate unappreciated or redundant information. An example would be to exclude conversation about business processes and people activities using a technology development structure. In this case, the omission would show up in the workshop as ineffective participation, frequent misunderstandings, and a lack of confidence for decisive action. Incomplete analysis will propagate when you observe people being cut off in conversation or being told to wait to speak. You might notice that people clam up when you really need them to describe situations and talk through problems in conversational thinking. You will get no response when you ask for agreement and get a blank look from people bewildered by the prospect of change.

You can make your JAD distinct from other interactive design methods by using a familiar language and avoiding rigid development disciplines which restrict discussion to a strange mono-logue which can inhibit the open conversation that would otherwise lead to the required knowl-edge exchange.

BUSINESS AND TECHNICAL PERSPECTIVES

It is in the best interests of each team member that the workshop agenda accommodates team characteristics and a documentation method to capture information to a prescribed level of detail. You will have greater success as session leader using a workshop process which allows simulta-neous consideration of business and technical perspectives. Furthermore, for the people usually invited to participate, you will find that business language is preferred for conversation when tech-nical jargon makes the eyes glaze over. Although some business jargon may cause a similar va-cant look, it is usually easier to resolve the mystery of what people do or want to do than how complex technologies work. Since the system includes both business and technical design, it is a matter of judgment to decide what is important to discuss. It probably does not matter that some people do not understand how technology works, it always comes down to what you need to know to allow people to work a system.

For an open discussion, you need to discover real problems and take abstract discussion to more definitive requirement information. It is preferable to start out with a business perspective pertaining to people involvement. On occasions, you will find it helpful to role play business rou-tine to describe the present environment in order to understand a current situation and discover the needs for change and the requirements to define the agent of change. In this way, business logic can be defined and agreed to along with a discussion for business and technical information. Then, in providing technical concurrence, the developer can document the information needed for implementation. Finally, as with business analysis, it is better to re-enact business procedure with new involvement of proposed system interactions and ensure design results are satisfactory and meet expectations.

PRIMARY AND SECONDARY LANGUAGE

For the above reasons, business language for procedure becomes a primary mode of conversation for workshop team members with a business background. Technical language becomes a second-ary mode of conversation in which ideas expressed in technological terms should be supportive and in terms of system development advice and technical concurrence whenever needed. A ses-sion leader will find it easier to demonstrate business concepts and situations using business mod-els and design scenarios reenacting business procedure and role playing the business professional rather than pretending to be a computer. Furthermore, to avoid difficulty, if your workshop is at-tended by a greater number of business specialists, you can use the premise that you can support a business language for most of the people most of the time and a technical language for some of the people some of the time.

From these perspectives, JAD is better implemented as a technique for business analysis rather than as a development methodology or development technology. It is a powerful and flex-ible approach for business people to explain things developers need to know to construct better business systems. Debate should be administered using logical and intuitive analysis structures without encumbering development methodologies and technologies which you, the session leader, and perhaps the team, would otherwise have to learn. All you have to do is learn how to implement JAD as a book building process in which you can work with others to capture business concepts, business design, and technology application design points of view.

JAD WORKSHOP ENVIRONMENT

The JAD workshop environment is summarized by reading the following headings in sequence, and then reading the explanatory notes. The customized structure mentioned in the chart is created and presented as a documentation kit which is further developed as a workbook and completed through a team activity in a workshop setting.

JAD Workshop Environment

A session leader–
Develops a structured approach for an interactive team meeting for the business system owner and workshop product consumer to create documentation consistent with a system development and implementation.

–works with a selected team of specialists–
Informed decision makers from the business community
Experienced in business practices and procedures
Skilled technicians with system implementation responsibilities

–using a customized throw away structure for the leader–
Orchestrate the players
Promote team evaluation of goals and objectives
Maintain a focus on business logic and system support
Provide a method to explore and test ideas and solutions
Convert abstract discussions into usable documents
Illustrate the resulting product and documentation

–assisted by session leader tools.
Manage a series of workshop preparation tasks
Customize a business structure and prepare workshop exhibits
Organize multiple and varied documents into readable materials
Transfer materials to and from other development tools

WORKSHOP
DOCUMENTATION
PROCESS

work-shop n. A room or a building in which productive work or manufacture on a small scale is carried out; an intensive seminar in some subject or study.

doc-u-men-ta-tion n. The assembling of documents; the using of documentary evidence to support original written work, or the technique of referring to such evidence in footnotes, appendices, etc. or having the evidence itself; the classifying and making available of knowledge of procedure.

doc-u-ment v. To support or supply with documents.

doc-u-ment n. An official paper; certificate; anything (*e.g., a workbook*) that gives information or supplies evidence.

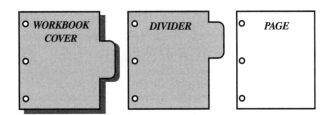

work-book n. A pupil's exercise book with printed problems etc. and space for answers; a book of instructions for procedure and operation; a book in which is recorded work accomplished or planned.

proc-ess n. A moving forward especially as part of a progression or development.

proc-ess v. To submit (something) to treatment, preparation, or process; to submit data to analysis.

CHAPTER SIX

🄹 JAD—A Book Building Process

RESPONSIBILITY FOR SUCCESS

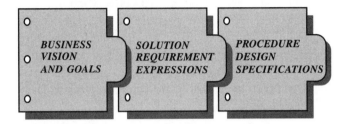

Successful workshops are planned carefully to suit the character of the business environment, the organization politics, and the goals of the executive sponsor to be compatible with a development methodology. A meeting starting without preparation will invariably degenerate into a series of uncoordinated activities which frustrates the team, demotivates involvement, and produces poor results. Even a most skilled session leader can come to grief if a meeting structure evaporates through poor planning and lack of foresight for eventualities. Yet compared to traditional methods, an unstructured and poorly implemented meeting might be more productive, if not the most comfortable experience.

The key deliverable is the workshop document. It must be prepared to support the structure and customary language for debate and inherently guide the session leader's role and team activities. Depending on the development life cycle methodology and the stage at which a workshop is held, a finished document may be a business concept, strategic plan, solution guidelines, or a requirements document for vendor analysis. It may be system development guidelines for a technology decision, including to buy, to build or both, or system specifications for a technology application. Indeed, a book building process may be for any thoughtfully analyzed subject to be documented. The structure of the document and the level of detail to be recorded should be decided ahead of a workshop and developed under the guidance of a session leader and supervision of a project manager or project leader.

For these reasons, a workshop session leader is responsible and indeed has a vested interest to provide instructions for adequate preparation and assuring completion. When things go wrong in a workshop, everyone bar none will look to the session leader for appropriate leadership for the next activity. In hindsight, the reason for an unfortunate experience will invariably show up as lack of readiness. If the session leader is not prepared for most eventualities, Mr. Murphy and Mrs. Murphy will be glad to take over the leadership role and the two Murphy children will throw in two cents to add disaster after misery.

GETTING STARTED

It is beneficial that people involved in the JAD process understand the capabilities and strengths of the analysis approach. A marketing presentation is required to bring managers and team members to a common understanding regarding expectations and resource requirements. Meetings and orientation presentations are necessary to obtain a commitment to proceed and acquire the resources to do the study. Good interaction with the executive sponsor is important for everyone to understand a proper sense of purpose and authorize qualified team members to debate the issues and decide the outcome. The key steps in the JAD approach are outlined as a book building process.

BOOK BUILDING PROCESS

The most effective way for a JAD session leader to gain acceptance and team confidence is to demonstrate the process and typical results from a workshop as part of an introduction presentation. This is done by showing the process in terms of a fill-in-the-blanks approach to documentation. The first set of blanks to select is a book cover with labelled dividers. The second choice in blanks is to select pages and forms for certain dividers. This presentation explains the process of selecting and further customizing form blanks for special needs and preparing materials prior to the meeting for team review and completion. It will be helpful to reference workshop experience and show completed documents from similar meetings. The preceding dividers and page inserts are typical of JAD business concepts analysis, requirements analysis, and specifications analysis book covers.

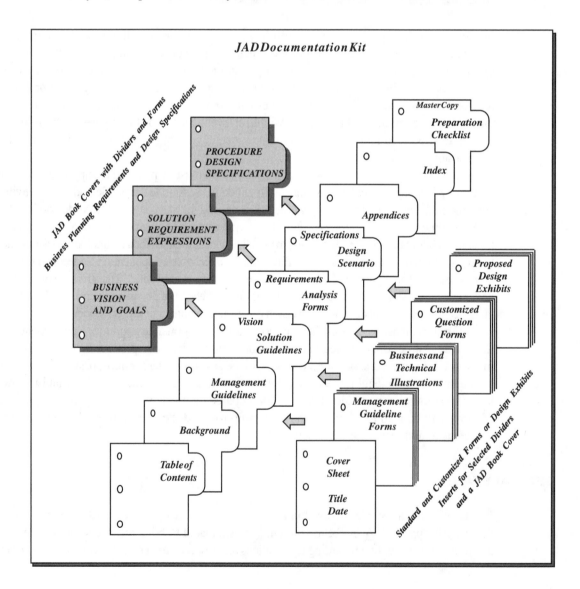

TEAM BUILDING AND DOCUMENTATION

During initial contact and conversation about the assignment, it should be possible for you, the session leader, to determine the type of workshop and assemble a sample fill-in-the-blanks book. By anticipating a level of content, you can suggest a book organization and then respond to individual recommendations for changes to the table of contents from the ideas and advice gained in further conversation. The first section of the book will invariably use typical JAD workbook dividers and standard forms and makes an excellent basis for subsequent adaptation.

Responding to individual contributions to develop a book structure will add to team acceptance for the book building approach and "buy" in for workshop participation and the documented result. Within JAD guidelines for structure and documentation standards, as session leader you will benefit by listening to, and considering, any suggestion for modification. At this stage, a small input to the document content and design can stroke an ego and pay dividends in greater cooperation when it is needed in the workshop meeting.

DIVIDER CONTENT FOR CONVERSATION

Although the sequence of your book content may not be the sequence of conversation for preparation, you will probably use the workbook organization to manage the order of discussion throughout a workshop. Each page is designed for an analysis topic with relationships for debate to other pages in the same or different dividers. You will need different dividers depending on the level of detail. When you use the Forms Based Analysis technique, you should select the *Analysis Forms* divider and customize the forms. For the Activity Based Analysis technique, you should select the *Design Scenario* divider and customize appropriate design exhibits. Preparation work includes the completion of a sufficient amount of questionnaires and sample materials for acceptable forms design or an adequate design scenario for workshop handout materials and team use.

A preparation checklist divider is placed after the index divider in a draft document and assembled as a master copy for the project leader. A *Checklist* divider need not be included in a team handout.

TABLE OF CONTENTS DIVIDER

The *Table of Contents* is the first divider of a workbook, usually with a cover sheet placed over it. This cover sheet provides the first area for customization in the title and proposed date. The topics list and agenda pages provide more fill-in-the-blanks spaces for completion. List your selected divider labels on the topics page and add other key topic headings as they emerge from conversation. In discussing the meeting agenda you can add key items to include as workshop activities. Agenda items and page numbers, dates, and workshop venue can be added as you decide these in workshop preparation.

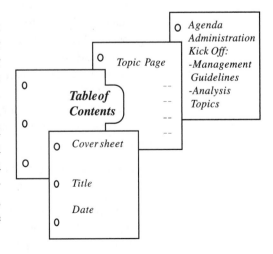

BACKGROUND DIVIDER

You can use the *Background Divider* to include a preamble about the assignment and workbook overview and team role. The information you put here will bring participants to a common starting point regarding previous activities, summary remarks, and the action plan to use a workshop. It is helpful for the reader if you include an outline of the workshop approach and team responsibilities on this page. In addition, as you discuss the assignment in these pages, it will enhance your knowledge and perception about the working situation.

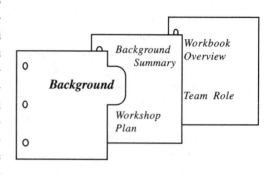

MANAGEMENT GUIDELINES

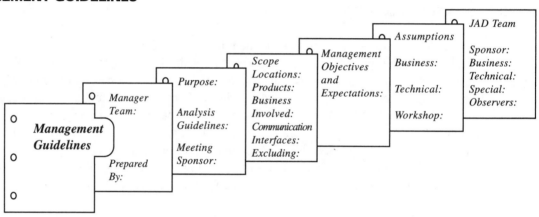

The above *Management Guidelines* pages contain the terms of reference for an assignment. For different development methodologies people will know this document by various headings, including Project Proposal Brief, Project Objectives Document, Project Definition, Executive Overview, Executive Summary, Feasibility of Requirements, Management Scope and Objectives Document, Project Initiation, Initiation Report, Opportunity Evaluation Report, Preliminary Analysis, Initial Study Report, Concept of Operations, System Abstract, et cetera. In popular JAD terminology, you should name it Management Guidelines.

For JAD documentation, you complete the above separate pages with the headings shown and insert them after the *Management Guidelines* divider. Each page contains a list of subheadings or statements pertaining to the information you need. Fill out the pages from conversation in your first preparation meeting for a workshop and continually revise them through further preparation. This process will also continue in the workshop meeting when the team members make contributions to reach consensus under each heading.

- *Manager Team* lists the names and titles of the managers and project staff who contribute to the terms of reference in the following pages and authorize the workshop participation.

- The *Purpose* page contains a statement for the intended outcome. It also outlines the *Analysis Guidelines* in a brief description for the workbook content. The intent for the system is often expressed as "Purpose of the Project." If a project has not been started, you can express it as "Purpose of the Assignment," or simply, "Purpose." When discussing the analysis guidelines statement, you should define the purpose of the workshop meeting and the level of detail for the team to achieve.

The *Analysis Guidelines* must be defined to match the structure designed into the workbook and the materials included for review. The guidelines may be restated as your preparation unfolds and new details are brought into the meeting agenda. To demonstrate value in participation the guidelines should also be explained in terms of using the document after the workshop. For authorization, this page usually includes the name and title of the sponsor or steering committee managers.

- The *Scope* page provides a list for inclusion and exclusion in the scope of the assignment. When you discuss scope, you can use a list of descriptive key word headings to organize the information. Typical subheadings include:
    - *Locations* where the system will be utilized or affect the business
    - *Product* or *Service* or *Information* types involved in the business
    - *Business Involved* in the system design for the above places and things
    - *Communication Interfaces* to other business operations or systems
    - *Excluding* related but unsupported business functions in this design

The above headings are typical for making a list of things which the team will consider in the scope of the design. The word *Locations* is used to define the business areas involved in using the system. The words *Products*, *Services*, or *Information* might be used instead to list the things the business area provides, or you might use more appropriate key words in a heading to suit the language of business. For example, the word Hospitals may be better than Locations, and the word Patients better than Products for an operational design for an emergency admissions system.

The *Business Involved* explains a list of things that go on in the locations included in the scope of analysis. Depending on the level of detail, you can express the list in terms of business concepts, business organizations, business functions, or business activities. For the above hospital example, a list for concept analyses could include Patient Care as an item for consideration. A list for organizational analyses could include Out Patients as an area for consideration. And a list for functional analyses could include X-ray as an activity for consideration. Whichever way you express the business involved, the items listed as involved should be included in an index and used to reference topics for more detailed analysis in the workbook.

The *Communication Interfaces* heading is optionally used to list the exchange of information to and from other departments or department systems. You can express these using full area names for manual interfaces or use acronyms for departmental systems with automated interfaces. For example, an Order Entry System may need to interface to the Pricing Department, or the Marketing Department personnel for a Price Book, or the PDQ Quotation System for an automated price.

While the above list describes the scope, items not mentioned may still be thought of, or sometimes expected and brought into the design by an implicit or assumed connection. For this reason, a definition of scope is more clearly defined when you list *Excluding* items after the above inclusions. In the Hospital example, although medical supplies are essential to treating emergency patients, Inventory Management could be defined as excluded from the scope. In another example, the functional scope for an Order Entry System might include the order pricing and tax calculations in the business functions list but exclude Sales Commission Processing which stated under the excluding heading identifies it not to be discussed.

In the workshop, you will find the list of exclusions very helpful to direct team participation and manage expectations for the result.

- The *Objectives* page lists management and operational goals to be achieved by changes due to business engineering and/or the installation of a new system. These can be stated as expectations in terms of benefits with qualitative or quantitative measurements. For example, an objective or expectation for an order processing system can be expressed as: Faster order turn around, or specifically, orders shipped within 24 hours. Objectives can be stated for a business or a technical perspective or both.

- The *Assumptions* page explains things which influence the design or constrain the system because certain rules or environments already exist or are understood in certain ways. These include:
  - *Business Assumptions* influence the character of the business design
  - *Technical Assumptions* establish boundaries on technological solutions
  - *Physical Assumptions* define the environment for a technology
  - *Workshop Assumptions* provide additional guidelines for the meeting

- *Business Assumptions* might include regulatory controls, professional guidelines, management policies, and industry trends. *Technical Assumptions* may describe established hardware, existing data base environments, design standards, and communication protocols. *Physical Assumptions* refer to operating environments and describe hours of operation, or special working environments in an industrial or business setting. They might describe an assumed use of certain or existing hardware and terminals. These notes usually refer to common uses and types and locations of technological devices. Physical considerations include printers or special equipment such as cash registers or hand-held terminals. The list can mention general technologies such as bar code readers, encoded identity cards, encryption, network circuits or network protocols, and key locks or other security devices.

    Occasionally *Workshop Assumptions* are noted; these might refer to a project plan or describe the methodology or standards for documentation. These assumptions may also describe the role of participants and review process for the final document. A workshop assumption might also describe the reason for including development technologies in the meeting and the role of specialist operators and use for various technical outputs. Other types of assumptions exist and vary with the nature of the business and technology application.

- The JAD *Team Members* page lists the names and titles of workshop participants. The names can be grouped under a workshop role heading for business or technical contribution to the design. Other people might be identified as part of the team using other role headings such as Expert Witness, Scribe, and Observer. In preparation, this page is considered after the scope and objectives have been discussed so that you can decide if the team selected is consistent with areas stated in the scope and if they have the required skills to assist the process.

    For the workshop, the list of names will be moved to the *Table of Contents* divider after the agenda page. It can then be used in the meeting sequence by way of introductions and administration.

SOLUTION GUIDELINES

The *Solution Guidelines* divider provides a place for illustrations which provide additional understanding and cross references to analysis topics. Depending on the level of detail, this can include key definitions, summary facts and figures in lists

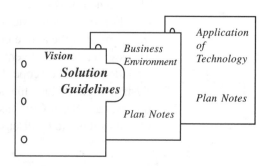

and charts, sketch diagrams of work areas, organization charts, or business functional overviews and activity lists.

The Solution Guidelines section is intended to illustrate a concept overview for a business environment with or without an application of technology. You can also use the Appendices divider to locate materials used less frequently but referenced nevertheless and included for complete documentation.

ANALYSIS FORMS DIVIDER

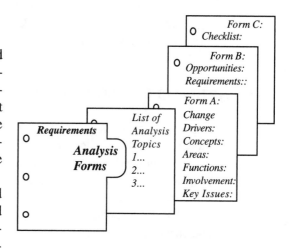

The *Analysis Forms* divider contains selected forms designed for issues debate and documentation for topics within the scope of analysis. This includes a forms sequence page to list the topics and provide a sense of order for the meeting. The design and number of forms required for a topic will vary depending on the level of detail required.

Information on one form is associated with detail on another. In this, the forms based technique is arranged to provide an analysis sequence to question and document design issues. You develop the sequence and forms design in preparation to be consistent with the workshop purpose and *Analysis Guidelines* for the information needed and level of detail required in the scope of design.

DESIGN SCENARIO DIVIDER

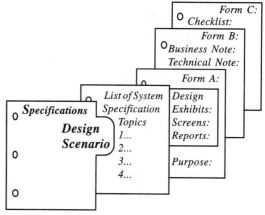

The *Design Scenario* divider is used to include proposed solutions and design exhibits for evaluation. These materials should be considered as paper model equivalents to a prototype system on paper. Design on one page is related to design on another as an operational scenario. For this, the JAD Activity Based Analysis technique is arranged to provide the analysis sequence and accumulate design information notes.

In preparation, you create a *Design Scenario* to be consistent with the workshop purpose and Analysis Guidelines for the information needed and the level of detail required in the scope of design.

APPENDICES DIVIDER

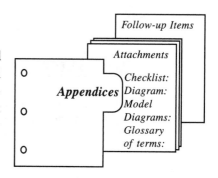

The *Appendices* divider is used to locate attachments and adjuncts to other sections where specific detail or general facts would be unsuitable. Attachments can include particular materials used by a team member with a specialist role. This can include your own JAD materials which may add an important point of view to the meeting but add little value to the document.

Appendices can include a glossary of terms, detail diagrams, and follow up items for resolution outside the scope of the meeting. Materials can be removed from or inserted to this section as they might be needed or generated during a meeting.

INDEX DIVIDER

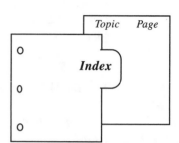

You can create a draft index for the workbook. The topic page index will be created when the workshop materials are published and inserted after the *Index*.

PREPARATION CHECKLIST DIVIDER

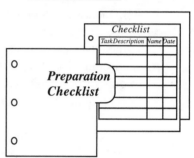

The *Preparation Checklist* divider is used to locate the list of preparation activities needed for a successful meeting. It is usually contained in one or more master copies used by the project manager and other people involved in getting ready for the workshop.

As you complete each activity you can review the list and check mark each task done.

JAD DOCUMENTATION KIT

With the realization that JAD can be regarded as a book building activity, it is appropriate for the session leader to use a tool kit to simplify the process. All that is required at this stage is a three-ring binder and a stock of dividers and preprinted forms with a basic design for a typical JAD workshop.

Considering the various materials used, the binder can be designed for common workshop needs. On the inside of the front cover, a half-size inside pocket is needed to keep brochure inserts, letters, and workshop supplies such as a name card and a marking pen. The preferred pen has a fine tip marker at one end and a yellow highlighter at the other. A slot for a regular letter-sized note pad for miscellaneous notes is optional for the inside back cover. For a professional look, your binder might be designed to display a full length title insert along the spine edge and a folding flap with a Velcro fastener to join the covers along the opposite edge and enclose the contents. The binder flap, name card, and pen might be printed with your company logo to add finishing detail to the kit.

This kit demonstrates your professional approach to organizing conversation into usable documents. You pick up your JAD binder and put a pen and a thesaurus in your pocket. You drink your coffee, chew on a mint freshener, and step out with your best smile to visit the people who can contribute their knowledge to start the working document which will keep you busy for a few days.

ILLUSTRATED JAD

In the preparation stage for an assignment with a bank, I had an hour and a half with the project manager to be briefed on their plan for a Global Payments System. I took notes on the pages in a binder from my JAD kit and selected a few preprinted pages for a possible workshop structure. We were to meet the executive sponsor that morning and on the way we were accompanied by a trainee session leader who sat in to observe.

The meeting started with the usual routine of introductions and exchange of information about the JAD process and about the project. I presented a brochure from the inside pocket and showed the preparation to date in the binder and took more notes from the comments made for the expectations for a successful meeting. We discussed the workshop process and executive kick off to start the meeting, and I provided a brochure describing the JAD concept and meeting involvement. We scheduled a time to return and review the typewritten document.

As we left the executive's office, the trainee pointed out that I had got away with poor staff work and that nobody else had ever taken handwritten work into such a meeting. We discussed this and agreed that the neat appearance of the overall package and the demonstration of a working document more than offset the potential for criticism. Indeed, we felt the materials had been appreciated for the show of quality and potential to deliver results from the start.

This approach to organization and packaging is not always valued for what it means to the JAD process. . . . One client spent a great deal of time deliberately removing items that might have been construed as a waste of budget funds, but that's another story. . . .

INVOLVEMENT FOR ANALYSIS

Bringing a book building approach to the team results in people considering workbook materials as the product of team effort. Accordingly, participants tend to focus attention to the JAD process and feel compelled to discuss subject material together. In this case, people become more proficient as business analysts and group results motivate thoughtful contributions towards documented design.

Voluntary participation comes from observing that the process works and joining in is for the sake of results. Like justice, progress must be seen and seen to be done. This means that progress should be perceived in understandable terms for the team to appreciate the workshop process. Using books to mark up progress is the easiest way of providing working materials and delivering a visible outcome. Several people will be involved in the meeting–how well they work together will depend on their reasons for being there and how well you empathize with the group. Understanding team politics will help.

CHAPTER SEVEN

🪑 JAD–Preparation for Success

JAD INVOLVEMENT FOR QUALITY

Implementing a JAD workshop involves a preparation phase and a workshop phase. Preparation for a meeting is crucial to the overall success of the workshop and team attitude for participation. The quality of preparation will be reflected in the fluidity of the analysis process and the value of documented results.

Success will depend on how well people work together and the ability of the session leader to develop team cooperation and a sense of responsibility for the result. Several people eventually contribute to the workshop purpose and all will have different reasons for being involved and have different objectives for the outcome. Reasons for participation originate in a sense of responsibility to discuss the issues and contribute to results pertinent to individual goals. The contents under a book cover and language used by workshop participants for documentation provide general guidelines for selecting team members. Using the Document Life Cycle model, books can be considered from a participation for quality point of view.

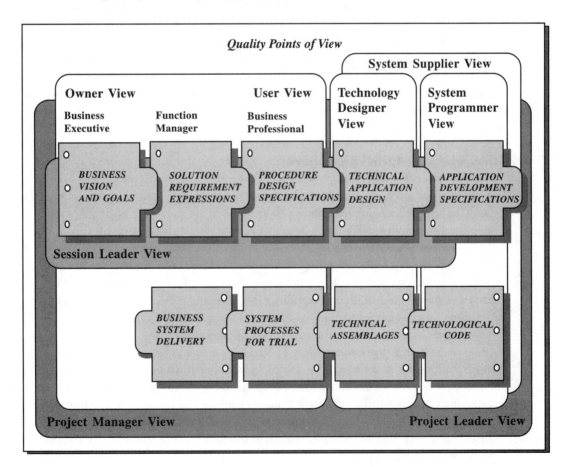

BUSINESS QUALITY POINTS OF VIEW

In the preceding model, corresponding levels of system development documents are illustrated in areas which typify responsibilities for quality. Individual points of view for quality will have a lot to do with job responsibilities and measurements for success. In a JAD workshop, several viewpoints for quality emerge as the team members describe different roles and responsibilities for success at work. Generally, business objectives for quality will be to do with an easy-to-use system which supports the daily operations and management reporting needs. Technology objectives for quality will have more to do with implementing a least cost system which is easy to design for user requirements, quick to assemble, and performs to expectations.

For business representation, a *Business Executive* point of view for quality will be that responding to or causing change for the continued financial strength and operational success of an organization. An executive will be interested in management controls and reporting information needed to manage existing and new business and observe trends in order to make strategic management decisions. In the context of JAD, the executive sponsor is responsible for providing vision, setting goals, establishing the guidelines for success, and authorizing and directing team effort.

The *Function Manager* point of view deals with the administration of business resources and monitoring service levels of the operations involved. In business planning, the manager is responsible for describing the business environment and issues of concern, defining information sources, and providing statements of direction for systems development including management policies needed for implementation. For procedure design specifications, a function manager may be the executive sponsor for a meeting and in this case provides the guidelines for success and authorizes team participation in detail design analysis.

A *Business Professional* point of view for quality focuses on the procedures and operations involved in conducting business. Business professionals are responsible for defining procedural activities and methods required to do business. As team members they describe specific information used in business operations and system interactions for department communications and work records and summary reporting.

TECHNICAL QUALITY POINTS OF VIEW

For technical representation, a *Technology Designer* or *System Supplier* view of quality deals with the selection and implementation of technological solutions to business problems. For a business application, this will be the assembly of computer hardware and software and the integration of new system functions and interfaces with other systems. A technology designer must understand how the JAD process assists design analysis and how to integrate business contributions with other information needed for systems development. A technology designer may also be a project leader with overall responsibility for development. For this reason, a designer should provide analysis guidelines for the outcome of a workshop and ensure the compatibility between team documents and various contiguous development processes.

A *System Programmer* view of quality concerns creating machine language to access information and make effective use of system capabilities with optimum and safe performance. A system programmer may not be as involved in the JAD process as the technology designer but has similar responsibilities regarding the use of a workshop approach for design information. A *System Supplier* with similar responsibilities and views of quality is also concerned with marketing, technical assistance, and training from support groups for their products and services.

JAD QUALITY POINTS OF VIEW

A *Project Manager* or *Project Leader* view of quality relates to implementing the scope of business system requirements within a specific time frame and managing budget funds while competing for skilled and available resources–all mutually constraining and conflicting criteria for achieving quality. A project manager usually has more business interests, while a project leader is usually stronger in technical knowledge. Perhaps one person with a different title, a project leader may be from a business or technical area and has the responsibility to understand JAD processes for business analysis and is able to integrate the technique into system development methods. The leader has the responsibility to coordinate JAD activities and ensure that team members have the experience and qualifications for good participation.

A *Session Leader* point of view for quality deals more with the implementation of an interactive design technique which ensures the involvement of all parties in comprehensive analysis of a business environment. The session leader is responsible for creating the workshop structure, the acquisition and organization of workshop materials, and the preparedness of team members to participate and contribute to the JAD process. The session leader is involved in all the preparation steps and interacts with all levels of business and technical representation. Ultimately the session leader is responsible for the success of the workshop and the ability for the team to debate the issues and contribute to a discussion document in such a way that it provides the information needed to enhance understanding for the development process.

The role of notekeeping will be supported by one or two people from either or both business or technical areas. In addition to their own views of quality, they are responsible for documenting business and technical decisions to a level of detail which is clear and appropriate for the next stage of systems development.

FOUR BASIC STEPS

The JAD process involves four basic steps to plan and prepare materials for the meeting and conduct the workshop. The first step allows the session leader to become familiar with the project and provides an explanation of the JAD approach for system developers. This involves a meeting with the project leader to discuss the development plan and how to utilize JAD to enhance the process. This step should start a draft document in the background pages as general notes, and in the Management Guideline forms to begin to write a statement of purpose. With notes for project purpose, the session leader can next talk about the level of detail expected from the meeting and outline the analysis guidelines on the same page as the purpose statement. Continued conversation provides notes on the following Scope and Objectives and Assumptions pages.

As the session leader becomes more familiar with the assignment, he or she uses any illustration which comes to mind to present an interpretation of the business environment as a model to better describe the situation. Invariably this leads to more discussion and jointly worked revisions to notes and illustrations. Existing illustrations may be found or new diagrams drafted for later use in the meeting.

Next, the forms and draft materials are organized as a workbook summary to take to the executive sponsor and use as a basis for discussion to ask questions, review the purpose, and clarify the guidelines for analysis. In this meeting, the session leader can introduce the JAD approach using an executive brochure, and the project leader can refer to the process already started in the workbook. He or she continues to demonstrate workshop involvement in reviewing the agenda, scope, and objectives pages to decide who can best participate in the meeting. People are usually selected from the areas mentioned in the scope for their experience skills and politically for their acknowledged support for management objectives.

Depending on the magnitude of the assignment and the politics involved, a business planning workshop could involve from five to twenty people in a one- to three-day meeting. A system specification workshop could involve four to fifteen people in a two- to four-day meeting. Getting the group of people involved to meet in one place at the same time is usually more of a challenge than the preparation. For this reason, the elapsed time is normally set by a workshop date chosen to match the availability of team members rather than the time to accumulate workbook pages. In some situations, this means that a meeting can occur within a few days or wait several weeks after the request for a workshop. The project manager should review the allocation of resources needed and the administration required to implement a workshop. Usually the project leader makes the phone calls to discuss the time and place for a meeting, prepares a covering letter for the executive sponsor to sign, and sends out invitations. Typically, the elapsed time to the workshop will be one to four weeks and includes a few preparation steps.

The second step is described as the *workshop orientation* for the session leader and team members. In this step, draft materials developed in step one are reviewed by certain team members and tested for acceptance and appropriateness for use in a workshop. This might involve a demonstration of the process and, as with previous staff work, it will probably result in a few edits and minor revisions to the structure and content. The main goal in this step is to ensure that the team understands the intent of management guideline pages and meaning in solution guideline illustrations. The session leader should also ensure that the team can work with the discussion materials using common language for debate.

For a business planning document, question forms provide the basic reference for discussion. Typically an orientation meeting is provided before the meeting. The workbook prepared so far is presented to team members who become acquainted with the process and fill out selected forms to the extent possible and return them for use in the workshop. For a design specifications document, an activity model provides the basis for discussion and the orientation takes place in interviews with function managers or department supervisors before the workshop. In this meeting, the session leader and the technology designer learn about area functions and business processes to create a Business Activity Model to outline system solution guidelines for discussion. For all workshops at various levels of detail, analysis structures are planned and adapted and workshop materials to be assembled are prepared using the book building process described previously.

The third step is described as *materials preparation* and is the time taken to create draft documents and workshop exhibits for discussion. For business planning documents, this will be the compilation of question forms filled out and returned by team members using the workbook and guidelines provided during the orientation meeting. For business design documents, this will be a procedure design scenario of screens and reports proposed by the technology designer using system requirements defined in previous business planning documents and work activity model solution guidelines prepared by the session leader. The latest revisions are assembled to be photocopied and bound with dividers for each participant to receive a workbook for the meeting. Overhead transparencies of each workbook page are prepared and taken with workbooks and any other presentation materials to the meeting room where a working environment is set up for the team.

WORKSHOP READY MATERIALS

The fourth step is described as the *workshop process*, and it is the time when the team is brought together to discuss the topics and workbook materials in the meeting. The agenda is implemented through workbook pages, and the process is explained in the first few pages of the document. Team analysis starts in the Management Guidelines divider. It is in these forms that the first revisions are made to document consensus as the team reviews previous contributions. With this initial workshop experience, team comments are used to continuously critique and change page contents. In the process, Solution Guidelines illustrations are presented to crossreference analysis materials. Presentation materials already used may be revised or added to. Through progressive discussion, the team provides context and content to make the workbook material realistic to common opinion. The results represent consensus for system requirements and design specifications. As the workbook pages change, the solution guidelines may need to be revised to be representative of and relevant to analysis and remain in tune with conversational documents. While the future system users focus on business requirements, system developers join in to support discussion and provide technical advice for alternative methods and cost considerations for business automation. Jointly the team becomes more involved and makes decisions about the business and technical solutions for systems development.

The process is repeated in a conversation loop to make solution guideline illustrations and all relevant documents more responsive to the business scope and objectives described in the management guideline pages. The session leader maintains discussion with questions and summary revisions to the workbook content using overhead transparencies and other presentation materials for all to see and comment on. If needed, the session leader or a participant might create new materials or additions on a supply of blank overhead foils or flip chart pages. As agreement is reached, the meeting document is improved by note keepers who write business or technical addendums in their own workbooks. The revised overhead transparencies and notes and other illustrations are then captured in a documentation system and printed immediately on overhead materials and periodically on paper to update team workbooks during the meeting. Shortly after the workshop, the document is published with a summary overview for review and approval to continue with the next development activity. The steps are summarized in the following chart.

JAD Process - Four Basic Steps

STEP 1 - **Management Guidelines**

STEP 2 - **Workshop Orientation**

STEP 3 - **Materials Preparation**

STEP 4 - **Workshop Meeting**

- **1 - 4 Days**

- **Structured approach and workshop process**

   - Question Forms Based Analysis, or
   - Business Activity Model Analysis

- **Session leader guidance**

- **Future system users define business design**

- **System developers define technical design**

- **Note business and technical decisions**

Workshop Process
Analysis loop

Define business situation

↓

Describe and test ideas and solutions

↓

Document requirements and specifications

Documentation loop

↓

Add complementing notes and illustrations

JAD WORKSHOP PROCESS

Using either a forms based or activity model based analysis structure, the workshop process is managed in a conversation and documentation loop shown in the above summary. Under the guidance of a session leader and using workbook references, people describe business situations. They explain change improvements and ideas to solve problems, and define requirements and specifications to be documented. Technicians provide advice about implementation alternatives and notekeepers document decisions reached through debate.

Generally, the workbook content is presented as the meeting agenda and the pages prepared on overhead transparencies are used to guide analysis. The session leader summarizes conversation and illustrates results by making revisions to presentation materials to show interim design as people direct additional comments for the team to reach consensus. The loop is repeated to achieve conclusions through conversation with the realization of team decisions through the evidence of revisions to workbook materials.

As work progresses, comparisons should be made to objectives stated for the business and a general understanding about team decisions will surface from the demonstration of results. In this, the analysis structure is used to validate results to expectations to substantiate team decisions for a quality design. Positive results are motivational, and the process becomes self-sustaining after a short start-up period. Through feelings of success, creativity emerges and new ideas blend into conversation. Additions and new results might be developed on a separate supply of overhead transparencies and flip chart pages.

The agenda and prepared organization for discussion and methods for documentation are designed to be mutually supportive. In addition to a structure for business analysis, the workshop process is used to organize the expression of thought into workbook pages and to compile the resulting materials into a useful format for systems development. Using the prescribed divider for conversation approach, workshop materials are maintained, and revisions and additions can be made in context to design ideas.

WORKSHOP DOCUMENTATION

The first key materials involved in the conversation and documentation loop will be the pages in the Management Guidelines divider. For business planning, most of the analysis materials involved in conversation are in the Analysis Forms divider. For business design they are in the Design Scenario divider. Additional notes and illustrations used to support analysis are placed in the Solution Guidelines or Appendices divider.

While the session leader maintains group memory using conversation summaries and revisions to presentation materials, actual notekeeping in the workbook should be supervised by a project leader. Depending on the type of detail and amount of information, one or two people will be asked to write business and technical decisions to a level of detail required for the development step. The documentation process is enhanced by capturing notes and illustrations in a notekeeping system for immediate printing of results for review and rework during the meeting. The completed workbook represents team consensus. Notes are recompiled and published for review and perhaps further revisions and subsequent approval.

The meeting is for the purpose of describing management and operational needs for information and defining requirement expressions and procedure design specifications within the scope of design. Most of the knowledge exchange should be from a business perspective. A recommended ratio of four business professionals to one data processing technician provides a good balance for information exchange.

WORKSHOP DOCUMENTATION

The ratio of business involvement to technical involvement changes over the development life cycle. In business planning and design analysis, one or more workshops might be needed—and the ratio remains about four to one. In the transition to technology development, the ratio reverses as future system users become less involved until a delivered system is available and involves the users again. During system testing the ratio may be equal or two to one in favor of system users who now have a specific role in system testing. This may or may not involve a workshop for quality assurance when business design as requirement input documents are reviewed for comparison to delivery outputs for system results. The JAD participation requirements are described in the following summary.

JAD Participation Requirements

- **Session Leader**
  Personable with good communication skills
  Experienced in the JAD technique
  Impartial and non-dictatorial leadership style
  Knowledgeable with business and some systems background
  Unbiased in guiding workshop administration
  Avoids designing business and technical solutions

- **Business Participation**
  Represents levels from management to administrators
  Exhibits sound business knowledge and background experience
  Tends to represent senior business people with a vested interest
  Contributes to business analysis, willing to define necessary details
  Assumes responsibility for system quality
  Has decision authority to promote new ideas

- **Technology Developer or Application Supplier Participation**
  Systems Analyst with responsibility to implement system technology
  Has current systems knowledge, technically competent
  Contributes to technical analysis and systems design

- **Business and Technical Scribes**
  Have subject knowledge and experience
  Have interactive discussion and notekeeping skills

- **Special Interest Attendees and Expert Witnesses**
  Quality Assurance Personnel
  Data Base Administrator
  Audit or Risk Analysts
  Systems Operations and Training Personnel
  Legal or Regulatory Consultants
  Union Representative
  Business Systems Architect

- **Observers**
  Quiet people in a watching and learning role

SELECTING TEAM MEMBERS

As the session leader, you will be involved with all the workshop participants and others involved in systems development. In the meeting, you will be very interactive with the team, posing questions, rephrasing responses, and noting summaries from several points of view to express consensus through documentation. Business representatives and system developers should also be involved in debate and provide ongoing conversation. Expert witnesses and special interest attendees may be called upon occasionally when particular advice is needed from specialist knowledge. Scribe participation will also involve ongoing conversation to clarify resolution of issues and create notes in the workbook. Observers should not be in conversation with anyone during the meeting.

Team knowledge is the primary factor for a successful meeting. For this reason it will be beneficial for you to consider team qualifications beforehand. The meeting will be intensive and the structure will quickly exhaust team knowledge if your team is inexperienced in business and technical topics. A session leader might influence, but would have no choice in the selection of team members. If there is any doubt about team qualifications or individual or group capabilities, you should recommend alternative or additional candidates or consider providing education and briefings before the workshop. The premise for successful participation is based on participants' experience in the areas involved, business topics defined in the scope of design, and the knowledge needed to understand management objectives and work through analysis materials to achieve them.

PERSONALITIES AND WORK STYLES

It is also beneficial that you consider individual personalities and work styles before you go into the meeting. It is more important to include people because of their experience and potential to contribute to the design product than exclude them because of personalities. A strong character will probably attempt to control the meeting or insist on discussing topics without due consideration to the meeting process. Your agenda should be capable of dealing with the issues in the scope of design. Ultimately, the session leader is responsible for the success of the meeting by managing the agenda for the sake of the process. In this you should be prepared for most eventualities and respond to people situations as they occur.

For many in the workshop meeting, the role of the session leader is not an important factor, or even one to be considered. Some participants will have their own agendas or be anxious to say whatever is on their mind. Generally, people will not cooperate with a process unless it appears to help them advance personal goals. The session leader must promote the organization for complete analysis and pace debate through each topic. Your ability to manage the meeting and assist the analysis process will be impacted if the planned agenda and meeting organization is disrupted by people unable to trust the process, or more directly, unable to gain trust in you.

PLAN TO AVOID TROUBLE

Foresight and planning will avoid trouble. It is better that you appreciate how key contributors recognize success before the workshop. This could involve interviews with selected participants before the meeting, or be covered in an orientation meeting or in the opening remarks for the workshop. As you discover how individuals measure success, you can explain how they can participate in the agenda and promote views for personal goals. In this way you establish expectations and attitudes for involvement as a team member and uphold your own role as a mediator and session leader for individual and group success.

TEAM SELECTION

Business team members should be selected for their ability to express ideas and make decisions. In a business planning workshop, the team will probably include executive and functional manager positions and people with a good knowledge of company direction and management policies. In a business design workshop, the team will probably include senior business professionals from management and supervisory positions and people with operational experience and good knowledge of business practices and procedures. While several people may be involved in a business topic, circumstances may require more than one person responsible for a decision. People with similar responsibilities from several divisional locations may work together for a team decision. In some situations, such as a person recently promoted from a different area, management decision responsibility and experience may not be available in the same individual. In these circumstances two people may be needed to attend to explain and resolve business issues.

In addition to business representation, information processing interests are represented in the meeting. Technicians should be selected for their project responsibility and knowledge of current and future strategic system technologies. Whenever possible, it is beneficial to match job levels and seniority between a future system user and a system developer so that the team can make joint commitments for results and be confident in follow through. Again, if decision responsibility and technical knowledge is not available in the same person, other people may be required to provide technical perspectives.

WORKSHOP NOTE TAKING

A key role in the meeting is fulfilled by one or two people who work as scribes and use their workbooks to document team decisions. In a business planning workshop, pages and forms are shown on overhead projectors to be revised by the session leader; one scribe will be sufficient to take supplemental notes. For typical workshop discussion, a business representative or project leader is usually responsible for documentation.

In a business design workshop, procedure specifications are considered in the analysis of business information presented as a suggested operational dialogue. In a design scenario, pages are shown as screens and reports on overhead projector material revised by the session leader. Two additional people are required to keep more detailed documents. For the perspectives provided in the meeting, notekeeping is best supported by two people experienced in business or technical terminology. The documentation role is dual and not one of merely recording. People selected for notekeeping should be qualified to express thoughts and question the issues and contribute to design while they document decisions clearly and correctly.

CONTRIBUTING CONVERSATION

Team members will be involved in an ongoing discussion to weigh business processes against business automation based on a potential benefit of technological design. Initially an idea should be promoted to become accepted amongst others when the information can be exchanged to determine the best idea for the best solution. This routine occurs in most situations and may span several levels of workshop detail. Occasionally, it will be necessary to include other contributors to provide specialist knowledge and information to help in understanding to reach agreement. These people might provide information from industry knowledge, auditing, data base design and administration, development technologies, system operations, vendor software, project management, technical training, union, government and legislation, legal, or any other specialist or consulting skills needed to complete the decision making process.

OBSERVERS

Other people may want to observe the proceedings for one reason or another and attend the meeting on the condition they do not participate in team discussion nor attempt to influence decisions or the discussion process. Typically a session leader in training provides assistance in the preparation for a workshop. In the meeting, a trainee watches the process and notes the proceedings to understand and become ready to implement a future JAD workshop.

WORKSHOP VENUE

Now that you have considered why people should be involved and planned what they will be involved in, all that remains is to decide where and when to meet and how to work together. The workshop location is a factor for success. A site away from the normal place of work is recommended for complete involvement in a meeting with few interruptions for the people who may otherwise be tempted to handle routine business.

Another good reason for providing a special place to meet is to emphasize the importance of the event and give recognition to the value of individual contributions and team effort.

CHAPTER EIGHT

JAD–A Meeting Place

ILLUSTRATED JAD

Many companies have access to training facilities and corporate office buildings away from the normal place of work. Some of these can be quite palatial and not commonly known about or normally unavailable to people involved in a workshop.

In an assignment involving an insurance company in Connecticut, a project manager took a workshop team to a management training center some ten miles out of the city. The location was idyllic–with spectacular views it was a perfect setting for creating a sense of remoteness from work pressures and for people to become creative thinkers and deal with situations otherwise thought of as beyond their scope.

The meeting started well because of the attention to detail for creature needs and comfortable surroundings to work in. The good feelings about the situation and workshop environment enhanced the team attitude which continued throughout the meeting. It ended successfully with a strong sense of accomplishment and good will. Well worth the effort and the relatively small additional expense of catering to people's needs.

ROOM ARRANGEMENTS

Apart from the setting, room arrangements are important for success. The room should have open space to accommodate up to fifteen or twenty team participants and, if needed, up to eight special interest people, and a work area for two support people. A larger room will be needed if several observers attend. A symmetrical horseshoe table arrangement for the team with additional tables and seating at the rear of the room will provide a good seating plan for those involved. Typically, each of the three sides for the team area should seat six people in comfort. Tabletops should have light colored surfaces with rounded edges and a front overhang or modesty drapes from the top to full length or three-quarters down. The tables should provide clearance for the chair dimensions and adequate leg room. Chairs should be the typical good office chair with moderate cushioning and comfortable support, perhaps with an adjustable back rest. Chairs with armrests are not usually recommended because of the extra width they take and potential for accidental nudges and finger crunches when people move. Basically, comfort is of the foremost concern.

From a working perspective, the horseshoe seating arrangement shown provides good viewing positions for team members to see each other and to look at the presentation area at

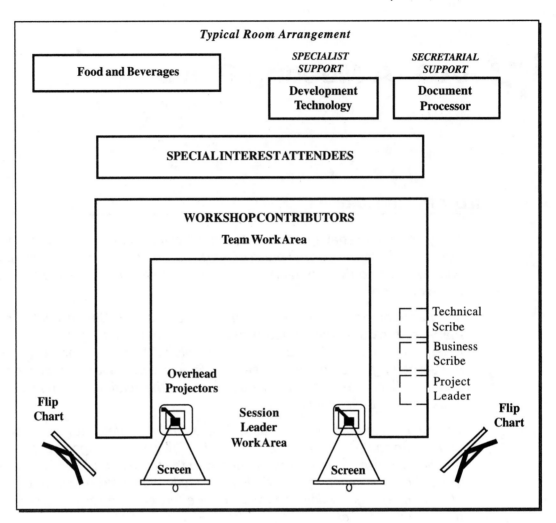

the front of the room. It allows any additional special interest people to see the discussion materials and to make eye contact with the session leader without disturbing the team. Support people working with a document processor or a development technology will also be able to listen to conversation and see the presentation materials generated from the team work area. Two overhead projectors at the front of the room aimed at screens, or preferably a wall-sized white drawing board behind the session leader, are needed for presentation materials. In addition, one or two flip chart stands, or wall chart pads at the front of the room are needed for temporary pen work and drawings.

WORKSHOP MECHANICS

The above illustration shows a typical seating arrangement for a JAD meeting room. Each team member receives a workbook, a tent name card, and a pen at his or her place at the conference table. Seating arrangements need not be preplanned except for the people involved in the mechanics of the workshop process. This includes the session leader who will be active with the presentation media, the project leader involved with people taking notes near the projectors, and optional support staff at nearby workstations.

The project leader and session leader now work together and use workbook and supporting materials to take participants through the prepared agenda. The session leader places the first overhead transparency of the book title cover sheet on the left overhead projector view and uses the image to gain attention and start the meeting with conversations about the assignment. Next, the table of contents is displayed on the right overhead projector to explain the workbook material in front of each participant. During this administration, the session leader should have time to ask people to write their names on the tent cards provided with the workbooks.

ESTABLISHED PROCEDURE

When the basic opening remarks are completed, the session leader then replaces the workbook cover sheet transparency with the workshop agenda overhead and explains the sequence of prepared workshop activities. If the meeting involves additional speakers, they can be asked to participate in the sequence shown in the prepared agenda. The process continues using one overhead transparency on one projector and displaying the next transparency on the other. The showing and replacing of sequential workbook pages is a presentation technique. In this way, one projector provides a previous group memory image while another provides a current work area and results image. Progressively displaying materials puts numerous discussion points into context while the team provides the comments you need to correct and complete the pages.

From the various comments made, the session leader can revise workbook materials shown overhead. A washable felt tip marker is recommended so that ideas can be reworked and documented easily. In this, several thoughts can be expressed and addressed in the process of reaching team decisions and consensus. While summary changes are made to presentation materials, the project leader should supervise note keeping as others provide supplementary notes to their workbooks. For each topic completed, the session leader can pass along the worked overhead transparencies to the project leader who may then bundle them with additional written materials and hand them to a secretary to update and reprint workbook pages. Typically, a good secretary will have already typed much of the displayed notes. Turnaround time for revised pages should be a matter of moments to provide refreshed overhead transparencies and a few minutes for team handouts during an appropriate break.

When participants use the JAD book building process in a workshop, administration mechanics will be quite straightforward and the above-mentioned equipment will be sufficient for a productive workshop. The pace of the meeting will vary and on occasions be quite fast. Workbook materials provide an easy-to-use environment in which everyone should keep pace and most share in conversational decision making. The quality of your facilitation role will be measured by how well you organize written thoughts to the basic references contained in your analysis structure. Your own pace of finding and adding to material for update with a felt tip marker or using handy wipes to erase mistakes and make changes should be fast enough for visual appreciation without delay to conversation. For this reason, only conventional equipment is needed and recommended to support your role of demonstrating consensus through presentation updates. Other equipment designed to support similar processes at an equally fast pace might be used if it provides an advantage to record keeping. An electronic white board with print capability could be used as an alternative to a flip chart. At some point, in presentation summaries perhaps, it might be beneficial to use an electronic slate placed on the overhead projector or a large display connected to a computer output.

ARE WE COMFORTABLE

A meeting is not a meeting without refreshments. Food and beverages are best set up at the back of the room or better in an adjoining hallway or kitchenette. Coatrooms and washrooms should be nearby. If possible, a JAD room could have access to a hallway or a meeting place with phones and casual seating arrangements to use during lunch and occasional breaks. The purpose of the meeting room is to hold conversation and work with several presentation media. For this, sound and lighting and comfortable surroundings are important factors for success. People need to see what is going on and hear what is said from many angles. Your voice should be clear to everyone and microphone assistance is not recommended for anyone. Overhead projector images should be in line of sight and large enough for easy reading. Lights need to be positioned and controlled to provide good contrast for screen images and flip chart drawings. Normal split lighting between front and back, and spotlights on table work areas should be sufficient.

WORKSHOP AGENDA

Managing group dynamics is the key to success for maintaining workshop pace and team involvement. Your role as facilitator must not be compromised by sources of distraction which may affect your ability to hear or be heard and involved in conversation. Although you might get used to annoyances, and treat them subconsciously—distractions become irritable to everybody and draw on much needed energy. These include noise, light, and heat all of which should be managed to comfortable levels. Access is recommended from the back of the room to reduce distractions caused in routine visits for caterers and other providers or guests to enter the meeting. Floor carpeting will soften the noises normally occurring from people traffic. Depending on size and exposure to daytime shifts in sunlight, windows may have to be covered with translucent or dark drapes to reduce the ambient light around overhead screen images and maintain good contrast for the viewing audience. Distractions from the front of the room can be particularly disruptive to the session leader's role. Any equipment here will be a source of noise and heat and apparatus should be limited to only essential items for presentation. Overhead projectors should be selected to be the same model with similar image patterns. They should be quiet or muffled and heat output should be directed to fan away from people and loose paper items on the table. Office equipment such as printers and photocopiers should be in an adjoining room, or at least located at the back of the room. Once you make arrangements try to keep them. As people settle into their surroundings it can be quite disruptive to the process, not to mention inconvenient, to change locations.

Based on your planning and preparation in the four basic steps you create a workshop agenda. The following sequence is typical for most JAD meetings.

JAD Workshop Agenda

Executive Sponsors Opening Remarks

Introduction and Administration

Analysis Process Overview

Management Guidelines

Analysis Topics

Action Items

Summary Presentation and Closing Remarks

STARTING THE MEETING

There is a certain amount of unpredictability in workshop activity and you should avoid being held accountable to expected agenda times. Day start, end, and break times and location details in the agenda footnotes are sufficient for attendance. Although the agenda will have gone out with the invitation letter, it is also in the workbook for you to start the meeting. For the workshop, the executive sponsor may want to open the meeting and introduce you and turn the meeting over to your leadership. Alternatively, you may introduce yourself and start the meeting using the first pages of the workbook to proceed into the agenda then ask the sponsor to make the opening remarks. You will now benefit from a previous meeting with the sponsor to discuss the points to make when starting the meeting. You might want to use the following list of remarks for your executive sponsor to prepare a few words to open the meeting and set the tone for the work assignment.

Points to Use in the Executive Sponsor's Opening Remarks

Significance of the Project

Move towards the future
Respond to changing market trends and customer demands
Improve service levels and operating efficiency
Establish a milestone in the business system development plan
Need accurate and meaningful management information

Selection of Team Members

Representing several key areas
Selected for individual skills and experience
Recognized as contributors to company objectives

Use of JAD Technique

Business-involved approach to systems development
Productivity increased through team consensus
Objective analysis facilitated by an experienced session leader
Maximum effort over minimum time
Business emphasis for user stated requirements

Expectations of the Workshop

Corporate and departmental business views included
Unique chance for creative and futuristic thinking
Improved interaction between staff activities and system function
Clear requirement and design specifications
Potential for rapid systems development

WORKSHOP PARTICIPATION

After the opening remarks, it is important that you to start up a conversational environment quickly and easily. To do this you can refer to the agenda again and review scheduled items to set expectations for the pace of the meeting and the time of the first break after topics in the Management Guidelines divider. You should explain that the team will spend most of the time discussing analysis materials after the first break up to a final review of action items and closing remarks.

Before you remove the agenda page, you should ask if there are any questions about procedure. As you move on you should also set an expectation for pace and meeting results delivery. These will be slow at first and more rapid as the meeting continues. Typically an executive sponsor does not stay for workshop details and leaves after the opening remarks or during the first break after the team review of management guidelines. If it is planned, you could mention the executive sponsor's return for a review of workshop results in the closing remarks. You can refer to the people involved in a summary presentation and the time you have allowed for materials preparation.

WORKSHOP ADMINISTRATION FOR PARTICIPATION

Next, to start conversational participation, you can show the team names list and point out your own name and clarify your own role as an unbiased workbook administrator. You can emphasize that you are not qualified to tell them how to do business or develop a system. Never break this promise. They should only expect you to conduct the meeting. Still referring to the list, ask the participants to introduce themselves and explain their role in the organization and what they expect to achieve by being involved in the meeting. After each introduction, or if a team member has made a significant point you want to amplify, you should add commentary to their remarks in a positive manner, and relate the goals to the meeting objectives and the methods you will use to facilitate the agenda for results. In particular, when the people assigned to notetaking introduce themselves, you should explain their role in the context of how you will administer meeting outputs. Once the participants have introduced themselves, you might remark on the overall team qualifications for a good result and thank them for participating. At this point if other people are present you can ask them to introduce themselves and clarify their reasons for being there.

The above introductions period is an important phase for you to exchange pleasantries and become familiar with the group. It is a time for you to make a mental note of posture and expression of individuals and team attitude. The exchange also gives team members an opportunity to understand individual roles and to see their own potential to contribute to the result. As you sense the tone of the meeting, you can also emphasize the opportunity to discuss the issues and clarify their responsibility to participate as a group.

In returning to the agenda to conclude the administration, you can mention the timing for work, the frequency of breaks, and the location of facilities near the meeting room. You may announce or ask about the food and beverages so that whoever made the arrangements can explain the plan. Finally, you should ask if there are any questions about the workshop administration. People will probably want to know about getting messages and rules for smoking. To avoid telephone activity in the room you can give out a phone number and invite the team to take calls through a message service to the meeting. However, you should remind the team to manage calls during breaks as long as a reply can wait. Smoking is not allowed in many locations and you should clarify smoking rules by asking the team to agree on the matter.

WORKSHOP TERMS OF REFERENCE

With the administration covered, you can turn to the background divider in the book and review the events up to the meeting. This is usually a brief mention or it may be a more formal discussion or a presentation in the agenda. No more than thirty minutes should elapse before you proceed to the next item on the agenda and discuss the terms of reference for the workshop. In this you display the divider page for the Management Guidelines and ask the team to turn the divider in their books to find the page. Using the workshop mechanics described above, you display each of the pages and take the time to reach and document agreement. This discussion will normally take you to the time of the first morning break.

After this, the next item on the agenda is to explain the analysis guidelines and apply them for the remaining discussion materials. At this time you should present the technique using an illustration which describes the relationship of forms for a business planning workshop or a relationship in work activity definitions for a procedure design specifications meeting.

Workshop mechanics are best explained in context of team roles and the support roles provided by system analysts and workshop notekeepers. Once explained continue to use the workshop technique for discussion and documentation.

Now you have established the environment for debate and the logistics are in place for good business analysis. The team has great expectation for the process and your skills in leading debate. You will have greater confidence in doing the job if you have a better understanding of basic JAD structures for concept analysis, requirements analysis, and specifications analysis loops shown in the Document Life Cycle Model.

ADVANCING BUSINESS PLANS

ad-vance v. To go forward; to progress, move towards completion; to cause an event to happen sooner than planned or expected; to suggest, propose; to advance a theory, progressive, in front of most others.

busi-ness n. Regular employment; profession; occupation; one's personal affair, concern, duty; something requiring attention.

plan n. A design for construction, layout, system, etc.; a *formulated scheme* setting out stages of procedure; *"a plan for the production of a book;"* a proposed or intended course of action.

for-mu-la n. A symbolic representation of composition, constitution, or configuration; a statement expressed in symbols showing the relationship of interrelated facts; form of words defining doctrine, principle, etc.; verbal phrase or any set form accepted as conventional; form of words for ritual or ceremonial usage.

scheme n. A detailed plan or system; a carefully constructed arrangement; a secret, dishonest or malicious plot; an official project or plan.

CHAPTER NINE

JAD–Business Vision Analysis for System Plans

FORMS BASED TECHNIQUE FOR VISION AND GOALS ANALYSIS

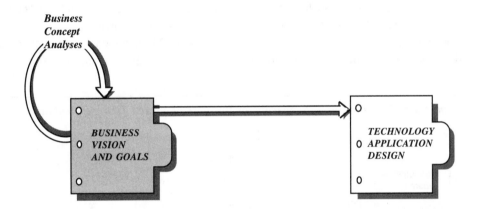

The concept of relating levels of systems design detail to a workshop technique is shown in the Documentation Life Cycle and Analysis Technique charts explained in previous chapters. The above summary illustrates life cycle documents involved in the *Concept Analysis* loop in terms of Business Vision and Goals and Technology Application Design. You can implement a Business Planning workshop to discuss business concepts, define business solution guidelines and first high level technical information using a Forms Based Analysis technique for business and technology plans.

ORGANIZATION FOR DEBATE

Described as a book building process, the JAD concept uses a piecemeal approach to discuss workbook materials in dividers for conversation. For Business Planning Documents, concept analysis is supported in the *Management Guidelines* and *Solution Guidelines* dividers. Following the JAD book building approach, the pages are organized to be in sequence for the information which defines the Vision and Goals for an assignment. The key to success is that the organization provides intuitive references to subject material and uses a familiar language for discussion. For the best results the session leader should review the form documents to ensure everyone involved in preparation activities is satisfied the arrangement is conducive to sharing ideas and exchanging information in a workshop setting.

To round out a business planning document, background information can be added to provide a general understanding about the assignment. These important sources of reference material are usually included in the Background and the Solution Guidelines dividers. Equally important but occasionally referenced materials can be included after the Appendices divider. Solution Guideline references provided as business model illustrations should be selected to relate to the Management Guideline pages used to start the debate. It will be easier to explain the technique using a diagram to illustrate the workshop approach for the analysis sequence and documentation process.

FORMS BASED ANALYSIS

In the following diagram, the main divider headings used in a workshop agenda are shown as a sequence of workbook pages. Pages usually involved in concept analysis are numbered in the order used. Pages without sequence numbers are usually recorded as appendices for the references and details needed for general conversation. All the materials should be referenced in the Index divider.

Concept analysis is based around the form pages in the Management Guidelines divider described earlier. These forms lead to documenting business vision from a general discussion about

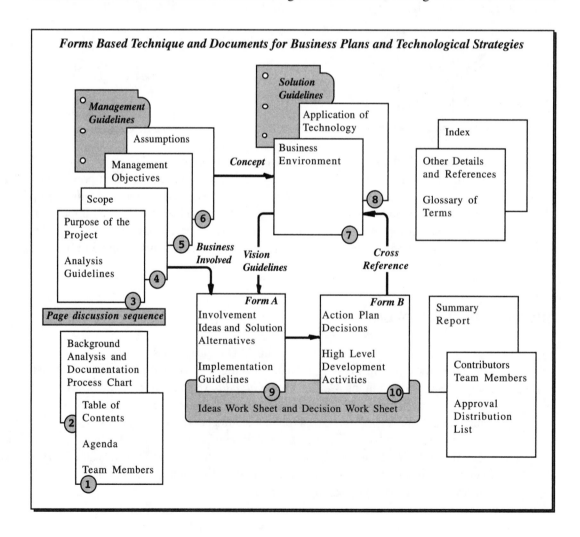

design decisions and other information to illustrate a business concept. Typical analysis is conducted and documented around the Management Guidelines and Solution Guidelines pages. Solution guidelines information is usually comprised of illustrations and supplementary notes to describe involvement as a working environment in which business and/or technological concepts can be shown supportive and applicable. Thoughtful analysis is best developed using an ideas and decisions work sheet to relate conversation as a point form summary to more detail. To complete analysis in notes for a business plan, a sequence for debate and a mechanism for documentation should be followed.

POINT FORM ANALYSIS

People from management levels may have fairly certain opinions about business concepts and applications for technology. Some people express ideas as if solutions are obvious and decisions made. In a business planning workshop for business concept analyses, solution guidelines are sometimes expressed as implementation requirements rather than ideas for evaluation and integration with other considerations for an overall purpose. Regardless of how ideas emerge, the session leader should follow the classic JAD communication model and illustrate current realities and demonstrate practical solutions from debate.

Information from workshop conversation about ideas as possible solutions will be very informative. In conversation related forms can be used to reference and clarify statements of scope, objectives, and assumptions. In this sense, when solution guidelines are discussed ideas can be explored to better understand the vision and to discover people's expectations for more acceptable change. Moreover, when general issues on these pages are decided, better direction for detailed plans will be obtained and unnecessary debate avoided when the focus on subsequent analyses is based on management direction.

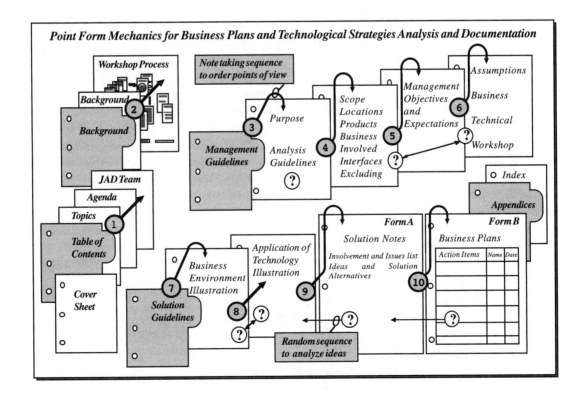

POINT FORM MECHANICS

The preceding mechanism involves only a few pages and the process is intuitive for most team members. Using the forms based analysis technique for business vision and goals, Management Guidelines forms are designed to organize thoughts about purpose and scope in concert with business objectives and vision for a result. Business vision is best illustrated in Solution Guidelines diagrams drawn to represent the proposed business and technical environments. Diagrams should be easy to understand with familiar language for the team to discuss solution ideas and make decisions and recommendations.

SCHEMATIC DIAGRAMS AND CLARIFYING NOTES

The various factors emerging from discussion and solution decisions are easier to sort out when work sheet forms are used to note issues and solution alternatives until several ideas have been discussed and consensus has been reached for a new vision. The technique to reach agreement is to document points of view and stated requirements as implementation alternatives on a work sheet page while ideas emerge and design plans are figured out. As results are demonstrated in note form and checked for realistic and acceptable theories in model illustrations, Solution Guideline diagrams and Management Guideline scope, objectives, and assumptions can be updated to complete the analysis and documentation. In ranking development alternatives, a design strategy will emerge explained in schematic diagrams and clarifying notes.

Analyzing solution alternatives will be complete when decision notes and illustrations are validated in terms of feasibility and commitment. These will represent management decisions for a business design with a strategy for people involvement and technology development. When information technologies are recommended, schematic illustrations usually explain a summary architecture for system hardware with high level outlines for an operational design shown as business information flows and labels for software applications. With design decisions noted, a list of implementation efforts and involvement can be reviewed as an action plan. In discussion, a second work sheet can be used to order various activities in terms of action items. Finally, as the activities are cross referenced to the overall design, people or areas responsible can be noted with dates to deliver results to the development process. To wrap up the meeting, the management objectives and expectations should be reviewed to validate the success of the result.

This level of workshop documents solution strategies and design recommendations to develop a new business environment with an action plan to implement business concepts with or without technological solutions. In another level of analysis, the JAD approach is adapted to discuss change opportunities and document more detailed descriptions of business processes designed to support vision and goals.

ILLUSTRATED JAD

In an assignment for a telephone company, senior managers were invited to a workshop meeting designed to discuss corporate strategies and plans for business in the 1990s. Strategies had been decided by company directors and the details of individual plans were to be worked out by area managers. As we developed the workshop approach, it was suggested that we use theme words already chosen to promote the goals for their corporate Vision 2000 project. These included five words all starting with the letter C to encourage ideas in concert with Corporate direction. Starting with the word "Customer" we listed the words on a poster-sized visual for group memory. We also documented summary statements from the corporate plan in the Management Guidelines and included the list of theme words on a page with other solution guideline illustrations.

In a one-day meeting, managers defined the scope of the assignment and key objectives and agreed to the need for mutual involvement in various business activities. During team discussion, we made reference to the theme as solutions and action items emerged for systems development. As the team described the issues, they were able to discuss ideas for business solutions and outlined a plan to develop a company-wide system for common business functions and shared information.

ADVANCING BUSINESS CONCEPTS

ad-vance v. To go forward; to progress, move towards completion, cause an event to happen sooner than planned or expected; to suggest, propose; to advance a theory, progressive, in front of most others.

busi-ness n. Regular employment, profession, occupation; one's personal affair, concern, duty; something requiring attention.

con-cept n. A thought or opinion, *vision*, general notion or idea, especially one formed by generalization from particular examples.

vi-sion n. The act of seeing or the ability to see; a picture formed in the mind; imaginative foresight (for the solution to a problem).

so-lu-tion n. The answer to a problem, the act, method, or process by which such an answer is obtained. (*Computer*) The act by which *technology* is *applied* to business problem solving processes.

CHAPTER TEN

ᒪᐧᒧ JAD—Change Analysis for Business
ᒣᓕ Plans and System Solutions

FORMS BASED TECHNIQUE FOR BUSINESS OPPORTUNITY AND PROCESS REDESIGN

When implementing the JAD communication concept, analysis starts in discussion about present realities to debate issues in terms of agreement for need to change with decisions and actions to implement change. Using the JAD book building approach and the preparation steps described earlier, people can better relate to a subject given a few pointers for conversation. In the case of

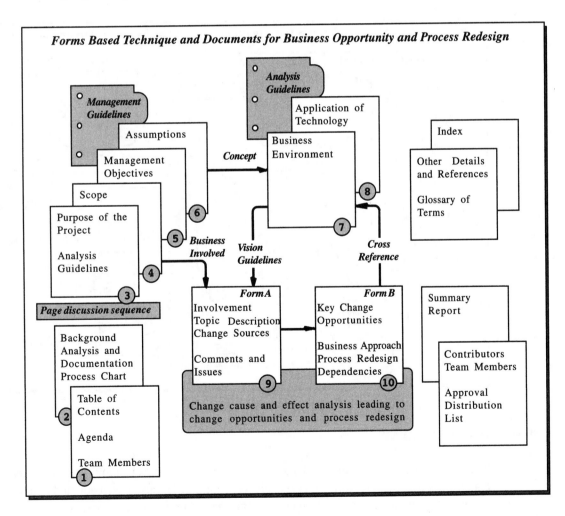

Forms Based Technique and Documents for Business Opportunity and Process Redesign

considering change, the session leader can refer to change cause and effect to raise topics for design analysis. In the preceding diagram, the work sheet analysis forms previously used to develop a plan become a more permanent record of design decisions. The involvement page is enhanced to list and describe change sources and then consider more definitive objectives and solution guidelines in terms of a new approach to business. In the following diagram, divider headings used in an agenda for business change analysis are shown with a sequence of workbook pages.

POINT FORM MECHANICS

Concept analysis is based on Management Guideline and Solution Guideline pages. The technique leads to documenting the sources and types of change effecting current business and detailed discussion about opportunities and decisions for a new business approach and process redesign. Solution Guidelines analysis is supplemented with change descriptions and related concerns to identify business opportunities and redefined business processes. Solution Guidelines and change analysis documents usually comprised of illustrations and notes to describe a working environment in which a new business approach or technology concept may be applied. For complete analysis, a sequence for debate and a mechanism for documentation are followed.

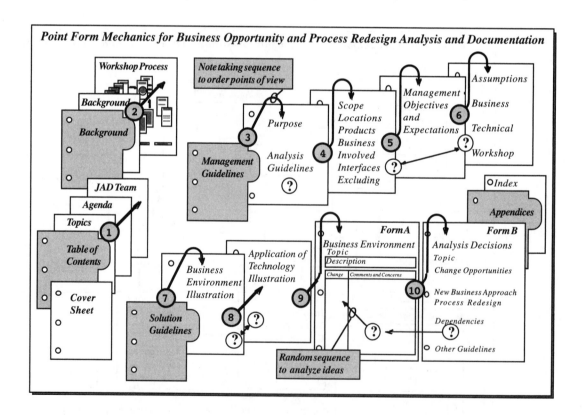

FORMS BASED ANALYSIS

The above mechanism involves only a few pages and the process is intuitive for most team members to follow. Using the forms based analysis technique for business vision and goals, the Management Guidelines forms are designed to organize thoughts about purpose and scope in concert with business vision and new objectives to respond to change. Business vision is best illustrated in Solution Guidelines diagrams drawn to represent proposed business and technical environments. Diagrams should be easy to understand with familiar language for the team to discuss ideas for change and recommend new business methods.

The above analysis structure supports discussion and exchange of information contained in forms and reference materials. Design analysis is conducted around two basic forms arranged to list change sources and opportunities for process redesign cross referenced to the concepts outlined as Solution Guidelines.

BASIC FORMS DESIGN

Two basic forms design provide an adaptive layout for analyzing change sources and process redesign opportunities. The forms can work for different topics and at different levels of detail. The first form is designed to describe an understanding of business concepts. It is used to document agreement about causes and types of change which affect or impact current methods to justify business redesign. The second form is arranged to document opportunities as expectations for new or redefined business processes. Analysis is balanced to further consider dependences and additional guidelines for practical change.

Typical Forms for Business Change Analysis and Process Redesign

BUSINESS CHANGE ANALYSIS   FORM A

TOPIC
Guidelines: Consider the above concept topic and provide a brief description. List key sources and types of change to analyze cause and effect in comments which explains the impact or issues about the business or raises opportunities.

DESCRIPTION   *(overview of the topic concept)*

CAUSE OF CHANGE	EFFECT, IMPACT, RISK FACTORS, CONCERNS, COMMENTS, ISSUES
(source or cause of change)	*(effect, impact, or risk due to change factors or things to know or be concerned about)*

PROCESS REDESIGN   FORM B

TOPIC
Guidelines: Consider the items and issues shown on the previous page to identify change opportunities. Explain what the change could mean and define business approaches and dependences to implement the change. Provide other guidelines and notes you feel would assist development.

FUNDAMENTAL CHANGE OPPORTUNITY
(principal change)

THIS MEANS
(alteration expressed as an expectation for results)

SUPPORTED BY A BUSINESS APPROACH
(process redesign to implement change)

DEPENDENCES
(requirements to implement change design)

OTHER GUIDELINES
(consequential needs and actions to support change)

For different levels of detail, the session leader can use one or more of either form to discuss the issues. At a high level for business concepts, individual forms may be sufficient to discuss key change opportunities in a brief meeting. Forms based techniques can be extended to multiple pages for additional information. For more detailed, longer than one day meetings, multiple forms can be organized to a topic index with the Analysis Forms divider to arrange material in workbook sequence. You can adapt the preceding forms to discuss and document fundamental changes and new approaches to business practices and procedures.

LOGISTICS FOR SUCCESSFUL BUSINESS VISION AND GOALS ANALYSIS

The JAD process uses four basic steps to prepare and lead a business analysis workshop. The logistics shown in the following chart explain typical steps and activities needed to use the Forms Based Analysis technique to define business vision and goals in terms of plans to implement new concepts and technology applications. In this, a business environment is documented as solution guidelines for a working system.

Usually, it takes a few days to one or two weeks of elapsed time from the outset to a workshop meeting. Preparation times shown are normally sufficient to customize a workshop approach, create the meeting agenda, and do the necessary staff work to prepare workbook and presentation materials for team discussion. For some situations, the elapsed time might be longer–it is a matter of judgment to decide what has to be done to implement the workshop technique. Preparation is the key to success, the activities shown provide a basis to get the right people with the right attitude and right materials all in the same place at the same time. From this perspective the main activities over a time frame are shown across the chart with participant involvements listed as role descriptions with key outputs for each step.

MANAGEMENT GUIDELINES

STEP 1 is described under the *Management Guidelines* heading and results in an itemized Preparation Checklist and a draft Management Guidelines document shown in the above chart for a Business Vision and Goals workshop using the Forms Based Analysis technique. The Management Guidelines step usually starts in a meeting where the project manager or project leader invites the session leader to present the JAD approach and discuss the assignment. At this time, the overall plan and how and when to use a workshop in the process are considered. From this discussion, the session leader can recommend an agenda and a book building process to develop an analysis technique for the situation.

Using a Business Vision and Goals book cover with dividers and typical forms to demonstrate structure for business plan analysis, a draft workbook is made by taking notes under various Management Guideline headings. Typical output from this stage will be an outline of purpose, scope, objectives, and assumptions about the assignment. All these points are captured under form titles and headings on separate pages described earlier as a book building process. Once the general terms of reference in the Management Guidelines have been defined, it should be possible to obtain or create draft business and technical illustrations to depict concepts and solutions. The session leader might have to draw basic diagrams in conversation to clarify understanding about a subject, and people might amplify the drawings or offer alternative illustrations. For typical workshop conversation, summary diagrams will be sufficient, but schematics may also be included which describe solutions in greater detail. Suitable diagrams should be included in the workbook after the *Solution Guidelines* divider. This meeting usually concludes in a discussion about the schedule and workshop venue, the meeting agenda and participants, and the preparation needed for success. Logistics are usually handled by the project leader or support personnel. A preparation checklist can be used to itemize the various responsibilities to prepare for the workshop.

EXECUTIVE SPONSOR

A key event is to meet the executive sponsor to discuss the background and confirm direction for the meeting. Staff work should be complete enough for the sponsor to review and provide additional points and approval to proceed. This is usually a short meeting of twenty to thirty minutes, although sometimes it can take an hour or more when detailed discussion is needed to advance to the next step.

APPROVAL TO PROCEED

For this level of workshop, the authority to proceed may be delegated to others. In some situations, there may not always be an opportunity to meet an executive sponsor–it may be sufficient that a project manager keeps the sponsor appraised of the situation. If there is a meeting, it will be an opportunity for the session leader to become acquainted and provide a brief description of JAD to explain how the process works, exchange views about what people want from the meeting, and discuss who should participate for the team to be successful.

Generally it is expected that notes will be taken from any conversation and made available in the next visit or workshop meeting. If a sponsor is involved and interested in reviewing materials, the session leader can demonstrate the approach by showing the staff work progress in a draft workbook. At this time, the sponsor may be asked to review the workbook and contribute content to make changes or additions to clarify the information as Management Guidelines. Using the pointers heard in conversation, the session leader should direct questions to the sponsor and adapt any staff work for an executive management point of view. Sometimes, it may be possible to work on the document in the meeting and the sponsor might welcome the opportunity to contribute to the process. In doing this, the session leader should demonstrate a willingness to listen and be responsive to the points made. Typically, a second visit would allow the executive sponsor to review the workshop agenda and workbook materials prior to the meeting.

The process does not necessarily have to be quick to start a workshop. For business plans involving new concepts, sponsors and managers may prefer to be more circumspect about providing information and want to work on documents in private or seek the opinions of others before giving an approval to proceed.

Once the Management Guidelines have been approved, the project leader can review the agenda and team membership required to contribute to the overall success of the meeting. The business concepts involved in the scope of design should be referenced to ensure that the team has the right background and appropriate knowledge for good participation. The team should be capable of contributing to the analysis topics and have the ability and authority to make decisions to implement change.

Although the attendees may have already been approached, a more informative invitation package can now be prepared containing administration details, agenda, and management guidelines for team review.

ORIENTATION INTERVIEWS

STEP 2 is described as *Orientation Interviews* for the session leader and workshop team. It results in a clarification of workbook materials before the workshop. This could involve an interview schedule, group discussions, or perhaps a steering committee meeting. For management lev-

Involvement and Outputs Using Forms Based Analysis for Business Vision and Goals

	STEP 1	STEP 2	STEP 3	STEP 4
ACTIVITY over 2-4 weeks...	Management Guidelines	Orientation Interviews	Materials Preparation	Workshop Meeting

INVOLVEMENT

	STEP 1	STEP 2	STEP 3	STEP 4
Session Leader	Develop JAD approach ¹/₂-1 day	Interview contributors ¹/₂-2 days	Organize workbook ¹/₂ day	Lead workshop analysis process ¹/₂-1 day
Project Leader or Project Manager	Integrate approach ¹/₂ day	Organize activities ¹/₂ day	Coordinate involvement ¹/₂ day	Supervise Documentation ¹/₂-1 day
Executive Sponsor	Approve and select team ¹/₄-¹/₂ day			Opening and Closing summary
Business Team Members	Contribute to direction ¹/₄-¹/₂ day	Interview meetings ¹/₂-2 days		Exchange knowledge ¹/₂-1 day
Developer Team Members	Customize forms ¹/₄-¹/₂ day	Contribute to content ¹/₂-2 days	Review workbook ¹/₄-¹/₂ day	Technical advice ¹/₂-1 day
Technical Support Project Leader		Review direction ¹/₂ day	Prepare to contribute ¹/₂-1 day	Technical analysis . . . Model
Notekeeping Session Leader Project Leader			Understand content ¹/₂ day	Note team decisions ¹/₂-1 day
Secretary, clerical Support			Start workbook ¹/₂-1 day	Update document ¹/₂-1 day

STEP OUTPUTS

Preparation Checklist	*Management Guidelines*	*Solution Guidelines*	*JAD TEAM WORKBOOK*	*BUSINESS VISION AND GOALS*
Itemized Activities	*Draft Scope and Objectives*	*Draft Business and Technical Illustrations and form notes*	*Basis for Critical Analysis*	*Revised for Approval*

DIVIDER CONTENT FOR CONVERSATION .... **BOOK CONTENT** ....

els usually involved, interviews will probably be the preferred choice to discuss vision information in a draft document.

Depending on the complexity of the assignment or the requirement for tactful involvement with others, draft materials can be further reviewed and supplied with new information. While this may be done only to keep people informed of the process, Management Guidelines will invariably be clarified. The extent of this activity is usually anticipated and coordinated by a project manager. If additional involvement is required, contributions from other business managers and system developers can be included from a few interviews or a steering committee meeting. In each new meeting the session leader will probably be required to sell the approach and gain acceptance for involvement. Occasionally, a delicate situation will arise and the session leader should look to the project leader for advice and guidance to resolve or preferably avoid any potential for conflict.

MATERIALS PREPARATION

STEP 3 is described as *Materials Preparation* and results in a completed draft workbook for the team to evaluate and revise during a workshop meeting. This is the staff work necessary to create draft documents and workshop exhibits and assemble them as a team handout. This includes partially completed forms from individual work and any other materials gleaned from or after orientation interviews.

Using the design in the forms structure, good business analysis starts in the time available in the first two steps. Before the workshop, the session leader can determine the need to discuss technology issues and if necessary include technological analyses in the meeting. Depending on the depth of business concept analysis, technology related topics may need to be included in discussion. The session leader should treat business design decisions and technology design decisions as separate but related issues. With a view that business direction and solution guidelines prescribe technological solutions, it is possible to discuss change opportunities with a greater focus on business objectives. In this way, people who need to decide on technology issues can review the Analysis Guidelines to prepare for their role and contribute to draft material in the workbook before a meeting. Indeed, providing business perspectives in early draft materials to technology developers allows them to ponder on technological direction and become more informed for the workshop.

By the time the session leader has reached the third step, the need for technological analysis will be more apparent. The issues about how to acquire and develop technologies will be better understood. With advice from a project leader or technology design analyst, the session leader should decide the best approach to include technological perspectives in the workbook with methods for debate and documentation. The role of the technologist is to understand business concepts and solutions direction from team consensus and provide the information and advice needed to make appropriate technology decisions. At this level of detail, the character of this has a lot to do with confirming that technological solutions are possible. For this reason, technologists prefer to use illustrations which verify decisions in terms of technical feasibility.

In preparation, when draft technology illustrations are reviewed, the session leader needs to determine how to share discussion time with technical representatives who want to use them in the meeting. For business concept analyses, such materials are best described as high level summaries with illustrations on paper to capture and convert business views into meaningful presentations of solution guidelines. At this stage, technical perspectives need only be included at a high level to provide concurrence with business views. For concept analyses, business representatives only need to be assured technologies can support the vision. The session leader should be able to summarize both business and technical points of view to document team decisions.

Preparation is complete when the Management Guidelines and Solution Guidelines materials are indexed to an analysis sequence and compiled as a workbook handout for each participant. This activity may take a few days, or it may be ready in one or two days and used immediately in a sequential workshop meeting. In addition to paper copies, an overhead transparency of each workbook page is needed for the session leader to present team contributions as discussion pages.

WORKSHOP MEETING

STEP 4 is described as the JAD *Workshop Meeting* which delivers revised documents and represents team consensus for a business plan and the solution guidelines to implement change. This is the time people are brought together to discuss the topics and materials contained in the team workbook. The book building process already started in preparation should be implemented throughout the meeting.

OPENING DEBATE

Starting with an overhead of the workbook cover sheet the session leader can lead the team through page order up to the purpose page in the Management Guidelines. In these pages, the team begins to focus on visions and goals analysis. By inviting critical assessment, discussion opens around prepared contributions. The session leader's role will range from making minor changes to content to being very involved in conversation and using communication skills to prompt and help the team reach agreement and document understanding. The participants will be glad to share in this technique as they see summarized debate in conversational and illustrative extracts.

While future business managers focus on business issues, system developers should support conversation with the provision of technological advice whenever needed to promote a better understanding about an application of technology. In this way, all team members become involved and jointly make decisions about business and technical guidelines for proposed change and business solutions. The session leader manages conversation to the prescribed scope and continues analysis so that solution alternatives become more responsive to the business objectives. Potential outcome of change is best understood when supporting notes and solution illustrations are updated to clarify and show conclusions in the context of overall purpose and objectives. The best technique to reach consensus is to document points of view and decisions as solution alternatives on workbook pages while ideas emerge and new business approaches are figured out. As results are demonstrated in note form and checked for realistic and acceptable change, the scope and objectives and assumptions pages may need to be revised to be current with new understanding.

In this level of workshop, the documented result is a business strategy and recommendations to engineer a new business environment and implement business concepts with supporting technologies. In the next levels of analysis, the JAD approach is adapted to analyze design change affecting area managers and business professionals. The technique is extended to multiple pages to discuss business requirements and define more detailed descriptions of business functions and system routines designed to support the vision.

ILLUSTRATED JAD

Difficulties about thinking futuristically have to do with leaving habits and traditional viewpoints aside while considering new perspectives. You cannot just ask people to clear their minds to think creatively. It's like saying, "Forget ev-

erything you know and tell me what you don't know." Typical JAD forms for change analysis allow you to develop good ideas to document future opportunities, but you might need an easy example on which to model discussion.

In an assignment for a Canadian Government department, I used a life situation to model analysis. Considering my son's education in words youth can understand, we used the following forms as a light-hearted example to promote deeper thinking about important business issues and the forces of change.

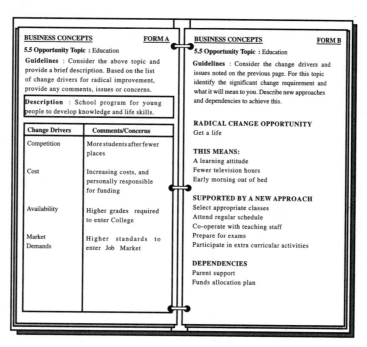

ADVANCING BUSINESS REQUIREMENTS

ad-vance v. To go forward; to progress, move towards completion; to cause an event to happen sooner than planned or expected; to suggest, propose; to advance a theory, progressive, in front of most others.

busi-ness n. Regular employment, profession, occupation; one's personal affair, concern, duty, something *requiring* attention.

re-quire-ment n. Something needed; something stipulated or demanded.

re-quire v. To stipulate; to place an obligation on; to need.

CHAPTER ELEVEN

JAD—Requirements Analysis for Business Plans and System Solutions

FORMS BASED TECHNIQUE FOR REQUIREMENT EXPRESSIONS

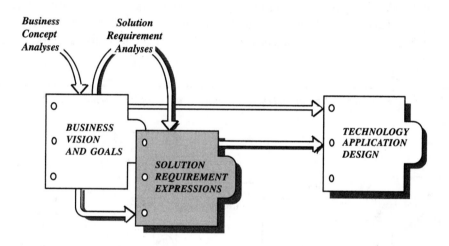

The concept of relating levels of systems design detail to a workshop technique is shown in the Documentation Level and Analysis Technique chart explained in an earlier chapter. The above summary illustrates the **Requirements Analysis** loop and life cycle documents involved in the migration of Business Vision and Goals information to become Solution Requirement Expressions and Technology Application Design. A Business Planning workshop can be implemented to discuss business plans and define first level business design and second level technical information using a Forms Based Analysis technique for solution requirements.

ORGANIZATION FOR DEBATE

Using dividers for conversation in a business planning document, requirements analysis is supported in the **Management Guidelines, Solution Guidelines,** and **Analysis Forms** dividers. Following the JAD book building approach, the session leader should promote an organization of question forms to repeat in groups for the topics defined in the scope of design. The key to success is that the organization provides intuitive references to subject material and the content uses a familiar language for debate. The greater detail contained in the analyses forms is further segmented by grouping subordinate topics in lists within a form. For completeness, topics are arranged to ensure that the sum of the forms represents the scope of analysis. For the best results, the session leader should adapt and design the forms to ensure the people involved in preparation are satisfied they are conducive to sharing ideas and exchanging information in a workshop setting.

To round out a business planning document, summary information can be added and a page provided for general understanding about the assignment in the Background divider. Important reference materials are included as Solution Guidelines, and more occasionally referenced materials are placed in the Appendices divider. The session leader and project leader select business and technical illustrations to illustrate solutions and relate analysis topics with forms used for debate and documentation. It will be easier to explain the technique using a diagram to illustrate the workshop approach for the analysis sequence and documentation process.

FORMS BASED ANALYSIS

In the following diagram, the main divider headings used in a workshop agenda are shown with a sequence of workbook pages. The pages usually involved in requirements analysis are numbered in the order used. Pages without sequence numbers are usually recorded as appendices for the references and details needed for general conversation. All the materials should be referenced in the Index divider.

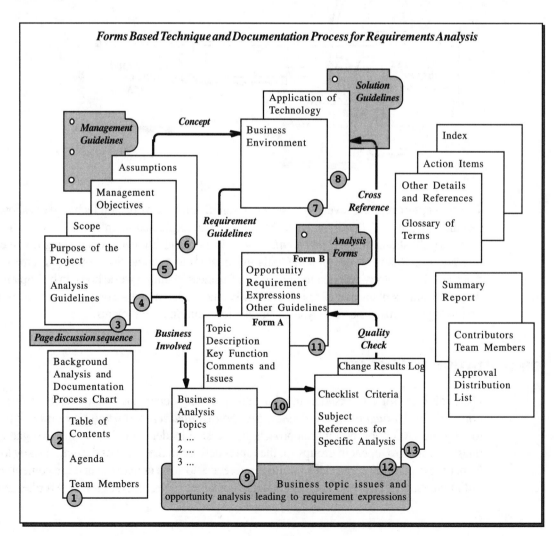

After the Management Guidelines and Solution Guidelines already described, the analysis structure continues to support discussion and exchange of information contained in forms and reference materials. To add clarity to organization, forms are preceded by a list of analysis topics matched to the business involved list on the scope page. Typical analysis is conducted around two basic forms. For accuracy and completeness, analysis is cross referenced to Solution Guidelines materials. For quality documentation and a greater level of detail, certain topics can be further cross referenced to optional subject materials on a third form providing specific analysis or design information attached to certain pages or appendices divider.

POINT FORM MECHANICS

All workshops start in a similar step to create a document with standard dividers up to and including Solution Guidelines. In a business planning workshop requirement expressions are documented in the Analysis Forms divider to differentiate between solution guidelines and the details recorded as requirement expressions. Forms similar to those used to list issues for Vision and Goals are redesigned to support more detail concerning business environments and solution decisions in a sequence shown below.

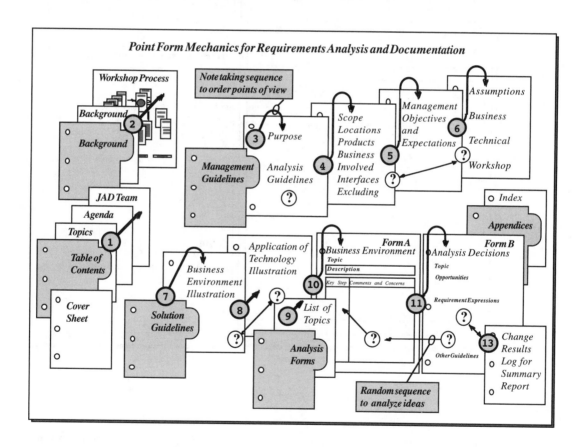

BASIC FORMS DESIGN

Two basic form designs provide an adaptive layout for analyzing business requirements information. The forms can work for different topics and at different levels of detail. The first form is designed to describe the reality of a present business environment; it is used to reach documented agreement on the issues which cause a need for change. The second form is designed to document opportunities as expectations for change and record statements of need as requirement expressions. These can be noted as direction for business vision for a system solution or in greater detail as information requirements for a system design. With these forms an immediate decision can be reached for action to implement a change or decisions and requirement expressions can be identified in priority for further analysis. In this way the workshop product can be considered independently or reviewed with other information used for an overall development plan. Business information and requirement expressions can be captured on forms repeated for a design sequence using headings and labels for different levels of detail using a basic forms design shown below.

Adapting Typical Forms for Various Business Analysis Detail

BUSINESS ENVIRONMENT   FORM A

(_____) TOPIC No. ___ _____.
Guidelines: Consider the above topic and provide a brief description of the (_____).List the key (____'s) to be analyzed and provide comments needed to explain strengths and weaknesses. Add the issues you want to discuss.

DESCRIPTION   *(overview of the topic)*

KEY(....)	COMMENTS AND ISSUES
(involvement)	*(things to know or be concerned about)*

REQUIREMENT DECISIONS   FORM B

(_____) TOPIC No. ___ _____.
Guidelines: Consider the items and issues shown on the previous page to identify the opportunities and potential benefits. Document the statements of (_____) for (_____) and provide other guidelines to assist development.

(CHANGE)
OPPORTUNITIES:

(benefit potential from change)

(NEW BUSINESS PROCESS)
STATEMENT OF (_____) FOR (_____):   RANK
(REQUIREMENT EXPRESSION)

(requirement expressions to implement change)

OTHER GUIDELINES

(consequential needs or actions to support change)

ADAPTIVE FORMS DESIGN

The forms can be designed through customizing the bracketed blanks for the working situation in titles, headings and instructional guidelines. The first bracket on each form is used to identify the topic and level of detail based on conceptual, organizational, or functional analysis. Forms are grouped in a logical sequence for analysis and each form is identified by an alphabet letter. Form A is designed to document present understanding starting with a topic title and brief description. If necessary, topic numbers can be used to relate material to an index preceding the forms. After the topic description, Form A uses two or more columns to list related subtopics and capture descriptive comments about the things to know or be concerned about. The second form records a further explanation of current strengths and weaknesses or issues about the subject of debate. The first column bracket is used to identify subtopics in key words which express the involvement and indicate the type of analysis. Using this format for concept analysis, the column heading could be "key items." For organization analysis this could be "key involvement," and for function analysis "key processes," or "key activities." When you customize the forms to suit a local or business language, the headings might be "key steps" or "key programs."

CUSTOMIZED FOR LEVELS OF DETAIL AND ORGANIZED FOR ANALYSIS

While Form A is customized for a level of detail for business analysis, Form B is customized for business design and technical requirements detail. The blanks on Form B should be customized to express the type of information to be gained from the meeting. This heading for what is to be recorded should probably comply with local terminology and language for a systems development methodology. Typical terminology might be continued from a vision and goals document using "New Business Approach" for a planning document, or "Statement of direction for plan" with the adjective "business," "technical," or "implementation" to describe a planning perspective. For business design, "Statement of direction for systems development" could indicate what is needed, or, "Statement of requirement for design" would suggest more detail. Depending on implementation activities, special labels might be used—"Statement of requirement for system enhancement" for a redevelopment document, or "Software features and requirements" to select a software supplier.

The forms should be customized to suit an analysis purpose in a format designed to record information needed for a development process. The paired forms are repeated and collated to the analysis items listed for discussion. The first choice for adaptation is to select a method to group topics. Typical analysis for a plan considers business concepts, business organizations, or business functions. The forms adaptation for detail creates an approach for debate. Generic terminology is normally sufficient in a forms structure and only a few additions will be needed to include special terminology in the headings and guidelines. To organize analysis, special subject labels can be used to describe the subdivision of topics or simply describe the organization as topic and subtopic. The following generic groupings might be used to sequence workshop topics for a more organized and analytical thought process.

> ### *Generic Hierarchy for Organized Thinking*
>
> Concept subjects and subject items which make up the whole
> Organizational units and functions which make up the whole
> Functional areas and processes which make up the whole
> Functional areas and business activities which make up the whole

The forms can be further customized for a special purpose and the final adaptation usually supports the appearance and instructional language. Appropriate hierarchical headings and labels are used for different analysis and documentation. A most commonly used sequence to organize discussion is found in a hierarchy of functions and related activities. Customized headings and labels provide specialty groupings for interest in particular subject matters or types of analysis. Organizational headings must be arranged to keep the intent of an agenda and the debating process intact. The following examples list typical analysis hierarchies for specialty topics and various levels of detail.

Typical Analysis Hierarchies for Specialty Topics

Business measurements and management decisions for productivity
Market segment and market programs to sell products and services
Product line manufacturing areas and assembly processes for production
Legislation and business areas impacted by new regulations
Business areas and administrative support for quality customer service
Principles and fundamental values which make constitutional policy
Empowerment degrees of freedom and responsibility ownership
Development life cycle with techniques and tools to implement technology

---

CUSTOMIZING FORMS

To customize the forms, the session leader must determine how best to document the issues and decision information needed for progress in development steps. At the business concept level, a basic forms design will probably work well enough with only a few cosmetic changes. The basic forms design should be improved when more information is needed to analyze requirements for business organizations or business functions. Adaptation at this stage usually includes the addition of columns and headings on both forms. Typical modifications add an "information used" column in the middle of Form A, and a new heading for "management and regulatory policy" is sometimes added to Form B. For subsequent review, a priority indicator to rank importance is often shown against decision statements on Form B. Sometimes a check mark column is placed after "other guidelines" to identify follow-up items.

When the forms are ready for the workshop, the Analysis Guidelines on the purpose page under the Management Guidelines heading must be reviewed to ensure that any knowledge to be gained using the forms design matches the instruction details provided for the team to follow in the workshop. In this way, when people read the management purpose and guidelines for the analysis they will also understand and anticipate the workbook content and process. Furthermore, when this page starts the meeting, the terms of reference will be reviewed in debate and expectations established for involvement. In the same way that forms ownership migrates to the information consumers during preparation, forms ownership also migrates to the information providers and decision makers during the meeting. The workshop process should become their own and they will expect it to be administered as outlined by the Analysis Guidelines stated at the beginning of the meeting.

MANAGING INVOLVEMENT

Information on one page is often cross referenced, or referred to, in page details nearby or on pages attached to different workbook dividers. Change of pace and change of direction will be frequent. In the workshop, participants and especially you, the session leader, need to maintain and project a sense of purpose and involvement. As you proceed to use the technique, it is quite normal for participants to lose track occasionally and perhaps display a lack of confidence in the process. This is especially true if difficult subjects or abstract concepts are involved. To avoid frustration, when you provide periodic progress reports you might have to be reassuring about results. You will always need to remind people about the process after an overnight break or after a long conversation which may not have apparently followed due process. In addition to the agenda and index, it is helpful to provide simple references to explain the evolution of workshop decisions. For this, the Forms Based Analysis and Documentation Process chart can be customized with page labels to illustrate your own workshop approach. And this should be used frequently in the meeting to mark up progress and summarize documentation results as they become available.

The Analysis and Documentation Process chart should be modified using equivalent headings for workbook dividers and pages and numbers for the analysis and documentation sequence. Typically, this diagram is placed after the background summary and just before the Management Guidelines divider. In this way the administration can be explained from the beginning and you can refer to the diagram whenever you need to remind people about the process and their progress in it. If any team members have been involved in workshop preparation, they can assist you in explaining the process to their peers. They will be compelled to confirm the effectiveness of the approach and value of team input. For these reasons, you will benefit from any staff work done by people involved in developing workshop discussion materials. The team will be more confident about working together and the meeting will be more effective because of it.

ORGANIZED THINKING

The Forms Based Analysis technique is supported by a topic and subject sequence and a relationship between materials. This includes a topic sequence for the forms and a subject sequence within the forms. Normally the sequence of forms can be used to track the agenda and pace the meeting. On average, the group will spend forty minutes to an hour on one set of forms for typical analysis headings with four to eight subtopics. Generally, the pace will quicken through the meeting. Because subject details vary, the team might work through two or three paired forms, or only one between breaks. Work can follow a prepared sequence starting with the first topic listed if it is the most important or establishes the basis for the remaining topics. Otherwise, you as session leader can pick the first discussion to be the least complex or best known and use it as an easy example to follow. You might place such a topic first or anywhere in the list to be selected by a team vote for the best subject to start on. Similar choices can also be made when you have to pace the meeting to an agenda deadline or allow the team to start or finish topics near to break times.

Typically, Form A lists several key subordinate topics related to form heading subject topic for debate. Subordinate items for discussion may or may not be listed in an ordered sequence on the form. Subject information is nearly always related in one way or another. For concept analysis, relationships may be indefinite, simply including subordinate items will be sufficient for the team to think about them in context of a heading. For functions and process analysis, relationships may be more certain and sequence more important to recognize order in a complete list or ensure a closed loop.

In the workshop, as more debate ensues and documented materials evolve, the team will validate the content and raise new points to reorder and complete items in a list. This is what should happen. In fact, you must encourage it for the thorough analysis you need to help the team discover the issues and problems which must be resolved for design quality and a better application of technology.

YIN AND YANG FORMS

To start analytical discussion, the first form, A, is designed to itemize related topics and capture opinions and concerns from previous interviews or meetings and several people later involved in the workshop. It documents observations and basic facts about work locations, work loads, current equipment, processing rules, and transaction types and volumes. In that Form A addresses a topic from critical and sometimes pessimistic perspectives, it usually provides a negative slant in noting problematic issues.

The second form, B, is designed to consider the issues raised in Form A. Based on opportunities and system possibilities to address the issues, this form is used to reach consensus for design decisions and actions needed to develop a new approach. In this way, Form B is more optimistic and usually promotes a positive view in that it documents opportunistic expectations for change.

During workshop time, there will be enough information on Form A for participants to consider and note opportunities and changes on Form B. With each form on an overhead projector to display conversational points, participants can follow the various thoughts as you write up ideas. They will reach consensus and make decisions in the course of debate. The relationship between a negative view on Form A and optimistic perspective on Form B will help formulate a note taking response to conversation. As session leader, you can judge by the character of expression and tone of speech which form and heading to use to document a point of view and use your own judgment as to when and what you should write about. Form notes follow a sequence for analysis and a mechanism for debate supports the process.

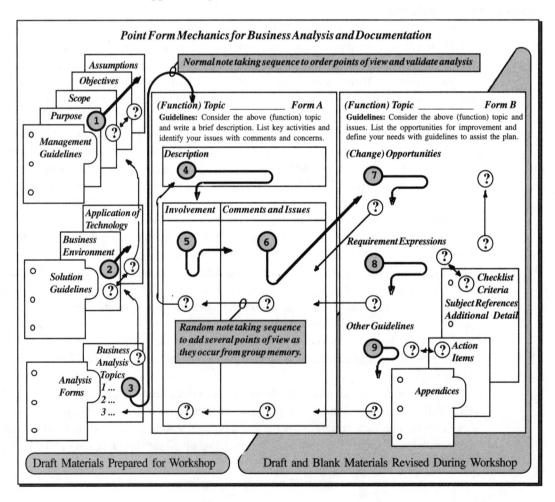

MECHANICAL FORMS

The above diagram illustrates sequential and random information as a forms dialogue. The process usually starts in conversation to reach agreement about the topic and description. Typically, conversation can be managed through the sequence of headings to result in requirement expressions. Once the headings are understood and the sequence established, the session leader can deviate from the usual track and note random thoughts until an issue is settled in final analysis. As the team works through the issues, new opportunities will be realized and new topics brought into debate. Information might be added to the forms in a random sequence and then the normal sequence used to validate the result. To maintain a piecemeal approach, overflow topics are separated onto new forms and notes reorganized into a new page sequence for a complete requirements document.

Form mechanics need not be fully understood by the team. Indeed, the mechanism may not be apparent since a relationship between one information and another need not be perfect. Using the principle of what you see is what you get, the team will rely on your judgment as session leader to take notes on overhead transparencies. Your purpose is to animate contributions to the pages and produce results in a documentation sequence.

TEAM REACTION

People respond to this approach for decision making in different ways. The course of a meeting will not change the way people are compelled to express ideas. Some people make an effort to follow the forms design and direct commentary to the headings shown. Others might not heed the process and contribute thoughts in casual conversation. Personalities, mannerisms, and various modes of expression notwithstanding, each person will want to be heard and have his or her point of view acknowledged.

In taking notes, the form sequence and pattern of information in the pages should be indicative for the session leader to notice a lack of continuity in related thoughts. The analysis routine imitates the JAD communication model: first, a topic description and key activities with opinions expressed as comments, concerns, or issues on Form A; second, an agreement for change expressed in terms of opportunities and finally, team decisions expressed as requirements on Form B. The pattern is subtle and easy to follow for most participants.

For consensus, it is sufficient that the human mind interprets the intent of the points made to finally explain a need as a requirement expression. People instinctively use projected pages and notes for group memory and they recall situations to relate the information you need to hear. Several points of view will emerge and you should be able to document most of the ideas on your current forms. To keep track and address several related issues, you can return to previous related work and clarify the information on different pages as points arise. To address unrelated concerns you can use an issues log to list ideas to be addressed when a relationship is more obvious, or simply later.

RESPONDING TO CONTRIBUTIONS

Using Forms A and B it is possible for you, the session leader, to distribute different perspectives across the pages and respond to almost any contribution. For people more comfortable talking through the details of the current system, you can translate their opinions into comments and concerns. For others more able to express why they want to change something, their views can be translated into opportunities. For those with a more direct view, you can paraphrase their points into statements of need. Similar results come from those who prefer to talk about how they want to use a new system. The session leader should respond to conversation about why things will not work or cannot be done by documenting a negative issue on Form A and then writing up a positive recommendation expressed as a requirements expression on Form B. For people who have already gone ahead to the positive, their idea can be written as an opportunity or requirement in language suitable for either. As this is done a corresponding comment or perhaps concern on Form A might have to be related.

Whichever way people get involved, they will all appreciate being heard and pleased to see the session leader make an appropriate note under a relevant heading. His or her ability to satisfy this common need will tend to neutralize any emotions which naturally emerge when people are encouraged to be critical, argue different points of view, and work hard to reach consensus. Responsiveness is crucial to team building and the continuation of the workshop process. Indeed the success of debate depends upon it.

As session leader, your own thinking in this way will help you focus on the assignment. It will ensure that you ask pertinent questions and keep you in tune and involved in conversation. As people lead into conversational topics, you can follow in form sequence and write down summary notes. While you might also start a conversation, the team will have the final word. You can follow points on current or past pages or use a blank form until you decide how to include the detail in the document. The mechanism in the above pattern allows the team to validate different points of view and confirm decisions. Working together this way generally promotes team involvement and consensus. It always results in more detailed analysis and a greater level of precision.

ANALYSIS PRECISION

Precision starts with a check that each business opportunity statement is relevant and team members are satisfied that stated requirements address the issues. To conclude a thought process, the team can be asked to consider constraints and suggest guidelines or management policies needed to assist or even implement the design solution. Typically, this kind of thinking will wrap up several issues under a topic heading. Precision is not confined to one set of forms or single topic issues, it also has to do with the overall result. As conversation is held about each topic heading, decisions should be cross referenced to a Business Environment or an Application of Technology illustration to validate the results in terms of fundamental premises for analysis. This will result in a clarification and sometimes the redefinition of concepts explained as Solution Guidelines.

Additional precision can be achieved using a checklist for comparison to important perspectives for success. A checklist can contain key management objectives in order of priority for the team to judge results in terms of strategic goals brought from previous analyses. Alternatively, a checklist might be used to promote key points about a concept so that the team can measure the result in compliance with certain principles. For workshop debate, the session leader can treat a checklist informally as a private list of issues used by a certain team member or systems developer as a reminder to ask particular questions. On a more formal basis, a checklist can be used as a visible part of the workshop process. Indeed, you might prepare a checklist before the workshop, or create an unplanned checklist from workshop conversation as it evolves or becomes necessary to facilitate team progress. Either might be used to simply round out discussion documents using another or different analysis form.

QUALITY CHECK

Checklist materials are designed and used to provide specific reference details or criteria which enhances team understanding about a business issue or tests the application of a concept. These materials might also provide business or technological details particular to a systems development process. In this, a checklist can be used to complete or validate expectations for business logic or verify decisions in terms of technological design.

Validating business design to expectations might include an alternative or a supplemental analysis technique to return information to the analysis forms. These may range from specific diagrams to a simple Pro's and Con's chart or more complex assessments using matrices or specific formulas to compare business variables. Technological verification to design usually involves additional analysis to test design decisions before implementation. Technical design checklist materials are usually used by team members who continue the work of systems development. Depending on complexity, checklist materials may be included in a discussion document or used as private reference material in professional use to create supplemental notes. Criteria used for design validation to expectations might be included in the document whereas criteria used for technical verification to test results is usually carried over to development documents.

For the next level of detail in a Process Design Specifications document, the JAD concept uses an Activity Based Analysis technique to define business operations so that reengineered business functions and processes are thought of in the character of work tasks. For the above Business Planning Documents this might take the form of a work checklist to validate design decisions. In this case, functional activities can be identified and workflow discussed to understand business further and define requirement expressions better. While the above mechanisms are flexible and easy to use, your job as session leader will be easier when you are prepared for good debate. To be ready and more successful, you should follow a procedure to design appropriate analysis forms and develop workshop materials for critical assessment in a workshop.

CHAPTER TWELVE

⫩⫨ JAD—Requirements Workshop Logistics

PREPARATION FOR A SUCCESSFUL MEETING

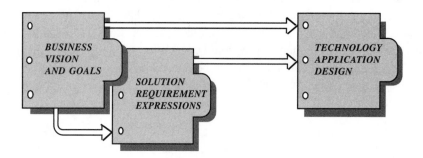

The concept of relating levels of systems design detail to a workshop technique is shown in the Documentation Level and Analysis Technique chart explained in a previous chapter. The above summary illustrates business planning documents as Business Vision and Goals and Solution Requirement Expressions and Technology Application Design. These book contents might be combined or kept separate to differentiate business concepts and process design detail in requirements analysis documents.

Generally, the scope of a Vision and Goals document described earlier is quite compatible with the scope of subsequent Requirements Expressions. Indeed, the Analysis Forms divider might simply be added after the Solutions Guidelines divider in the same workbook. In this case, an existing workbook can be continued to the next meeting for new information. Alternatively, existing Management Guidelines might be used again to refocus objectives and assumptions and restate the Analysis Guidelines on the purpose page to describe a greater level of detail in a new workbook. Several analyses included in the scope of a larger business plan would probably use separate books. A new book can also be started when other analyses have progressed to the point where a workshop would confirm understanding in the early stages of development activity.

The JAD process uses four basic steps to prepare and lead requirements analysis in a workshop setting. The logistics shown in the following chart explain typical steps and activities needed to use the Forms Based Analysis technique to define business concepts, business organization, or business functions and process design with solution guidelines and system requirements.

Usually, it takes one to four weeks of elapsed time from the outset to the workshop meeting. Preparation times shown are normally sufficient to customize the workshop approach, create a meeting agenda, and do the necessary staff work to prepare a workbook and presentation materials for team discussion. For some situations, the elapsed time can be

Involvement and Outputs Using Forms Based Analysis for Requirement Expressions

ACTIVITY over 2-4 weeks...	STEP 1 Management Guidelines	STEP 2 Orientation Meeting	STEP 3 Materials Preparation	STEP 4 Workshop Meeting
INVOLVEMENT				
Session Leader	Develop JAD approach 1 day	Introduce forms technique $1/2$-1 day	Organize workbook 1-2 days	Lead workshop analysis process 1-3 days
Project Leader or Project Manager	Integrate approach 1 day	Organize activities 1-2 days	Coordinate involvement 1-2 days	Supervise documentation 1-3 days
Executive Sponsor	Approve and select team $1/4$-$1/2$ day	Opening remarks		Opening and closing summary
Business Team Involved	Contribute to direction $1/$ -2 days	Approve forms organization $1/$ day	Originate and return forms $1/$ -2 days	Exchange knowledge 1-3 days
Developer Team Involved	Review plan and customize forms 1-2 days	Draft technology application plan 1-2 days	Compile draft workbook $1/2$-3 days	Technical advice 1-3 days
Technical Support Project Leader Systems Analyst	Review solution guidelines $1/2$ day	Review solution direction $1/2$-2 days	Prepare to contribute 1-2 days	Technical analysis . . . Model
Notekeeping Session Leader Project Leader			Understand content $1/2$ day	Note team decisions 1-3 days
Secretary, Clerical Support			Start workbook $1/2$-1 day	Update document 1-3 days

STEP OUTPUTS

Solution Guidelines

- *Preparation Checklist*
- *Itemized Activities*

- *Management Guidelines*
- *Draft Scope and Objectives*

- *Analysis Forms*
- *Question Forms in Analysis Sequence*

- *JAD TEAM WORKBOOK*
- *Basis for Critical Analysis*

- *REQUIREMENT EXPRESSIONS*
- *Revised for Approval*

DIVIDER CONTENT FOR CONVERSATION . . . . **BOOK CONTENT** . . . .

longer. It is a matter of judgment for the session leader and project leader to decide what has to be done to adapt and implement a workshop technique. Preparation is the key to success, and the activities shown provide the basis to get the right people with the right attitude and right materials all in the same place at the same time. From this perspective, the main activities over a time frame are shown across the chart and participant involvement listed down the chart with role descriptions and key outputs for each step.

MANAGEMENT GUIDELINES

STEP 1 is described under the ***Management Guidelines*** heading and results in an itemized Preparation Checklist and draft Management Guidelines pages shown in the previous chart listing activities to prepare for a workshop. The Management Guidelines step usually starts in a meeting in which the project manager or project leader invites the session leader to present the approach and discuss the assignment. At this time the overall plan for the project is considered as well as how and when to use a workshop in the process. From this discussion, the session leader can start the book building process to develop an analysis technique for the specific situation. Depending on the availability of prepared materials, previous plans should be reviewed for direction and integration of known solution guidelines and design information from the support team involved.

STARTING A WORKBOOK

With a typical workbook as a starting point, the session leader should assist in any adaptation to the analysis structure to gain the information required at this stage of systems development. Using a Requirement Expressions book cover, dividers, and typical forms to demonstrate structure for requirement analysis, you can create draft materials in this meeting by reviewing existing or taking notes under the Management Guidelines heading. Typically, the output from this conversation will be an outline of purpose, scope, objectives, and assumptions about the assignment. All these points are captured under form titles and headings on pages described earlier as a book building process. This meeting usually concludes with a discussion about the schedule, the workshop venue, the meeting agenda and participants, and preparation needed for success. Logistics are usually handled by the project leader or other support personnel. You can use a preparation checklist to itemize various responsibilities to prepare for the workshop.

The next key event in the checklist is to meet the executive sponsor to review workbook materials and confirm direction for involvement. Before this meeting and depending on the complexity of the assignment or the requirement for tactful involvement with other people, draft materials can be further reviewed and supplied with new information. While you may do this only to keep people informed about the process, you will inevitably clarify management direction. To the extent that political activity can be anticipated, this is usually coordinated by the project team leader. If additional involvement is needed, it could include contributions from other business managers and system developers from interviews in one or two days, or in a steering committee meeting. Each new meeting will probably require you to promote the approach and demonstrate results to gain acceptance for involvement. Occasionally you might recognize a delicate situation and look to the project leader for advice and guidance to resolve or preferably avoid any potential for conflict. For a typical assignment, at this level, review activity need not be extensive. Indeed, once the project leader has a draft document, as session leader you may not be involved while other people work on materials independently or until events are covered when you can resume preparation responsibilities.

STAFF WORK REVIEW

At some point you can decide that staff work is complete enough for the sponsor to review and provide additional details and approval to proceed. This is usually a short meeting of twenty to thirty minutes, although on occasions it may take up to an hour or longer if more detailed discussion is needed. For an efficient interview, you as session leader should explain the meeting as an opportunity to become acquainted, to explain the process, and to exchange views about what the workshop should cover to be considered a success. After your sponsor has explained what is needed, you can provide a brief description of the process and review the agenda. You might also demonstrate the approach as a draft workbook with evolving staff work.

You should be sensitive to different work styles and protocols and make allowances for the time needed to proceed to the next step. At this time, if your sponsor is willing to review the workbook and contribute to the content, you can make changes or additions to clarify the information in the Management Guideline pages. Using pointers from conversation, you can direct your questions to adapt your staff work to a management point of view. While people contribute to the process and as you respond, you should be able to note key points in the workbook during the meeting.

Sometimes, a manager may prefer to be more reflective about providing information and might want to work on documents in private or seek the opinions of others before giving approval to proceed. In these situations, you can review workshop plans in the first meeting, generalize discussion to the process and team participation and arrange another meeting to start the preparation. For other situations, you may be required to lead a review meeting or attend a steering committee meeting in which managers jointly reach agreement about the direction for the assignment. Typically, you would also see the sponsor a few days or just prior to the meeting to review the workshop agenda and peruse the discussion document.

TEAM ROLES

Once the Management Guidelines have been approved, you can review the agenda and explain the role of the sponsor to kick off the meeting and mention some things for typical opening remarks. In addition, you can discuss the team qualifications required to contribute to the overall success of the meeting. For this you should review the scope and refer to the locations listed and functions involved and the detail required to confirm the right people are invited. The team must be capable of contributing to analysis topics and have the ability and authority to change business functions. For this, you can review the objectives and expectations to ensure that the team is selected for the right background and appropriate knowledge for good participation.

At the same time or shortly after a management review, those involved should adapt the analysis forms design for the topics in question. This includes the session leader in conversation about the detail required for the current development step and the type of information the team will be able to provide. Using typical questionnaires for adaptation, you can customize the structure by creating a sequence to relate analysis topics and stylize the forms to include commonly used, or, in some cases, specific terminology.

Although attendees may have already been approached, the project leader can now prepare a more informative invitation package containing administration details, the agenda, and Management Guidelines for team involvement. In addition to the topics outline in the scope page the analysis topics index can be included for people to understand the workbook organization and consider the draft material before the meeting.

FORMS OWNERSHIP

While the session leader promotes the idea that the basic forms design must be administered in the meeting, it is also important that the ownership of the forms is perceived to transfer from the session leader to team members. It is very important to gain approval and general acceptance for the forms design. In doing this, the team will consider the meeting their own and instruct the session leader about the best way to facilitate debate and how to achieve documentation objectives. To do this the providers and consumers of workshop decisions must be identified. These are usually the project initiators and business managers and project leader and technology developers respectively. As analysis forms are adapted to particular needs, the session leader transfers ownership of the forms design to generate a team approach for the meeting. Those involved will be all the more confident about the workshop process. In this prepared materials will be thought of as assistance for the meeting and team decision making processes. The idea of transferring forms ownership to the team will be appreciated by everybody and the positive feeling about the process will infuse good attitudes for participation.

WORKSHOP REHEARSAL

When, as session leader, you are satisfied that the forms based analysis can be administered in a workshop, you should practice the process on a trial basis with a business representative or a systems analyst or both. Using the goals and objectives in the approved Management Guidelines and information referred to in the Solution Guidelines and Analysis Forms, review the workshop agenda and use the workbook in a brief rehearsal. Your test need not be extensive—you should be satisfied that the process works and that you have sufficient materials to support analysis. It should prove the approach effectiveness for debate. You must also consider the flow of materials for workshop administration and the language for good documentation. To provide examples, you can use discussion material provided at this time, or any sources which add knowledge to the forms.

Before the next step, review the approach with the project leader and others to uncover potential hazards. These include conversations about department politics, team qualifications, individual work styles, and personalities. Considering these factors will help you determine your support role to assist the process. As you become familiar with the assignment, constraining items might surface which could effect workshop implementation. These will have to do with resource availability and the lead time to become ready for the meeting. Your first choice should always be to bring the most in context material to the table. This will invariably require assistance from others who possess the wisdom and experience you need to know about.

Your underlying strategy for implementing a successful workshop is to make the people assisting you use the workshop process while they review or prepare materials ahead of the meeting. There should be no radical change between your approach to preparation and your workshop technique. To the participants, the workshop should appear as an extension to work already done. In this they will continue to assist you, but this benefit will elude you if you cannot go through preferred involvement and preparation steps. You will have to make choices to optimize the help people provide in the time available.

WORKSHOP LOGISTICS AND INVOLVEMENT ALTERNATIVES

STEP 1 can ususally be completed in one day or within two days. However, to implement an orientation at a comfortable pace, a few days should elapse before the next meeting. A few days, or perhaps two weeks, is sufficient to implement the logistics normally required to bring a group of people together for an orientation meeting. The meeting is used to introduce and start the analysis forms review and create a draft copy of the first opinions expressed about the subject. This can be done in a separately scheduled meeting or, to reduce travel time and costs, orientation can be accomplished in one or more conference calls instead of a meeting. Either way, follow up calls will improve things and documents should be exchanged between those involved. A few days will be needed to prepare and compile notes and documents for the workshop from materials gathered in a preparation step.

Workshop logistics can be organized and implemented in different ways to suit different situations. Typical preparation steps for a workshop are implemented separately over a two- to four-week time frame shown. *STEP 1* is similar for all types of workshops and results in tangible outputs in the form of a draft workbook and an activities checklist to outline the responsibilities involved for a successful workshop. After the orientation, workshop steps can be administered differently for logistical needs and special circumstances.

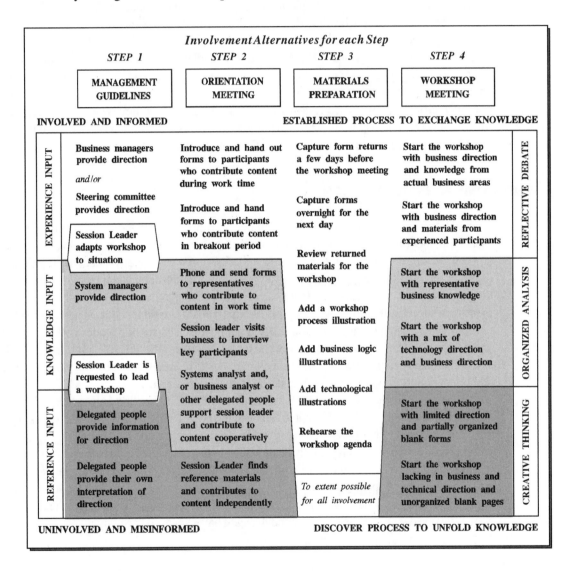

	STEP 1 MANAGEMENT GUIDELINES	STEP 2 ORIENTATION MEETING	STEP 3 MATERIALS PREPARATION	STEP 4 WORKSHOP MEETING	
	INVOLVED AND INFORMED		ESTABLISHED PROCESS TO EXCHANGE KNOWLEDGE		
EXPERIENCE INPUT	Business managers provide direction *and/or* Steering committee provides direction Session Leader adapts workshop to situation	Introduce and hand out forms to participants who contribute content during work time Introduce and hand forms to participants who contribute content in breakout period	Capture form returns a few days before the workshop meeting Capture forms overnight for the next day Review returned materials for the workshop	Start the workshop with business direction and knowledge from actual business areas Start the workshop with business direction and materials from experienced participants	**REFLECTIVE DEBATE**
KNOWLEDGE INPUT	System managers provide direction Session Leader is requested to lead a workshop	Phone and send forms to representatives who contribute to content in work time Session leader visits business to interview key participants Systems analyst and, or business analyst or other delegated people support session leader and contribute to content cooperatively	Add a workshop process illustration Add business logic illustrations Add technological illustrations	Start the workshop with representative business knowledge Start the workshop with a mix of technology direction and business direction	**ORGANIZED ANALYSIS**
REFERENCE INPUT	Delegated people provide information for direction Delegated people provide their own interpretation of direction	Session Leader finds reference materials and contributes to content independently	Rehearse the workshop agenda *To extent possible for all involvement*	Start the workshop with limited direction and partially organized blank forms Start the workshop lacking in business and technical direction and unorganized blank pages	**CREATIVE THINKING**
	UNINVOLVED AND MISINFORMED		DISCOVER PROCESS TO UNFOLD KNOWLEDGE		

Involvement Alternatives for each Step

COST SAVING OPTIONS

Costs and time factors will probably weigh into choices for logistics. In the above chart, the *Classic* JAD route is shown in the top line for maximum business involvement and most effective preparation. Depending on the pace and opportunity to meet people, it may be required to reach a workshop taking different paths. It will be a matter of judgment for those involved to respond to the situation along the alternatives shown. The best involvement is seen to start in the top left of the chart across to the top right. The most typical involvement combines knowledge and experience inputs to prepare materials for organized analysis. In this range, team involvement in preparation leads to the discovery and accumulation of information to be exchanged in the meeting. When cost factors override these benefits, the least advantaged and least cost path is shown in the lower path. In this, the workshop starts with blank forms and as they are used in conversation, the process to uncover knowledge is discovered.

BREAKOUT TIME FOR PREPARATION

In an approach to save travel expense, the orientation and remaining steps can be scheduled into one meeting by adding an extra day to the agenda. This is the least impacting alternative and uses a breakout session for an equivalent amount of preparation in a shorter lead time. Using this alternative, the extra time in the first day is used to provide an orientation in the morning with a breakout period in the afternoon. During the breakout period, individuals fill out the forms by themselves or in small groups. When they have completed the forms to the extent possible, they return them to be typed and compiled as a team handout. In this way *Step 3* is completed overnight and the workshop in *Step 4* is implemented on the day after the orientation. The effort involved is not much different to that used following separate steps and it achieves similar results in a shorter time frame. These logistics allow you to complete a workshop within a week or take two weeks in all. The approach is quite plausible and preferred for some situations.

AGENDA TIME FOR PREPARATION

In another cost saving approach, a breakout period is not utilized and a workshop orientation and workshop meeting is combined into a single agenda. Using this alternative the orientation amounts to an introduction in the opening remarks, and a review of management guidelines and the solution guideline pages. After this, the session leader completes the blank forms on behalf of the team from the comments they make to each page displayed on the overhead projectors. Implementing a successful workshop using this alternative is more dependent on session leader ability to focus debate using communication skills to get results. The session leader will have to rephrase and paraphrase from conversation and write comments from the several opinions heard. Then, to reach consensus, each summary should be treated as if it were written by the participants and the document edited through more conversation to reach agreement.

This approach leaves little time for reflective thinking. In fact, the only time available is in the agenda. And this may not be sufficient to establish the best conditions and attitudes for good participation. Without the benefit of prepared contributions from more experienced knowledge sources, a team will probably not be ready and possibly be unwilling to discuss the issues. There will be fewer prepared materials, and debate will be more stressful and less effective. The first part of the agenda will be a time consuming learning experience for everyone when materials are out of tune with the subject or the team is unfamiliar with the content and the concepts. In any event, useful results will not emerge until everybody is involved, and the session leader and the team have achieved harmony in the process.

TEAM MATURITY

It usually takes five to six hours for team maturity to develop to the point when there is general agreement about new concepts and the basics for analysis. Even with the advantage of being involved in preparation, you will also require workshop time to understand the direction the meeting takes. In the classic JAD approach, using a separate orientation meeting you benefit from an understanding brought to a workshop and the team can reach appropriate maturity in conversation and participation early in the agenda.

Without an orientation, the same realization and ability to work together will have to be established using valuable workshop time. Furthermore, while you are involved in a similar learning time you will also have to find or create the materials which reflect your understanding for others to focus analysis. Until you do, conversation will be fragmented and may be tense. It will be awkward for you and the team to be involved in conversation and difficult to make sense of all the information. You can easily avoid these problems by preparing workshop ready materials to orchestrate the meeting towards tangible and documented results.

While a meeting without an orientation is possible, it does require greater skill and support from the people involved in preparation to be successful. Even without planning and prepared materials, this alternative is an improvement over a brainstorming session. This choice for logistics is quite reasonable in situations when you want to explore new ideas in a short time frame and discuss ideas and issues without necessarily finding the answers. It can be implemented with less risk when analysis topics are prioritized and selected for attention during the meeting. In this situation, it will be better to make the team aware that results should be considered as recommendations to be reviewed in due course. Indeed, it will be necessary to set reasonable expectations from the beginning to reduce the pressure for results and early successes.

POTENTIAL TO SUCCEED

Using the *classic* JAD approach and depending on the availability of people, all the steps can occur in a one- to four-week period. This should be enough time to develop materials for debate in a format conducive to exchange knowledge and increase understanding. Time is well spent if you

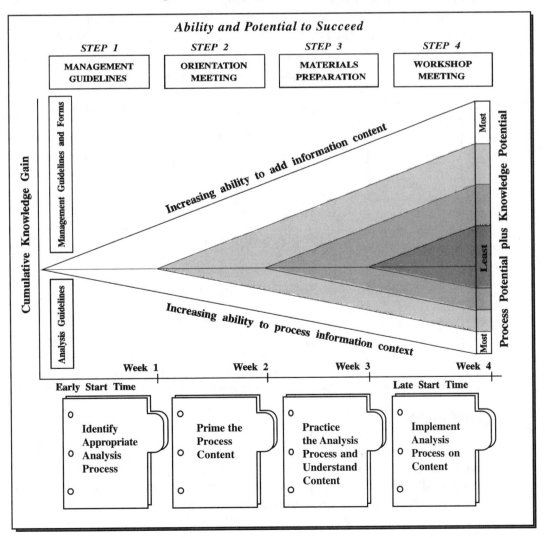

prepare yourself to lead the session and become able in the process. Your ability to do this and potential to succeed increases with an early start in step one.

ORIENTATION MEETING

STEP 2 is described as the *Orientation Meeting* for the session leader and the workshop team and results in the clarification of draft materials and a distribution of workbook materials to people able to contribute to the process. In the preferred scheme, shown in the top line of the previous Involvement Alternatives chart, *Orientation* and *Workshop Meetings* are scheduled apart by a few days or within a week or two. Usually a project leader has the authority to work with the sponsor and schedule people and arrange the venue. The following agenda sets out a typical sequence of events. During the orientation meeting, you should introduce the approach, review draft management guidelines, and distribute the analysis forms to business representatives to take away or use in a prearranged breakout period. This meeting may only take an hour to review the content, or it may take two to three hours if presentations are included in the agenda and revisions are made to the Management Guidelines in workbook materials.

For an orientation meeting, you can modify the following typical workshop agenda for your sequence of events. This should include time to explain the approach and start team involvement in business analysis. When Day 2 is separated by a few days you can use the same agenda page to resume the meeting process at the business analysis topics. If Day 2 starts more than a few days after the orientation or you meet new team members, it may be beneficial, or indeed necessary to remind people of scope and objectives in a review of Management Guidelines.

Orientation and Workshop Agenda

Day 1 — Executive Sponsor Opening Remarks

Project Overview

Introductions and Administration

Workshop Approach

Management Guidelines

Analysis Guidelines and Materials Overview

Introduce and Distribute Forms

Day 2 — Review Document Progress

Business Analysis Topics

Action Items

Summary Presentation and Closing Remarks

OPENING REMARKS

Most meetings start with the executive sponsor providing opening remarks. Optionally, this can be followed up with the project manager or the project leader saying a few words about the project. After this, the session leader should introduce the meeting agenda to explain the timing and basic administration for the meeting. This should include a few minutes for you to ask each participant to introduce themselves and provide an overview of their work responsibilities, and explain what he or she wants and expects from the meeting to consider it a success.

In personal remarks, the session leader should make the participants feel at ease and know they will enjoy the success they are looking for through participation. If someone identifies a topic and it is in the agenda, you can let them know their interests will be included in conversation. If the team sees it as an omission, include it in the agenda. If it is not in the preparation, highlight the item on the issues chart or at least make a mental note about it for recall during the meeting.

Next, describe the workshop approach and demonstrate the workbook content as an input for change through team involvement in the meeting. Explain the approach as a book building process from team contributions. You can further explain the value of prepared material from staff work and why individual help is now needed to work on the forms before the next day's workshop. As you proceed in the first day orientation agenda, present the Management Guidelines in conversation to define the assignment. Managers who contributed to the guidelines may choose to stay while participants review the pages and reach agreement on the issues. As you promote conversation about the pages, make notes to add or clarify the information. After this and for the most part, the team will understand the scope and objectives for analyses at this point in the agenda. It will probably be time for the first coffee break.

Next, and prior to working on the forms, the team should come to an agreement about the basic concepts involved in achieving the desired result or realizing the solution guidelines through business reengineering. New concepts developed for business or technical perspectives and ideas represented in the Solution Guidelines must be discussed and thought of in the context of more detailed analyses. As you review draft concept materials you can update them through conversation and relate various ideas to subject information in the analysis forms. Once you all have a better understanding of the business environment and application of technology illustrations, participants will be more comfortable about being involved in future conversation. You will find it easier to relate to the references needed to facilitate debate and reach consensus.

Purposeful forms design and meaningful preparation is usually sufficient for analytical work. However, to make forms more acceptable, it is still possible to add or make small modifications as they are used by the team. When there are no more questions about orientation materials, you can introduce the analysis forms and assign them to individuals or to small groups with topical knowledge. If you have sample information in the same format as the analysis forms, you can demonstrate what is expected to be done. You can then go over the administration for the team to return their work and end this agenda item with any final questions about the process. In the time remaining, or in the breakout period before the materials are returned for compilation, you should continue to work with the team and provide any assistance needed.

MATERIALS PREPARATION

STEP 3 is described as *Materials Preparation* and results in a draft workbook compiled for team use in the workshop meeting. Materials preparation is the staff work time taken to create draft documents, design exhibits, and assemble them as a team handout. This includes the partially completed forms from individual work and any other materials created or provided during or after the orientation meeting.

In the time available in the first two steps, preparation for good business analysis is supported in the basic forms structure. Before the workshop you can determine the need to discuss technical solutions and how to include technology analysis in the meeting. Depending on the depth of business analysis, business function analysis often includes technology related materials. In any case, you can treat business engineering and process redesign decisions and technology design decisions as separate but related issues. With a view that business problem definitions and solution directions prescribe a technological solution, it is possible to complete workshop preparation with a greater focus on business objectives. In this way, the people who need to decide on technology issues can review the Analysis Guidelines and prepare for their role and contribute to the draft material in the workbook before the meeting. Indeed, draft materials worked during preparation should be available to technology developers so they can review and determine technological direction and be more informed for the meeting. The team will expect technologists to be ready to provide advice.

By the time you have reached *Step 3* the issues about how to develop a technology should be better understood and the information needed for technology development analysis structures will be more apparent. You will need advice from the project leader and technical design analyst to decide on the best approach to include technical perspectives in the workbook method for debate. The role of the technologist is to understand the accumulation of requirement findings and solution direction from team consensus and provide the information needed for more detailed technological design. At this level of detail, the character of this has a lot to do with providing confirmation that a technological solution is possible. For this reason, a system developer will want to use illustrations which verify requirement information in a context of technological design. You should review draft technology illustrations to understand how you will work with technologists and involve them in workshop conversation. In this way it is possible for technologists to create special materials and add to them in the course of knowledge exchange. For a business planning workshop, such materials are best discussed as summary information. For the benefit of non-technical people, they are best worked on paper illustrations used to capture and convert business views into meaningful technological design with comparisons to specific verification criteria. If an issue is raised at a detail level, it can be addressed and brought back to the summary level for general conversation and consensus. With this approach, summary details can be lifted out of discussion and documented agreement can be reached on higher level issues which are potentially the more important to resolve and complete in the workshop.

TECHNICAL PERSPECTIVE

While technology solutions are chosen and developed to respond to business needs, business design will be influenced by constraints imposed by technology. Technical perspectives should be included in workshop discussion to provide concurrence with business views and explain any influence technologies might impose on a business environment. Business representatives will want assurance that technology will support objectives without being inflexible or too constraining. As shown in the Workshop Disciplines Chart in an earlier chapter, technological perspectives are best represented in languages supportive of the actual issues in debate. To reach consensus, a systems analyst might have to explain a technical issue using particular illustrations representing specialist points of view. In this case you as session leader may have to facilitate debate using business perspectives in the forms and technical perspectives on separate illustrations provided. Usually, it is necessary for you to summarize both points of view in documenting design decisions.

Using the JAD book building approach, business and technology illustrations can be included in the workshop handout. Such materials range from sketch diagrams to detailed schematics. They can be hand drawn or generated output from analytical or system development tools. For this reason, and if it is practical to do so, technological development tools might be used in a workshop to generate discussion materials or demonstrate results of discussion during the meeting. Following the example of providing separate clerical support to create workbook revisions, you can include a specialist support role to generate revised technical analysis materials. Using this approach, the team will be able to keep sight of the issues and decisions which effect a change. And, the results of detailed computer assisted analyses will be less disruptive to a train of thought if they are introduced by the session leader at an appropriate time to rationalize decisions once the necessary information is available.

The materials preparation step is complete when forms and supporting pages are indexed to an analysis sequence and compiled as a workshop document for each participant. This activity may take a few days or be done in late afternoon time for a next day workshop. In addition to paper copies, overhead transparencies of each workbook page are needed for the session leader to present team contributions in debate.

WORKSHOP MEETING

STEP 4 is described as the ***Workshop Meeting*** in which people deliver a revised document representing team consensus for business and system requirements. The workshop meeting is the time to bring people together to discuss topics and materials contained in a meeting workbook. The book building process is implemented from the beginning of the agenda to the end. Starting with an overhead transparency for the book cover, the team is led through sequential pages. Depending on the preparation alternative chosen to reach a workshop, material will be discussed in greater or lesser detail. Even though people may have already read the Management Guidelines, everyone will benefit in reviewing it to be reminded of the assignment. Following conventional meeting protocol, review the agenda and analysis guidelines to focus discussion. If you covered most of these points in an Orientation Meeting, there should be few changes so that you can quickly move to more detailed discussions in the Solution Guidelines and Analysis Forms.

Using business illustrations in the Solution Guidelines to cross reference analysis topics, the team starts a critical assessment and debate around contributions provided so far. Your role as session leader will range from making minor changes in content to being very involved in conversation and using your communication skills to help the team reach agreement and document understanding. The participants will be glad to share in your technique in which you summarize debate in conversational and documented extracts. While future system users focus on business requirements, system developers can support design conversation in providing technical advice for alternative methods and costs for automation. In this way, all team members become involved and jointly make decisions about business and technical solutions for systems development. You manage the conversation to an acceptable scope and continue the process until the requirement notes respond to the business engineering objectives described as Management Guidelines. As you make progress you can gather up overhead transparencies and supplemental notes to be typed for immediate return as new overheads and periodic inserts to workbook pages. At key stages of design, or at the end of the day, you can affirm team decisions using a Change Results log to list apparent change for a summary report to management. While you might do this to edit design detail in review, you will validate change results to expectations and inevitably strengthen team comfort and commitment to emerging design plans.

After the analysis work on the forms, you need to review and assign responsibilities for unresolved action items. To wrap up the meeting, you can review the stated management objectives to validate successful results of team work. In closing you should thank the team for participating and recognize the people who prepared discussion materials for their contributions to the success of the process. Your thanks should also mention clerical support for typing workbook pages. Finally, you should thank the sponsor for the direction for the assignment and wish the team continued success as the project moves into development.

WORKSHOP PRODUCT

In these workshops, documented results compile vision and goals and requirement expressions for a new business environment in design detail for what a system should do. For the next level of detail, the JAD concept is adapted to work in a system specification language for the look and the feel of manual and automated processes for people to design the way they would like to operate.

ADVANCING PROCEDURE SPECIFICATIONS

ad-vance v. To go forward; to progress, move towards completion; to cause an event to happen sooner than planned or expected; to suggest, propose; to advance a theory, progressive, in front of most others.

pro-ce-dure n. Act or manner of proceeding; a prescribed way of doing things; a particular course of action.

spec-i-fi-ca-tion n. Act of specifying; detailed items required for a project to be carried out.

spec-i-fy v. To name or mention explicitly; to include in a specification.

CHAPTER THIRTEEN

JAD—Procedure Specifications Analysis for Business Design

ACTIVITY BASED TECHNIQUE FOR DESIGN SPECIFICATIONS

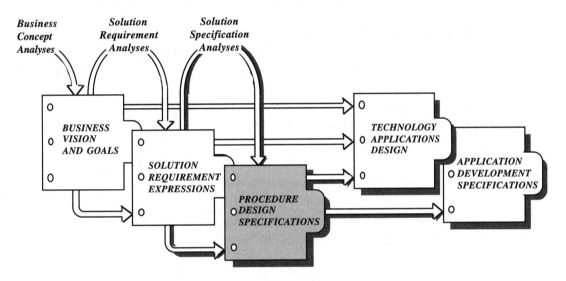

Using the previous Documentation Level and Analysis Technique chart to relate design information the above summary illustrates *Solution Specifications Analysis* and life cycle documents involved in the migration of Solution Requirement Expressions to become Procedure Design Specifications with Technology Application Design and Development Specifications. You can implement a Business Design workshop to discuss business requirements and define second level business design and third and fourth level technical information using an Activity Based Analysis technique for business procedure specifications.

ORGANIZATION FOR DEBATE

Using the dividers for conversation approach for a system specifications document, business design analysis is supported in the *Management Guidelines, Solution Guidelines,* and *Design Scenario* dividers. Typical design detail to describe an operational specification is documented in a design scenario divider. Depending on the level of detail, the Activity Based Analysis technique can also be used to check precision in a business planning document and add detail to requirement expressions in the previously described *Analysis Forms* divider.

Following the JAD book building process, the session leader should promote an organization of design scenario exhibits to show business operations and system transactions defined in the scope of the project. In this approach, business design specifications are considered using work definitions to differentiate analysis topics by the character of typical business activities. In doing this, an operational design can be animated by a list of verbs and nouns which abbreviate requirements as solution guidelines in a Business Activity Model. Your key to success is to provide intuitive references to subject materials and use a familiar language for debate. For the best results, manipulate the verb and noun list until it becomes representative of business operations for a design scenario conducive to sharing ideas and exchanging information in a workshop setting.

To round out a procedure design specifications document, summary information can be added to provide background and general understanding about the assignment in the Background divider. Business Environment and Application of Technology illustrations and important reference materials from previous analyses can be included in the Solution Guidelines divider. Occasionally referenced materials are located in the Appendices divider. From preparation, include a proposed design scenario in the form of business information as an operational dialogue presented for analysis on suggested screens and reports in the Design Scenario divider. It will be easier to explain the technique if you use a diagram to illustrate the approach for your analysis sequence and documentation process.

In the following diagram, the main divider headings used in a workshop agenda are shown as a sequence of workbook pages. The pages usually involved in specifications analysis are numbered in the

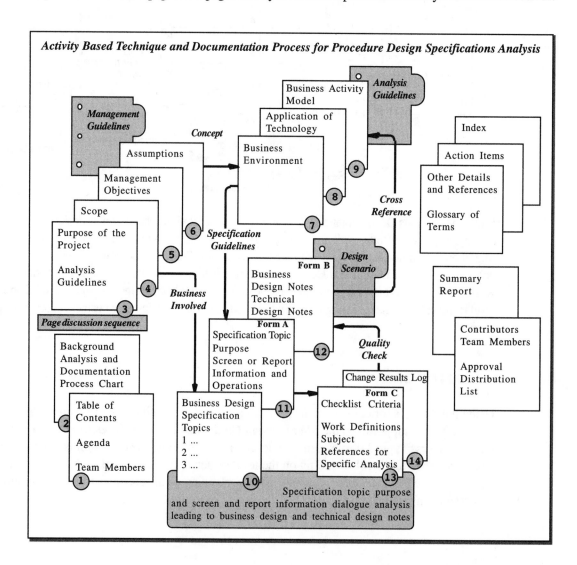

order used. Pages without sequence numbers are usually recorded to the appendices for the references and details needed for general conversation. All materials should be referenced in the Index divider.

After the Management Guidelines and Solution Guidelines already described, the analysis structure continues to support discussions and exchanges of points of view about design exhibits and reference materials. To add clarity to organization, a design scenario is preceded by a list of system specification topics matched to the business involved in the scope. Analysis is conducted around a Business Activity Model presented as the last page in the Solution Guidelines. Using this, certain business tasks can be grouped for which selected design exhibits are examined in the context of supporting work characterized by an appropriate Work Definition. For accuracy and completeness, analysis is cross referenced to other Solution Guideline material and design requirement decisions are summarized by the words in the Business Activity Model. Analysis decisions are noted on screens and report exhibits with attached business and technical design notes. As results emerge, design change should be logged periodically to validate business engineering and process redesign objectives.

POINT FORM MECHANICS

All workshops start with a similar step to create a document with standard dividers up to Solution Guidelines. In a Business Design workshop, requirements and specifications are documented in the Design Scenario divider. Forms are designed to illustrate a proposed operational scenario with design notes compiled to have a similar appearance as an operator's guide for a system. A Business Activity Model is used to provide an abstract to better understand process redesign in a point form document in which work flow and business automation is related for analysis. Point form mechanics follows a sequence shown below.

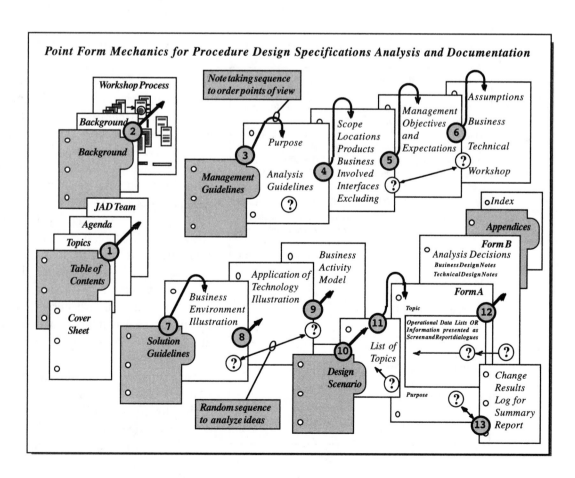

ADAPTIVE FORMS DESIGN

In this approach, two basic forms are organized to analyze business design specifications. The forms work for different topics and at various levels of detail. Form A is arranged to document specification decisions for business information in the manner of system interactions for an operational dialogue as it would appear to people operating a quality system. Form A is the work area to be used to present design scenario materials on an overhead projector for team discussion. Form B is not necessarily shown as an overhead image for team review. It is organized to capture workshop results as business specifications and technical detail to clarify design requirements and provide the knowledge needed for actions involved in further systems development.

The two forms provide a relatively free format area in the workbook to contain numerous design scenario exhibits and various levels of illustrated and documented detail. While the forms are separate for presentation and note taking, they are usually combined on one or two pages repeated for specification topics.

Typical Specification Analysis Forms

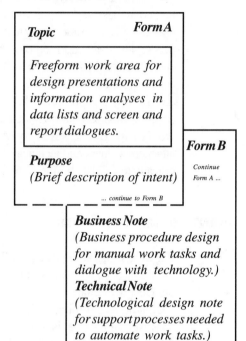

Typical Business Activity Model Form

> **BUSINESS ACTIVITY MODEL**
> BUSINESS ROUTINE AND AUTOMATION
> **Guidelines**: Consider the following Work Definitions and describe business activity in a summary list of verbs and nouns for manual and automated tasks to do work. Use an appropriate Work Definition to group characteristic tasks in a plausible sequence for efficient and effective work flow. From the list, project an activity summary to the attached analysis forms to engineer work as an operational system.
>
> WORK DEFINITIONS   MANUAL AND AUTOMATED TASKS
>
> A. WORK ENVIRONMENT   *(Activity Verb and Noun list to describe business tasks in a work flow sequence characteristic of work definition headings shown.)*
>
> B. RECEIVED WORK
>
> C. INITIAL PROCESSING
>
> D. WORK MANAGEMENT
>
> E. WORK IN PROCESS
>
> F. RESULTS PROCESSING
>
> G. COMPLETED WORK
>
> H. WORK REVIEW

ORGANIZED FOR ANALYSIS

At a higher level, business engineering analysis uses a list of topics in a relational hierarchy with a forms index to bring sequence and structure to a meeting agenda. For process redesign analysis, a list of business tasks brings order to debate with a Business Activity Model to convey sequence and relationship in a list of verbs and nouns which outlines the system.

While an organization list provides sequence and structure, it also provides a point form document to assist group memory. Using the forms based technique this is portrayed in topic groups. Using the activity based technique, this is better reflected in task groups for the way future system users would like to be involved with a working system.

To convey representative group memory and to bring sequence and structure the Business Activity Model shown must be understood and applied for comprehensive systems design. To do this, work flow is considered in terms of managing business using a work tray utility.

CHAPTER FOURTEEN

JAD—Work Trays for Business Procedure Analysis

ACTIVITY BASED ANALYSIS

Activity based analysis allows people to consider process redesign in the way they want to work. There is usually an element of satisfaction or dissatisfaction in the way things are done. As session leader you need to discuss this to discover needs for change. Following the JAD Communication Model, your workshop approach should illustrate sufficient understanding of the present and realize change through innovative design. When a Business Activity Model is used, tasks in a verb and noun sequence initially describe current procedures in a draft design scenario. A proposed design scenario can change tasks and sequence. The final list reflects accepted business design after successive analyses when a design scenario becomes a business engineering solution.

Through progressive debate a proposed design scenario is redefined as the team contemplates ideas and suggestions for requirements and procedures for practical business design. To demonstrate understanding and method in evaluating ideas you as session leader keep in tune with an evolving design scenario through frequent updates and additions to the work flow summary shown as verb and noun combinations. For this reason, as you use a Business Activity Model, it becomes a means for thorough analysis and quality design documentation. In the dynamics of using it for analytical guidance, it indicates progress and becomes a topical agenda for the meeting. It is a checklist and reference document for the logical relationships which validate operational design and ensure the factors for a good system are considered first in the analysis of business procedures.

Required tasks for various business routines can be arranged by the application of structure inherent in sequential work. People often relate work flow and management practices to references known by many in the way work trays establish procedure. For this reason Work Definitions for activity analysis are based on describing the "In Tray," "In Process," and "Out Tray" utility. The arrangement is predisposed to a logical relationship in which questions are raised to facilitate analysis. The definitions are flexible and adaptable to analyze various business situations for technical and non-technical solutions. Business people understand work definitions for work trays and invariably use an appropriate interpretation for objective but creative analysis.

WORK TRAYS FOR BUSINESS ROUTINE

Work trays are commonplace in active business areas. The concept of staging work using labelled trays is acceptable for most people to describe business routine. Over the years, conventional wisdom has named staged work using popular and practical tray titles: "Received Work" for the "In Tray," and "Work in Process" for the "In Process Tray," and "Completed Work" for the "Out Tray".

By extending tray labels to describe typical activities using pending status codes to manage a work backlog, it becomes

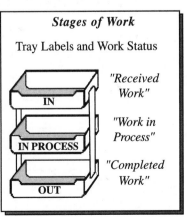

Stages of Work

Tray Labels and Work Status

"Received Work"

"Work in Process"

"Completed Work"

possible to characterize work types at different stages. In a further structure of work definitions, various manual operations and automated work can be described to distinguish the analysis for people tasks and automation as external and systems design.

WORK TRAY ANALYSIS

When the above work tray concept is applied and the work definitions used for business analysis, a relatively easy approach is presented for people to consider a proposed design scenario. Insightful points of reference are gained to define business policy, procedures to determine system requirements for business operations, and the specifications to operate technology designed to streamline and automate work.

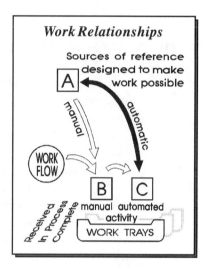

Each tray is considered in turn and the work involved is defined to outline manual and automated tasks. As design is specified sources of reference which make business activity possible is also considered and defined. Combining the three points of view makes the system whole in a relationship shown here as [A] [B] [C]. While each work tray is designed separately, the design might be reused or added to for the reference sources which in total defines the work environment for the trays.

CHARACTERISTIC WORK

In the following illustration, business activity is staged through work trays in which an analysis structure is characterized by eight work headings to differentiate the manual procedures and automated processes. Structure is identified using alphabet letters A through H. Physical work directly associated with work trays is highlighted in headings [B] [E] and [G]. Automated work is shown in [C] as Initial Processing on work received at the In tray and [F] as Results Processing on

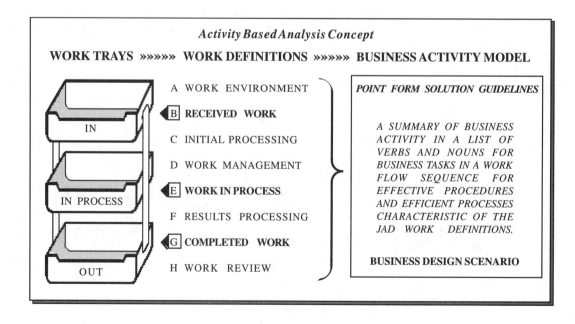

work at the In Process tray. The remaining definitions characterize management involvement in upholding business as a Work Environment in [A], Work Management in [D], and Management Review in [H]. The work trays and work definitions are considered together to create a Business Activity Model in a verb and noun list to analyze a business design scenario.

STRUCTURED BUSINESS ANALYSIS

JAD work tray definitions are designed to convey logical work relationships to facilitate the analysis of business routine and the application of technology to process information. While work routines become evident from an observation of work tray tasks, logic relationships in business routines and automation are not so apparent. The following diagram illustrates how to consider business analysis in relating workflow tasks and business information management tasks into and out of a business area. The enclosed area surrounding work flow represents the extent of business design defined as scope in the Management Guidelines for an assignment. Business information and work flow are shown in two levels described as operational controls and operational tasks. Work is processed in the operational task layer through the work tray utility with management influences exercised from operational controls to direct business processes.

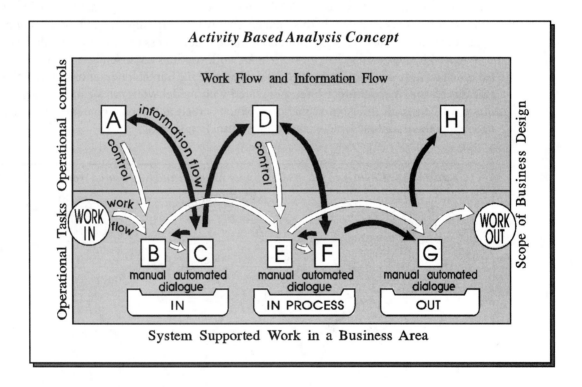

ACTIVITY IN VERBS AND NOUNS

For each work heading, verbs and nouns are listed to indicate activity in terms of the tasks needed to support a desired result. Management perspectives in definition [A] head the list, with tasks to manage information sources and business controls which define a work environment. Using the above business analysis model, information references and controls are applied through manual and automated information dialogues designed to support various activities associated with each work tray. These are presented as work tray tasks that occur each time people interact with business and operate technology designed for business.

The In tray has a verb and noun list for $\boxed{B}$ and $\boxed{C}$ to relate manual and automated activities. After received work, another business management perspective is presented in a task list $\boxed{D}$ to monitor and assign work. Here progressive work status is tracked and a pending backlog assigned for completion to the work held at the In Process tray which also has a verb and noun list for $\boxed{E}$ and $\boxed{F}$ for manual and automated work. A Business Activity Model is complete when activities are listed to send concluded business onward from the Out tray $\boxed{G}$, and finally management tasks using business analysis and operational reports in $\boxed{H}$.

WORK DEFINITIONS FOR CONVERSATION

To analyze business logic and define system design specifications, the workbook divider for conversation approach is extended to use work definitions for discussion. When JAD work definitions are used to characterize work trays, word associations can be used to prompt conversational topics which describe business activities and relate manual and automated tasks to a Business Activity Model. Each work definition provides fundamental ideas to analyze solution guidelines for tasks which in total defines a business environment. Work definitions $\boxed{C}$ and $\boxed{F}$ add perspectives to automate information dialogues; these need not be considered for an all-manual system designed for people to do all the work. These work definitions characterize automation and are used to define tasks done by a technology application when business procedures are changed. In this, manual In tray tasks $\boxed{B}$ might be redefined or eliminated by automated tasks listed for $\boxed{C}$. Similarly, manual In Process tray tasks $\boxed{E}$ could be changed or replaced by automation listed for $\boxed{F}$. As work routines are discussed business specifications can be defined with an operational perspective for human interactions with technology. For this reason, manual procedures associated with model work trays can be analyzed to include a technological design scenario in which screen and report contents are arranged in characteristic design for typical computer information systems.

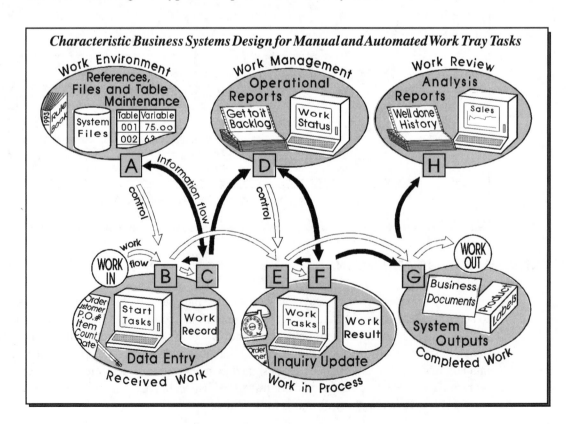

CHARACTERISTIC BUSINESS SYSTEMS DESIGN

Just as certain business functions are characterized by work tray activities, typical computer system processes can be characterized by basic information management functions. As tasks responsive to business needs are considered typical design can be matched to work definitions as procedures and technology engineered for work trays. Characteristic operation control designs include data maintenance for work controls and reporting for operations management and business analysis. Typical operational task designs include data entry to start work, inquiry update to process work, and system outputs to complete work.

POINT FORM SOLUTION GUIDELINES

It is easier to use customary language for systems analysis when key words are used to depict business activity rather than technological illustrations to map systemized processes. A list of words to describe characteristic activity is less likely to intimidate business people. This approach allows non-technical people to become focused and lucid as they explain familiar business processes and explore design opportunities for improvement. At first, the list illustrates system procedures people know from working through familiar business routine. In debate, a design scenario evolves to become representative of new and redesigned processes. Throughout the meeting, the list contains sequence for agenda and relationship in a point form analysis document which provides group memory to more detailed system specifications.

While opportunistic change may be significant in the detail, it is unlikely and probably impractical to obliterate time-honored business activity. Despite change, required work must still be done. People will appreciate the idea of keeping business intact as familiar tasks are engineered to analyze work routines and recognize redundancy and change procedures and design automation for a more efficient work flow.

A verb and noun Business Activity Model does not have to be complex or precise, nor do it have to be grammatically correct. Since conversation contains inconsistencies and written language is interpretive, wordiness can lead to misunderstanding. Simple is clear. It is more important that few words provide meaningful summaries of intent. Actual words depend on the people involved and their normal use of language. Because a first draft illustrates the current environment, it should not be difficult to use representative point form to provide an overview of the present system. Since the Business Activity Model concept supports both current and future system perspectives, a first draft can also include recommended changes and automation. Indeed a point form systems abstract is only complete when the key words illustrate proposed solutions and the team understands the design and the procedures involved.

BUSINESS ACTIVITY MODEL EXPLAINED

When the Work Definition concept is applied to discussions of work, people responsible for managing work so that people who do work can participate in decisions to design business policies and procedures. Even when detailed discussions and complex subject materials are used people see familiar references in a task list which must go on for good business. Change and automation becomes evident as task descriptions are moved and listed to work definitions for manual or automated activity. Because the activity list summarizes the existing and transforms it to a new and changed business environment, future system users and system developers become clear and realistic about business and technical design decisions. The model should be comprehensive for the scope of design and show an understandable sequence of manual and automated tasks for the work involved. As people realize the potential of automation in their own terms, design ideas are more acceptable and consequential change less disruptive and easier to implement.

This approach succeeds when design discussions are focused separately and completely for each work tray and discrete stages of Received Work to Work in Process are followed through Completed Work in the overall scheme of things. Although the concept is applied in eight work definitions, fewer relationships need be thought of at a time when tasks are considered to be clustered to individual work trays. In the following charts, generic work descriptions lend themselves to illustrate characteristic system activities. In applying these definitions the best words can be selected and composed to describe operational controls and tasks as necessary for work which all in all defines a business system. Using these words to model business creates a road map to relate design ideas and gather appropriate discussion materials as a workbook document for an effective meeting.

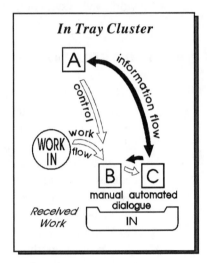

IN TRAY CLUSTER

When Work Definitions A B and C are clustered, the basis to analyze work in the In tray is formed. Starting with definition A , business needs can be studied for references and sources of information which make a work environment possible. With this definition the controls needed to identify and manage work according to management policy and business practice can be considered. Definition A also allows you to consider work due in or information about future work due into an area.

Work environment topics for system design should only and need only include the tasks to manage source references and information relating to work activities in the scope of design. For Received Work, manual references and automated information sources are specified as they could be used by people involved in obtaining and starting work. In this, automated sources of information are designed to be applied by computer processes or presented in system dialogues to assist work flow.

Definitions B and C characterize work received at the In tray. Using definition B for Received Work, typical data capture processes using screen dialogues designed for data entry with automation to streamline work arrival activities are considered. Definition C reviews business automation and information processing in terms of file creation and record keeping. The benefits of replacing manual activities with practical automation to improve record keeping with status codes to track work are explored. As consensus for automation is reached, manual work listed for definition B is reviewed and new procedures needed for people to interact with technology are considered. To round out this work tray design, also study how to generate work arrival notifications and other automated system outputs resulting from information recorded about work received. Periodically, as a system design evolves, the tasks under definition A should be reviewed to ensure that references and operational controls provide the environment needed to streamline received work.

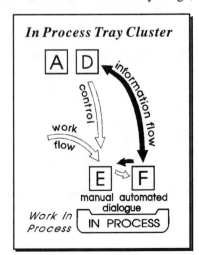

IN PROCESS TRAY CLUSTER

When Work Definitions A and D , and E and F are clustered, the basis for analyzing the In Process tray is created. This is similar to the In tray cluster with additional design to manage various work assignments and tasks duly needed to complete work. Starting with definition D , operational in-

GENERIC WORK DEFINITIONS

In this approach team debate is focused on business analysis by examining the work flow shown in double lines in the center chart. Shown as a solid line, information is analyzed to support business and provide system users with a dialogue for work routines including the operation of technology. The following work definitions provide generic guidelines to characterize a business design scenario as point form tasks structured to animate and analyze procedure specifications.

A WORK ENVIRONMENT - BUSINESS CONTROLS

Information and controls about work to be done at some future time is provided from planning sources, other locations and within the business area.

The information is maintained in a priority sequence and work controls are periodically reset or adjusted.

The control information is used to manage the business and provide operator guidance to receive and complete the work.

B RECEIVED WORK - SYSTEM INPUTS

Work and related resources come into the business area from other locations.

Guidance and control information is used to receive the work.

As work and resources arrive a unique identification of each is entered into the system.

C INITIAL PROCESSING - RECORD KEEPING

The system records the time of reporting, does the necessary processing including validation of data input and creates or updates associated records.

Information is logged to track the work and record the status of various work activities.

The system automatically provides control information operator guidance, initiates changes and notifications, produces printouts, updates history, etc.

D WORK MANAGEMENT - MONITOR AND ASSIGN

Managers and personnel regularly monitor planned and received work to determine what can be done and re-establish priorities and assign resources.

Access is provided to information and instructions to complete the work.

E WORK IN PROCESS - INQUIRY UPDATE

Business area personnel proceed to work on various jobs that have been assigned.

Guidance and control information is used to complete the work.

Progress on the work is periodically reported to the system for administrative feedback and planning.

F RESULTS PROCESSING - RECORD KEEPING

The system records the time of reporting, does the necessary processing including validation of data input and creates or updates associated records.

Information is logged to track the work and record the status of various work activities.

The system automatically provides control information operator guidance, initiates changes and notifications, produces printouts, updates history, etc.

G COMPLETED WORK - SYSTEM OUTPUTS

Documents and labels are provided as needed to identify and describe completion and authorize disposition.

Completed work is routed to holding or other locations.

Actual work departures are recorded as necessary.

H WORK REVIEW - MANAGEMENT REPORTS

For comparison to previous periods, the system provides:
- *Departmental work summaries*
- *Measurements relative to business targets*
- *Cost and quality performance metrics*
- *Service levels*
- *Error rates*
- *Resource utilization information*
- *Statistical and trend analyses*

formation needed to review work backlogs and the sources of reference information needed to guide work processes are considered. Information used to monitor work flow is usually more dynamic than typical controls and static information references specific to a work environment. Control references are also involved in handling work; for this reason work definitions $\boxed{A}$ and $\boxed{D}$ are shown together to provide static and dynamic information to assist Work in Process to completion. As a session leader, you design manual references and automatic information sources as they should be used by people attending to collective or personal work backlogs. As designs emerge, you can review the tasks under work definition $\boxed{A}$ so that business references provide the information and operation controls needed to streamline work.

MANAGING WORK FLOW

In the Activity Based Analysis Model, work flow is shown at an operational task level with operational controls to manage procedure. Operational controls are used to guide work flow and provide references to measure business progress. In this, definition $\boxed{D}$ is used to analyze business requirements to track work through the In tray to the In Process tray to various stages of completion. With this definition, the information people need to know to manage work flow and best assign available resources can be considered. Definition $\boxed{D}$ can be used to consider manual reports or automated views of business information for people to do work and monitor activity and performance in different areas. Also, methods to assign work and information presentation techniques to provide access or guide for the details needed to process work in the In Process tray can be evaluated. Using definition $\boxed{E}$ for Work in Process, physical involvement due to accepting work for completion can be analyzed, including typical data capture processes using screen dialogues designed for information inquiry and updates with automation to streamline work processing activities. With definition $\boxed{F}$, business automation and information management can be studied in terms of file search and record keeping for progressive work results. As agreement is reached about automation, tasks listed for definition $\boxed{E}$ can be reviewed to consider new procedures to work with technology. To round out design, the need to generate work status or completion notifications and other automatic system outputs resulting from information recorded about work in process should also be considered. Periodically, as design emerges, review the references defined for the work environment to ensure they provide required information and operational controls for a complete process.

OUT TRAY CLUSTER

When work definitions $\boxed{A}$, $\boxed{G}$, and $\boxed{H}$ are clustered, the basics emerge for analyzing work in the Out tray. This cluster is similar to the In tray cluster, but designed for sending work on instead of receiving work. Starting with work definition $\boxed{G}$, business requirements to create or support physical outputs which leave the area after the work is done in the In Process tray can be analyzed. For Completed Work, manual and automated information sources are analyzed as they could be used by people involved in concluding work responsibilities. Using this definition, consider also various methods and information used to authorize and record work disposition. Definition $\boxed{G}$ is concerned with physical work outputs from completed work processes. Automated system outputs are considered as information interfaces designed under work definition $\boxed{F}$. Finally, management reports for

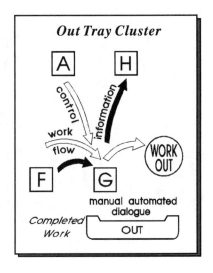

operational measurements and various business results and other required information listed under work definition ⌐H⌐ can be discussed.

PAPER MODEL PROPOSAL

As a result of listing key words to illustrate work, the Business Activity Model can be used to prepare draft documents and workbook materials for a meeting. The key words illustrate the system as a paper model and provide realistic references for discussion. In the workshop, as session leader, you will benefit from preparation based on the same model. You will have greater confidence in opening the meeting if you worked with the people involved in preparing a design scenario, and you understand the proposal before calling for debate.

CHAPTER FIFTEEN

JAD–Specification Workshop Logistics

PREPARATION FOR A SUCCESSFUL MEETING

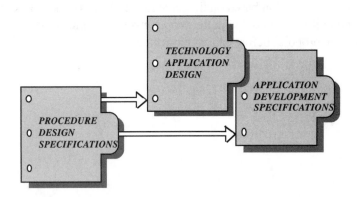

The concept of relating levels of systems design detail to a workshop technique is shown in a Documentation Level and Analysis Technique chart explained in a previous chapter. The above summary from that chart illustrates business design documents as Solution Requirement Expressions with Technology Application Design and Development Specifications. While business and technical detail might be combined, the books are usually kept separate to differentiate business procedure design and business automation design.

Vision and Goals and Solution Requirement Expressions analyses might be documented separately or combined as one book, Procedure Design Specifications are usually documented separately. This workbook is arranged like a Requirements Expression document except that the Analysis Forms divider is replaced by a Design Scenario divider after solution guideline illustrations. Previously used Management Guidelines can be used with redefined and more focused objectives and assumptions. The Analysis Guidelines can be restated on the purpose page to describe the increased level of detail in the design analysis forms.

The JAD process uses four basic steps to prepare and lead a workshop for business process redesign analysis. The logistics shown in the following chart explain the typical steps and activities needed to use the Activity Based Analysis technique to define business design specifications for an operational environment in concert with documented business concepts and business function requirements.

Usually, it takes two to four weeks of elapsed time from the outset to the workshop meeting. Preparation times shown are normally sufficient to customize a workshop approach, create the meeting agenda, and do the necessary staff work to prepare a workbook and presentation materials for team discussion. For some situations, the elapsed time can be longer—it is a matter of judgment for those involved to decide what has to be done to implement the workshop technique. Preparation is the key to success, and the activities shown provide the basis to get the right people with the right attitude and right materials all in the same place at the same time. From this perspective, main activities over a time frame are shown across the chart, participant involvement is listed down the chart with role descriptions and key outputs for each step.

Involvement and Outputs Using Activity Based Analysis for Procedure Design Specifications

ACTIVITY over 2-4 weeks...	STEP 1 Management Guidelines	STEP 2 Orientation	STEP 3 Materials Preparation	STEP 4 Workshop Meeting
INVOLVEMENT				
Session Leader	Develop JAD approach 1 day	Outline workflow 1/2-1 day	Organize workbook 1-2 days	Lead workshop analysis process 2-4 days
Project Leader or Project Manager	Integrate approach 1 day	Organize activities 1-2 days	Coordinate involvement 1-2 days	Supervise Documentation 2-4 days
Executive Sponsor	Approve and select team 1/4-1/2 day			Opening and Closing summary
Business Team Involved	Contribute to direction 1/2-2 days	Visit Area Supervisor 1/2-1 day	Contribute Materials 1/2-2 days	Exchange knowledge 2-4 days
Developer Team Involved	Integrate plan requirements 1-2 days	Draft System Design Scenario 2-5 days	Compile draft workbook 2-4 days	Technical advice 2-4 days
Technical support Project Leader System Analyst	Review solution guidelines 1-2 days	Review Solution direction 1/2-3 days	Prepare to contribute 1-2 days	Technical analysis . . . Model
Note keeping Business experience Technical skills			Understand content 1/2-1 day	Note team decisions 2-4 days
Secretary, Clerical Support			Start workbook 1/2-1 day	Update document 2-4 days

STEP OUTPUTS

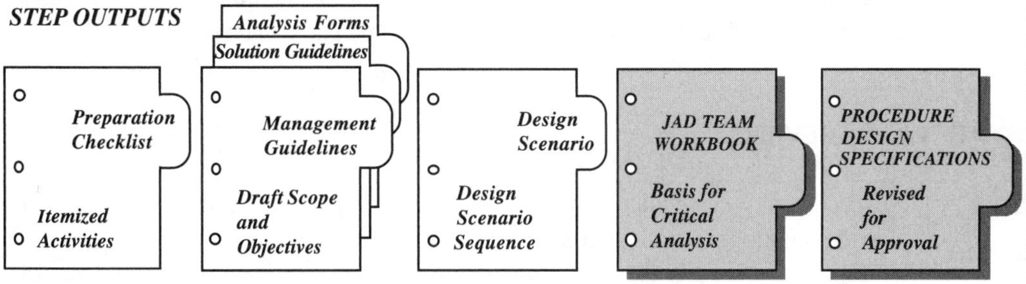

Analysis Forms / *Solution Guidelines*

- *Preparation Checklist* — *Itemized Activities*
- *Management Guidelines* — *Draft Scope and Objectives*
- *Design Scenario* — *Design Scenario Sequence*
- *JAD TEAM WORKBOOK* — *Basis for Critical Analysis*
- *PROCEDURE DESIGN SPECIFICATIONS* — *Revised for Approval*

DIVIDER CONTENT FOR CONVERSATION . . . . **BOOK CONTENT** . . . .

MANAGEMENT GUIDELINES

STEP 1 is described under the *Management Guidelines* heading and results in an itemized Preparation Checklist and draft Management Guidelines pages shown in the above chart with activities to prepare a workshop. The Management Guidelines step usually starts in a meeting in which the project manager or project leader invites the session leader to present the JAD approach and discuss the assignment. At this time, the overall plan for the project is considered as well as how and when to use a workshop in the process. From this discussion, the session leader can start the book building process to develop the analysis technique for the situation. Depending on the availability of prepared materials, previous plans for direction should be reviewed and known solution guidelines integrated with design information.

STARTING A WORKBOOK

With a typical workbook as a starting point, the session leader should assist in any adaptation to the analysis structure to gain the information required at this stage of systems development. Using a Procedure Design Specifications book cover and dividers and typical specification forms to demonstrate structure, you can create draft materials in this meeting by reviewing existing or starting new notes under the Management Guidelines heading. Typical outputs from this conversation will be an outline of purpose, scope, objectives and assumptions about the assignment. All these points are captured under form titles and headings on pages described earlier as a book building process. This meeting usually concludes with a discussion about the schedule, the workshop venue, the meeting agenda, and participants, and preparation needed for success. Logistics are usually handled by the project leader or other support personnel. A preparation checklist is useful to itemize various responsibilities to prepare for the workshop.

The next key event in the checklist is to meet with the executive sponsor to review workbook materials and confirm direction for involvement. It is important to follow required procedure for a successful workshop, and as with any assignment, it might be prudent for tactful involvement with other people to review draft materials before you meet the sponsor. While you may do this only to keep people informed about the process, you will inevitably clarify the purpose in the Management Guidelines. To the extent that political activity can be anticipated it is usually coordinated by a project team leader. If additional involvement is needed, it could include contributions from other business managers and system developers from interviews over one or two days, or in a steering committee meeting. Typically, each new meeting may require you as session leader to promote the approach and gain acceptance for involvement. Occasionally you might recognize a delicate situation and look to the project leader for advice and guidance to resolve or preferably avoid potential for conflict. Review activity need not be extensive. Indeed, once the project leader has a draft document, the session leader may not be involved while other people work on materials independently or until certain events are covered and you can resume preparation responsibilities.

STAFF WORK REVIEW

At some point you can decide the staff work is complete enough for your sponsor to review and provide additional details and approval to proceed. For this level of workshop, a sponsor may have been involved in an earlier business planning workshop. If management direction is clear from previous work, you might only need thirty minutes to define the purpose and agenda. If this is the first meeting, and depending on complexity, it might take up to an hour or longer when more detailed discussion is needed. For an efficient interview, you as session leader should explain the meeting as an opportunity to become acquainted, to explain the process, and exchange views about what the workshop should cover to be thought successful. You could probably demonstrate the approach as a draft workbook and evolving staff work.

Although this approach works at a different level of detail than business planning, you will probably experience similar politics to reach an agreement to proceed. If you already have momentum from previous planning it will be easier. You should nonetheless consider different work styles and protocols and allow for the time needed to advance to the next step. At this time, if your sponsor is willing to review the workbook and contribute to the content, you can make changes or additions to clarify the Management Guidelines. Using clues from conversation, direct your questions to adapt the staff work to a management point of view. While people contribute to the process and as you respond, you should be able to note key points in the workbook during the meeting.

At this level of detail, people may be cautious about providing information and want to work on documents in private or seek the opinions of others before giving approval to proceed. In this situation, the session leader would review workshop plans in the first meeting, generalize the discussion to the process and team participation, and arrange another meeting to start the preparation. For other situations, you might lead a review meeting or attend a steering committee meeting in which managers jointly reach agreement about the direction for the assignment. Typically, you would also see the sponsor a few days or just prior to the meeting to review the workshop agenda and peruse discussion materials.

TEAM ROLES

Once the Management Guidelines have been approved, as session leader you can review the agenda and explain the role of the sponsor to kick off the meeting and mention certain things as typical for opening remarks. In addition, people should consider the required qualifications to contribute to the overall success of the meeting. For this, review the scope and refer to the locations listed and functions involved and detail required to confirm the right people are invited. The team must be capable of contributing to analysis topics and have the ability and authority to change business procedures. Review the objectives and expectations to ensure that team selection has the right background and appropriate knowledge for good participation.

Although attendees may have already been approached, the project leader can now prepare a more informative invitation package containing administration details, the agenda, and Management Guidelines for team involvement. In addition to the topics outline in the scope page, the analysis topics index should be included for people to understand the workbook organization and consider materials before the meeting.

ORIENTATION

STEP 2 is described as the *Orientation* for the session leader to understand the basic workflow and document a more detailed agenda in terms of the analysis structure. This usually starts in a discussion with the project leader to outline the workflow as a Business Activity Model using JAD Work Definitions to sequence tasks and animate work tray procedures. With a draft list of typical business activity, the session leader will benefit by a visit with area personnel to confirm it relates to the business routines to be analyzed.

The purpose of task sequence is to describe a plausible design scenario by which business operations and business automation can be defined. Once a Business Activity Model is drafted you can begin to relate solution ideas as a business design scenario and start specifications analysis. Indeed, the task list provides an ideas road map to arrange business and technological design discussions and understand the details of emerging solutions. As you continue this discussion, you can ask for proposed design exhibits in the form of screens and reports to support business tasks identified in the list. JAD work definitions provide the needed references to order discussion materials and compile draft design specification pages.

DRAFT DESIGN SCENARIO

In the following chart, a Business Activity Model is shown as a point form solution guidelines document to list business manual and automated tasks related to an arrangement of work definitions. This document provides key word associations for the team to understand the details and validate task words as logically and syntactically correct for various processes. In this the team can be involved in analysis for an efficient work flow sequence and systems design without being engrossed in the detail. Business tasks are related to workbook pages in a compilation of design exhibits with attached business and technical notes. At this stage, as people become oriented to the situation, they can draft a solution guidelines document to provide a basic index in key words to outline design scenario tasks and identify discussion materials for analysis.

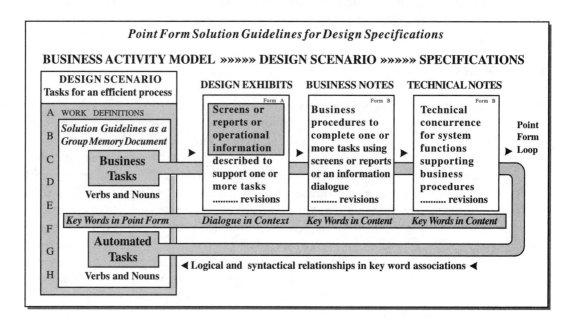

DESIGN ANALYSIS BASED ON KEY WORD ASSOCIATIONS

Analytical discussion is based on appropriate key words for business engineering intent and process redesign. The key word discussion loop provides the knowledge bridge for design specifications analysis which in turn, is based on a team review and revisions to suggested design exhibits. Start with a plausible systems solution in the context of purposeful change. Success depends on providing insightful interpretations of required tasks for a complete business design represented in the word associations needed to bridge the knowledge gap which separates the understanding of process redesign and technology application design.

The session leader should be able to identify appropriate language for work flow using the basic JAD Work Definitions as key word indicators. To draft a design scenario, you will also need to express automated work in key words which can be more easily identified if you consider characteristic systems design for manual and automated work tray tasks. While previous charts illustrate design relationships for work trays, the following chart details characteristic screen and system functions for work definitions. With this background, people should be able to find suitable vocabulary to outline tasks for a design scenario sequence. As you hear different points of view from different experience and with mixed perspectives for change, you will have to decide on an appropriate sequence consistant with proposed solution guidelines.

CHARACTERISTIC SCREEN AND REPORTS AND DATA PROCESSING DESIGN FOR WORK DEFINITIONS

The following chart describes characteristic system features for work tray definitions as typical manual and automated processes you would recognize in a business design scenario and present in point form verbs and nouns to model activity. Characteristic screen and system functions for each work tray include manual and automated dialogues for work flows shown as an open double line and data processing shown as a solid line for information flow.

A WORK ENVIRONMENT - MAINTENANCE
Reference Sources to be Applied in Work

Business parameters to manage processes
Routing and authorization controls
Formula variables for business calculations
Resource information and work assignment criteria
Work due information or forecasts from other areas
Operator guidelines and error help functions
Access controls to system data and functions

B RECEIVED WORK - DATA ENTRY
Information Dialogues to Start Work

Menu selection to access system functions
New information about work received into area
Updates to existing information from other areas
Criteria and instructions to start a work process
Information access to respond to incoming inquiries
Incoming message display from network systems

C INITIAL PROCESSING - RECORD KEEPING
On-line or Batch Data Processing

Validation edits and data completeness tests
Operator guidance and error messages displayed
Calculations using formulae and defined variables
Data and status code record keeping
Log work events for administrative feedback
Log audit and statistical information
Archive information for historical records
Electronic outputs and notifications for received work

D WORK MANAGEMENT - OPERATIONAL LISTS
Summaries to manage work backlog

Work listed by status codes for follow-up action
Messages alerting or identifying work situations
Dynamic work lists with access to record details
Work load figures and resource assignment options
Work information with sort options to review detail

E WORK IN PROCESS - INQUIRY UPDATE
Information Dialogues to Complete Work

Update screens to add information to input records
Data updates to complete a work process
Search and sorting criteria to retrieve information
Inquiry screens to research business problems
Menu screens to access inquiry and update screens
Request procedure to release or create system outputs

F RESULTS PROCESSING - RECORD KEEPING
On-line or Batch Data Processing

Validation edits and data completeness tests
Operator guidance and error messages displayed
Automatic system interfaces provides new data
Calculations using formulae and defined variables
Data and status code record keeping
Log work events for administrative feedback
Log audit and statistical information
Archive information for historical records
Electronic outputs and notifications for completed work

G COMPLETED WORK - GENERATED OUTPUTS
Physical Results of Completed Work

Routing information to address and label products
Information records to acknowledge work departure
Print work departure notifications
Media transfer of information

H WORK REVIEW - TREND ANALYSIS
Business Information Sources

Summary and detailed reports
Analysis tool and information graphics presentation
Adhoc inquiry tool for user defined business reports
Operational and statistical information log
Audit and event tracking information log
Report schedule with routing cover sheet

Technology Application   Information Dialogue

Work Environment — References, Files and Table Maintenance — System Files
Work Management — Operational Reports — Work Status — Get/Put Backlog
Work Review — Analysis Reports — Well done History — Sales
Data Entry — Received Work — Start Tasks — Work Record
Work Result — Inquiry Update — Work in Process — Work Tasks
Completed Work — Business Documents — System Outputs

WORK IN   WORK OUT   control   Information flow   Work flow

MATERIALS PREPARATION

STEP 3 is described as *Materials Preparation* and results in a draft workbook compiled as a team handout for the workshop. This is the time people involved in systems planning and development take to provide documents and create design materials to be compiled as design scenario exhibits. Solution illustrations from previous planning results can be included with a draft Business Activity Model to outline the understanding of proposed solution ideas. For workshop ready discussion documents, gather solution ideas and analysis materials in the form of sample screens and reports provided from either, or both, system developers and computer literate business representatives.

While a Business Activity Model is listed to reflect the character of business process design, it should also reflect the character of business automation design and relate both for complete analysis. Design solutions can mix totally new ideas requiring significant modification alongside familiar ideas requiring only slight alteration. For this reason and depending on the scope of change requirements, design scenario materials may be obtained from specialists proposing radical change or experienced system users only interested in enhancements. In preparation, people should understand the purpose of proposed change and recognize characteristic business systems design as manual and automated work tray tasks to match solution ideas with appropriate key words for analysis. Design exhibits might be provided from system analysts or future system users and range from previously unknown and perhaps unusual design to the more conventional.

CHARACTERISTIC DESIGN LABELS

Session leader purpose in recognizing characteristic systems design is to label representative tasks people know to be fundamental to business routine. In this way, participants become tuned to required business involvement and capable of discussing proposed solutions in terms of new procedure. As you sequence verbs and nouns to list what you understand as workflow tasks you can also anticipate conversation about a proposed design scenario. The above chart illustrates typical sequence to organize related characteristic screens and data processing design to work definition tasks.

For a typical work area, a task list is usually, but not always, represented in a single A to H sequence. While the relationship of workflow and information flow should be inclusive, it is only necessary to suggest a sequence in a verb and noun list. When work flow crosses areas and departmental boundaries, multiple occurrences of work definitions can be used with key words and codes to identify special

BUSINESS ACTIVITY MODEL
BUSINESS ROUTINE AND AUTOMATION

Guidelines: Consider the following Work Definitions and describe business activity in a summary list of verbs and nouns for manual and automated tasks to do work. Use an appropriate Work Definition to group characteristic tasks in a plausible sequence for efficient and effective work flow. From the list, project an activity summary to the attached analysis forms to engineer work as an operational system.

WORK DEFINITIONS   MANUAL AND AUTOMATED TASKS

A. WORK ENVIRONMENT . . . . .Business Controls
    Data Base - Finalized Loads
    (Security Controls)
    (Barcodes)
    Lift Types
    Preprinted Tags Beginning of Turn
B. RECEIVED WORK . . . . Foreman
    Review Loading Layout
    Assign Resource for Turn
    Determine Loads to be Processed
    - Request / Print Loading Layout
B. RECEIVED WORK . . . . Shipper / Crane Leader
    Review Finalized Layout
    Locate Correct Lift for Return / Reload
    Select Loads / Request Tags
C. INITIAL PROCESSING . . . . System
    Validate Authorized Access
    Display Finalized Loads
    - Print Loading Layout
    Sort / Print Requested Tags
    Identify Print Location
    Update Data Base
B. RECEIVED WORK . . . . Crane Leader
    Pre-locate Materials and Tag/ Retag Lifts for:
    - Truck / Rail / Interplant Truck for Barge
    Report Tagging Status Complete
D. MONITOR AND ASSIGN . . . . .General Inquiry
    Loading Layout
    - Truck / Rail / Barge
    Load Display (Truck / Rail / Barge)
E. WORK IN PROCESS . . . . Changes
    Customer /Office Originated Changes
    Substitute Materials Process)
E. WORK IN PROCESS . . . . Crane Leader
    Approve / Reject Vehicle Equipment
    (Reject Vehicle Process)
Continued . . .   Identify Report
    (Substitute Materials Process)

logistics and ownership of business operations and system functions. In the following example for a Vehicle Loading System also described in the appendices, the business activity model includes procedures identified to work areas and job descriptions.

TYPICAL WORK DEFINITION QUESTIONS FOR BUSINESS DESIGN ANALYSIS

The following chart lists typical questions you could ask using JAD Work Definitions for conversation. Starting with questions about business controls, you should be able to discuss design specifications for source references to support business procedures and system routines. You can cluster your questions to determine processes and information dialogues for each work tray considering work management perspectives for efficient and effective work flows.

A WORK ENVIRONMENT - BUSINESS CONTROLS

Do you need to be aware of work which is due into your business area

Where can you find information about work you will have to do

What sources of information are available to you about the work due into your area

What information sources contain controls or guidelines about work to be done

How are work controls and guidelines maintained

B RECEIVED WORK - SYSTEM OUTPUTS

What events or information changes start a work process in your business area

What information must be recorded to acknowledge or log work arriving in the business area

What unique information references the work sources containing controls or guidelines to receive the work

Can other sources of information provide assistance in the process of receiving work

C INITIAL PROCESSING - RECORD KEEPING

What checks and formulas are needed to validate or create information about received work

Under what circumstances is control information used to provide operator guidance

Where is work receipt information stored

Are codes assigned to identify received work and track work status

What procedures could be triggered automatically because of received work

D WORK MANAGEMENT-MONITOR AND ASSIGN

Is it necessary to monitor work progress and assign resources to complete the work

What information do you need to identify work situations

Is it necessary to adjust priorities or reassign resources to the work backlog

Who needs to be aware of the work backlog

What would be the best method to access available information about the work identified for further action

E WORK IN PROCESS - INQUIRY UPDATE

What information must be recorded to complete assigned work

What events or information combinations trigger a change to work status

Can other sources of information provide assistance in the process of completing work

F RESULTS PROCESSING - RECORD KEEPING

What checks and formulas are needed to validate or create information about work in progress

Under what circumstances is control information used to provide operator guidance

Where is work progress information stored

Are codes assigned to identify work progress and track work status

What procedures could be triggered automatically because of processed work

G COMPLETED WORK - SYSTEM OUTPUTS

How is completed work prepared for distribution

Do you need to follow special instructions to complete work

Is it necessary to label or attach documents to completed work

Should you log work as it leaves the area

H WORK REVIEW - MANAGEMENT REPORTS

What reports do you need to provide operational and trend evaluations

Is operational information gathered in the process of completing work current and available for reports

Do you provide mandatory government or corporate reports

Can you access the information you need for historical analysis

WORKSHOP MEETING

STEP 4 is described as the workshop meeting in which people deliver a revised document representing team consensus for business procedures and system design specifications. This is the time to bring the team together to analyze design exhibits in a meeting workbook. The book building process is implemented throughout the meeting. Starting with an overhead transparency for the book cover, the session leader directs the team through a review of related pages. Following conventional meeting protocols, the agenda uses the introduction and background pages including the workshop process chart to start the meeting dynamics and explain the process. This sets the tone to review the Management Guidelines and focus ideas for the Solution Guidelines and Business Activity Model in the remaining workshop discussion time spent reviewing proposed solutions on the Design Scenario forms.

In this, you will need to explain the Business Activity Model as it applies to providing key word associations for analytical thinking and how it provides a summary to the detailed system design specifications. Having introduced the workshop approach as a book building process, you should now explain the analysis technique in a short presentation using the Characteristic Business Systems Design chart with the Generic Work Definitions chart. As you explain the process, you can refer to the draft Business Activity Model and illustrate how it works to list and relate design topics. At this time you can also use the Point Form Solution Guidelines for Design Specifications chart to explain the documentation support process.

CRITICAL ANALYSIS IN POINT FORM

During critical analysis of various ideas compiled as sample solutions, the team can define new processes and automation design through revisions and additions to business and technical notes in which key words in content are transcribed to more detailed specifications. As you progress with design ideas and scribes take specification notes, you should also identify new key words in context and transcribe them in additional point form back to the model.

An overall Business Activity Model is developed to illustrate solution decisions as a group memory document to promote design ideas and understand emerging analysis in the sense of logical and syntactical relationships found in key word associations. In an actual workshop illustration of the previous example, process redesign is represented in revisions, additions, deletions, edits, and many sequence changes to the list.

As you follow the process, checkmark related analysis items to indicate progress. You can focus appropriate debate using typical questions shown for the above JAD Work Definitions to consider design analysis for efficient work flow and effective information dialogues.

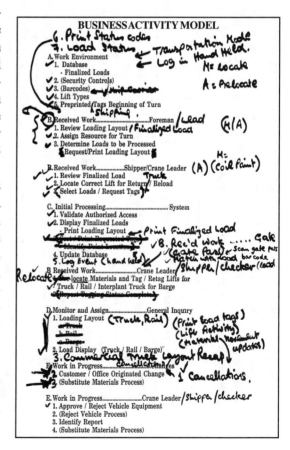

DESIGN SCENARIO FOR CONVERSATION

In the workshop agenda the session leader uses characteristic work definitions in turn to raise discussions about the details of various tasks inclusive for design. Briefly presenting the Generic Work Definitions chart on one overhead and the draft Business Activity Model on another to remind the team of the basis for analysis. For each work tray cluster, review the design scenario topics from the top of the list and call for discussion based on workbook page headings and content. Putting the JAD concept charts aside until you need them again, show the related design exhibits on an overhead projector. Allow someone, usually the page author or the project leader, to explain the substance of a proposed design. Starting at the top as the task list unfolds, note summary design decisions as modifications to screens and reports. Accordingly procedural design is shown in point form animation prescribed by the A to H work definitions.

Because you lead discussion in task sequence and tasks are defined and redefined, the Business Activity Model evolves as a dynamic agenda to manage conversational topics and pace analysis. While you revise screen and report contents and update the Business Activity Model, other designated business and technical notekeepers record more detailed design on page equivalents of the presentation materials.

Your role will range from making minor changes to page content to being very involved in conversation and using your communication skills to help the team reach agreement and document understanding. The team will be glad to participate in your technique in which you summarize debate in conversational and documented extracts. While future system users focus on procedures and system dialogue specifications, technology developers support design conversation in providing technical advice for alternative methods and costs for automation. In this way, all team members become involved and jointly make decisions about business process redesign specifications and technology application design for systems development.

WORKSHOP RESULTS

The project leader would manage conversation to acceptable scope as the session leader continues the process to make the design scenario respond to business engineering objectives described as Management Guidelines. During the meeting, you have some responsibility for the overall quality of documentation and should periodically review the details. Although business and technical notekeepers are involved in conversation, you might ask them to read out their notes occasionally. If you have not already done so, use key words from this discourse and revise the task list to confirm the rationale of team decisions in observing logical and syntactical relationships in key word associations. As you make progress, gather up overhead transparencies and supporting pages to be typed for immediate return as new overheads and periodic inserts to workbook pages. At key stages of design, or at the end of the day, you can affirm team decisions using a Change Results log to list apparent change for a summary management report. While you might do this to edit design detail in review, you will validate change results to expectations and inevitably strengthen team comfort and commitment to emerging design plans.

After the analysis, work on the forms you need to review and assign responsibility for unresolved action items. To wrap up the meeting, review the stated management objectives to validate successful results of team work. In closing, thank the team for participating and recognize the people who prepared discussion materials for their contribution to the success of the process. Your thanks should also mention documentation support and the clerical production of workbook pages. Finally, you thank the sponsor for the direction for the assignment and wish the team continued success as the project moves into development.

ᛉᛯᛘ SESSION LEADER SKILLS

ses-sion n. The sitting of an assembly for official business; a single meeting of such a body; period of time spent in some activity.

lead-er n. Someone who acts as a guide; a directing head or chief; someone who or something that leads a body of moving troops, animals, etc.; someone or something that holds first place; a conductor of a musical group, esp. of one in which he also performs.

skill n. Ability to do something well, especially as a result of long practiced experience; a particular technique to *implement* something, *(the work calls for skills); tact*, to manage a person with skill (Old Norse Skil, *Discernment*).

im-ple-ment n. A tool; a thing or person, serving as an instrument.

im-ple-ment v. To carry into effect, e.g., to implement a promise.

tact n. Understanding of how to avoid giving offence and how to keep or win goodwill.

dis-cern v. To see, to *observe*, or make out through any of the senses; to perceive with the mind, discrimination, insight, perception.

ob-serve v. To perceive, notice, come to know by seeing; to note attentively; to comment.

CHAPTER SIXTEEN

JAD–Implementation Checklist

WORKSHOP READY SESSION LEADER

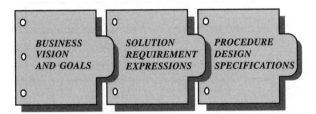

While JAD is described as a communication technique, the key to being ready is to recognize JAD as a process to utilize fundamental principles for business analysis using discussion and documentation structures. The process can be used to bring people with different skills together to analyze various subject matters and reach agreement on a number of points of view. A session leader manages the process and follows procedure to be ready to facilitate debate and document business solutions to a prescribed level of detail. Throughout this, communication skills play an important factor for success, especially in the workshop period when discussion must be managed effectively to gain consensus and document decisions. A more durable measure of success is to value documented results over the merits of personal charm and charisma in reaching consensus. While

---

JAD Process - Four Basic Steps

STEP 1 - **Management Guidelines**

STEP 2 - **Workshop Orientation**

STEP 3 - **Materials Preparation**

STEP 4 - **Workshop Meeting**

- 1 - 4 Days
- Structured approach and workshop process
  - Question Form Analyses, or
  - Business Activity Analyses
- Session leader guidance
- Future system users define business design
- System developers defined technical design
- Note business and technical decisions

Workshop Process
Analysis loop

Define business situation

↓

Describe and test ideas
and solutions

↓

Document requirements
and specifications

Documentation loop

↓

Add complementing
notes and illustrations

---

both are important, session leader management skills and communication abilities are less challenged and more rewarded when the approach is based on a reusable and results-oriented process. It is beneficial to manage the details of the following steps using a checklist.

KEY STEPS AND CHECKLIST ITEMS

The following checklist is designed to list the details needed to implement an easier workshop. The logistics relate various steps for business planning and design meetings shown on previous charts as Involvement and Step Outputs. As you plan a JAD, people take responsibility for preparation, and as you JAD your plan, you can check your progress to target dates.

Initial meetings in *STEP 1* include formal and informal discussions as people become acquainted with the process. Similarly, you become familiar with the assignment and people look to you for advice to devise a workshop agenda. It is acceptable for you to take charge and explain the approach and demonstrate it in practice. This leads to an expectation that you will direct the process, which you can administer from a checklist.

While you may have already covered the first few items in discussions and presentations, you can check any items done and explain the rest as you entrust responsibility to others for completion. When you explain a checklist in this way you demonstrate organization and competence. It leaves a sense of comfort that the necessary details will be addressed and everyone will be ready for a good meeting.

Business Area: _____
Project/System: _____
Workshop Date: _____

TASK	TASK DESCRIPTION - PAGE 1					DATE	NAME
010	**STEP 1** INITIAL PREPARATION AND COMMITMENT						
020	Identify and assign checklist responsibilities.						
030		Name	Initials	Responsibility	Phone		
	Support Team:						
040	Discuss project with project manager or project leader.						
050	Identify workshop approach for analysis and strategy for achieving usable documentation for next implementation step.						
060	Identify executive sponsor.						
070	Project manager schedules meeting with executive sponsor and user management to present JAD executive overview and obtain commitment to proceed.						
080	Prepare for presentation to the executive sponsor including overview of any prepared materials in a workbook.						
090	Continue draft materials in Management Guidelines or schedule meeting(s) for completion.						
100	Outline responsibilities of the executive sponsor and obtain commitment to the workshop and team requirements for success.						
110	**STEP 2** WORKSHOP PREPARATION ACTIVITIES						
120	Identify workshop team members and select workshop dates for participants. Book session leader, documentation support and meeting room facilities and presentation equipment.						
130	Schedule appropriate orientation interviews, meetings or site visit.						
140	Select and book the workshop location with room for team seating in horseshoe arrangement.						
150	Arrange for breakfast, lunch and appropriate refreshments for breaks (and other optional catering/reception etc.)						

TASK	TASK DESCRIPTION - PAGE 2		DATE	NAME
160	Book rooms for out-of-town participants and session leader.			
170	Identify spokesperson for optional workshop summary to executive sponsor on final day.			
180	Define documentation support requirement and book resources.			
190	Review and clarify project terms of reference in Management Guidelines with project leader.			
200	Determine exhibits and documents needed to supplement background/solution guidelines/appendices divider contents to assist understanding business/system analysis materials.			
210	Optional progress report for executive sponsor to review management guidelines and finalize team list.			
220	Determine use of ranking criteria with optional weighting factors to prioritize team results.			
230	Brief executive sponsor for short kick-off/opening remarks and wrap-up/closing remarks (prepare/add presentation foils as necessary).			
240	**STEP 3** ANALYSIS PREPARATION			
250	BUSINESS PLANNING	BUSINESS DESIGN		
260	Determine analysis sequence/forms hierarchy and customize pages.	Create Business Activity Model for proposed design scenario.		
270	Optional site visit and/or meet key business representative to review situation and forms design.	Visit work area/business site. Review Business Activity Model as responsive to work processes.		
280	Distribute questionnaires with covering letter and selected exhibits or meet selected team members to fill out forms.	Arrange preparation of optional photographs of work processes matching involved business routines.		
290	Complete scheduled orientation meeting. Provide orientation materials and questionnaires to participants including those unable to attend an orientation.	Determine sample screens, reports and forms to match tasks listed in the (A-H) Business Activity Model.		
300	Follow up questionnaires/forms and compile results as a workbook.	Follow up screen/report exhibits and compile as a workbook.		

TASK	TASK DESCRIPTION - PAGE 3	DATE	NAME
310	**STEP 4** WORKSHOP MEETING LOGISTICS		
320	Review scribe(s) responsibility/role and arrange clerical support and appropriate documentation equipment. Coach clerical role for timely document delivery as overheads and workbook inserts.		
330	Order overhead transparencies for type of printers and copiers.		
340	Assemble presentation materials and prepare an overhead foil of each page of the workbook for session leader.		
350	Prepare a copy of workbook in a binder with appropriate dividers for each workshop member including observers.		
360	Book conference room and facilities for meeting. Ensure the following materials will be available for session: 2 overhead projectors, 1 flip chart with paper, blank overhead foils (for session leader and scribe), one copy of workbook on overheads and one on paper for session leader, marking pens for foils and flip charts, packing/masking tape, spare bulbs for projector, name tents and pens for each of the participants.		
370	Arrange other necessary supplies for the session dates e.g., PC workstation, printer, printer cables, power extension cord, table, photocopier,		
380	Prepare workshop introduction presentation.		
390	Review additional presentations and schedule presenters.		
400	Arrange optional education and demonstration of proposed equipment for participants.		
410	Distribute Management Guidelines, Workshop Agenda, and Invitations containing logistical information to all workshop participants. Specify appropriate workshop casual or business attire.		
420	Verify room setup and test equipment prior to use, if possible.		
430	Complete scheduled workshop.		
440	Complete documentation and prepare optional summary report. Distribute documents to involved parties for review.		

However, leave nothing to chance. Count on things not being done. Expect and tolerate that if you check on a task it could be done and you need not have checked. Conversely, if you trust that even the simplest thing will be done without follow-up, you will find it not done, or it will be wrong when you need it most and regret not having checked it before.

Each of the different workshop types and procedures for specific levels of detail have been described in previous chapters. While the checklist itemizes appropriate steps for business analysis, it also lists the things to be organized and managed for the physical things needed to do a good job.

PREPARATION AND COMMITMENT

Typical troubles seem to occur when people implement interactive workshop processes. As session leader, it should not be difficult to follow the lead of those requesting assistance. You should be able to reflect similar enthusiasm for a project in conversations as you recommend and start an appropriate book building process.

Certain difficulties emerge as you consider required resources from the business areas concerned. People often underestimate the value of participation and withhold skilled professionals in consideration of supporting essential business. Any misunderstandings now will result in unqualified people attending a meeting. Because of this, a team will have difficulty dealing with the issues and lack the authority for decisive action. A simple test for needed experience is to judge the age factor. As you discuss and document the purpose, scope, and objectives, check that participants have basic credentials for where they come from and for what they are able to discuss.

MATCHING TEAM QUALIFICATIONS

Another trouble in team selection occurs when sponsoring managers want to present knowledge with uncompromising authority, or they want to preside over team activities. For certain levels of detail, you should explain that it might be more appropriate for a sponsor to start a meeting and optionally assist the Management Guidelines review. For most situations, you can leave the details for the team to resolve and present in a summary presentation. This approach is appropriate to defuse rank and possible intimidation. There will be occasions when a sponsoring manager is a welcome addition for encouragement and team focus. Alternatively, you can adapt analysis structures and workshop agendas to occupy management levels in selective debate and take increasingly detailed Solution Guidelines from one workshop to another. In this you can match similar knowledge for efficient workshop processes and participative debate for effective results. It is a matter of judgement for you to decide how to match people skills with business planning and design analyses and when to schedule managers for opening remarks and closing reviews. In your professional role for JAD, explain the various options and techniques available to advance business concepts and recommend a suitable agenda to optimize team involvement.

WORKSHOP PREPARATION ACTIVITIES

In the next phase of implementing JAD, you add content to workshop discussion materials and review the analysis technique. Typical troubles occur deciding the level of detail for analysis, and later, the provision of ideas and sample solutions to prime workshop discussion materials. A good way to sense a required level of detail is to relate proposed workshop documents to current development activities as people judge their position on the JAD Document Life Cycle Model.

RUSHING INTO ANALYSIS

For each type of workshop there will be a range of knowledge involving various subject matters and levels of detail within. System developers usually become engrossed thinking about implementing a system and want to work on the details as they look for answers to define technological design. Being responsible for implementation, they usually have in-depth knowledge of potential solutions and development efforts involved. With a sense of urgency for results, and although the business may not be fully defined, people tend to work on detailed plans and specifications associated with technology application design and development. This situation usually results in the belated discovery of business actions previously thought unimportant, or simply not thought of. As the details surface, development might remain in design a little longer with revised plans in terms of what to develop and when to implement.

Another reason people anticipate rapid results is that many technicians, and indeed business people, suggest that solving business problems is not so tough. Moreover, people tend to underestimate the value of written knowledge and think it redundant to document anything which might be thought obvious. For these reasons, you could be asked to lead a workshop to analyze system specifications when the business requirements have yet to be defined. You may be asked to lead a workshop for requirements analysis when business concepts are not well documented, if at all understood. For the most part, people judge their place on the Document Life Cycle Model well enough to select an appropriate workbook. This appraisal should be sufficient to determine a responsive analysis technique for good discussion. Furthermore, you need not decide an exact fit since these workshop techniques have the flexibility to analyze business detail at various levels. You should expect that materials will change about 30 to 40 percent in revisions and additions to clarify understanding and prepare accordingly. Because acquiring knowledge is progressive and validation is an expected part of the process, retroactive revisions occur to about 10 to 20 percent of documented knowledge and previously held undocumented opinions.

FACILITATION CONSULTING VERSUS INFORMATION CONSULTING

While you may have to figure out the level of detail to determine how best to analyze subject matters, you almost always have to discuss how to obtain draft materials to prompt discussion. Contributions to prepare a workbook originate from a number of sources. Your key contacts can help, and you will probably want assistance from the same people asking you to work for them. Alternatively, you might be directed to people who have the knowledge you need. In any event, it may seem odd that you need staff work from the very people wanting you to help them. Indeed, some mistakenly understand that you will provide information in a consulting role and answer certain questions. In reality your job is to question them to facilitate analysis which you can do better without subject knowledge to give. The professional role of facilitator should be clearly defined as the administrator of a process for people to be more thorough in business analysis, and everyone must understand that good results depend on the quality of knowledge brought to the meeting. A session leader might have to mention that general business knowledge is sufficient to facilitate thoughtful debate and document design decisions. You may have to add, in reassurance, that your own ignorance of business details is preferred for objective questioning and an unbiased drive for good results.

In a few situations, you might encounter people reluctant to provide information before a workshop. Indeed, some may not support your request to provide items of discussion and information before a meeting. Reasons for this vary—you might become aware that people have already answered previous surveys. In any case, you should not expect cooperation for similar or repeated activities. Sometimes you are given documents to read, or you have to work with others involved in previous or scheduled interviews. It may be sufficient and a better response to local politics that you accept the status quo. You should check into the history of previous work and take advice to coordinate your own preparation.

ARE WE REALLY COOPERATING

While people look to you for direction to use the process, you will have to spend some time talking about things already known. You need to hear this to choose a workshop structure and provide any advice about the logistics to prepare for a successful meeting. In reality, you become ready for them as they become ready for you. This may surprise those who may simply expect a workshop to start and a session leader to begin without a prepared agenda. This is the least advantaged option shown in the lower path on the Involvement and Alternatives chart. It is a common perception and you should make an attempt to dispel the notion. Left unresolved, this issue can lead to a difficult workshop or a disappointment. In any event it is prudent to document expectations for discussion results.

As long as people see you strive for common goals and mutual success, you will probably experience cooperation. While you use the Involvement and Outputs chart to select the level of detail and use a JAD Checklist to assign responsibilities, it should be easy to plan the required preparation. Willing team work should start as soon as people recognize the benefits of team involvement and just being better informed to exchange and discover knowledge. You may need to illustrate these benefits using the Ability and Potential to Succeed chart so that people will understand how you want to work the process. As you request assistance, you may encounter objections to do with logistics and sequence. You should be able to deal with these worries as you recommend and discuss the best path to follow when you explain the different approaches shown on the Involvement Alternatives chart.

Other reasons might underlie apparent lack of cooperation in preparing draft materials. As session leader you should know that although people might be willing to discuss ideas and want to participate, you simply have to work to gain required knowledge. It is not spontaneous and it requires practice. Even with the right encouragement, people remain reluctant, perhaps fearful of being wrong or showing ignorance, or even fearful of being right and being perceived as too clever. This becomes more acute when you need draft discussion material in greater detail. When precision is thought important, people become even less forthcoming with ideas and suggested solutions. To overcome this, you can explain that several authors enjoy anonymity in contributing materials. Moreover, you only use suggestions to examine ideas and demonstrate alternatives. To explain this you might show the approach on the JAD Communication Model chart to illustrate that you only need expressed opinions to start discussion. You can point out in good JAD tradition that if an idea cannot be put on paper from a well informed source, an educated guess will do, and if an educated guess is not available, a happy guess will do just as well. You only need plausible examples of intent to refine through constructive criticism and contributions from knowledgeable participants.

ILLUSTRATED JAD

As you entrust preparation work to others, you might experience that people with development responsibilities become referees of your process. As you write a checklist for things to be done, other people with politics in mind make arbitrary decisions to save time and prevent certain items, or do something else more purposeful to sell or use a systems development methodology. Candidate items for revisions to your plan usually involve meeting people to communicate expectations and solicit information which would establish workshop rapport. On one occasion an associate spent a day preparing a workshop for a client and attended a progress review meeting. When he reported back, I was shocked at the number of items undone and not done. Reality dawned as he gave me a reasonably well prepared document and said he had done the best he could, and all things considered felt pretty lucky to have gained anything useful as a discussion document.

WORKING ON LOGISTICS

Given that you have the right sponsorship in all regards, and have prescribed the right approach to satisfy most eventualities, you might be tempted to relax in the confidence of things going well. Indeed, once you start successfully you should be all the more vigilant to maintain early expectations. As you continue checklist **STEP 2** you will have to manage your own time and activities as people contrive the coincidence of team members, session leader, documents, equipment, food and beverages in a meeting room. It can be quite a task to make this happen. Fortunately, people recognize you have little authority in the matter of team selection and when to hold a meeting. While you may advise others to allow time for preparation, workshop dates are often selected by sponsoring managers. Depending on importance, urgency, and management support, a workshop date may be set and instructions sent for participation. In this, other people call participants and make arrangements for all concerned.

For the next checklist item, consider your own involvement to meet participants and how to orient others to the situation. You might use the chart showing Involvement Alternatives for Each Step to identify how much you can do before a meeting to benefit good debate. For the most part, you should have the freedom to follow recommended procedure. You will usually meet people to prepare a discussion document. However, an orientation meeting may not be allowed and difficulties emerge in your plan to visit places when others also want to meet people. Consequently, you might be excluded from the process, and although you may promote the idea of establishing team rapport for yourself, others may want to do it for you. To overcome this difficulty, you might be able to meet one or two people as others continue an interview schedule. In the end you may have to accept, but not rely on, the judgment of others as you discuss the situation whenever you can before a meeting. You will have to catch up as quickly as possible to overcome differences of opinion and assessments of those involved. People undoubtedly will assist your plan if they use the book building process and contribute draft materials to a workbook, and you should be positive about any supportive actions before and during the workshop.

WORKING IN A HOTEL

Another preparation activity is to select a good location to meet. Difficulties become apparent when you depend on others to provide the things you need for a workshop setting. For most people concerned, it is better to be near, but not actually on, business premises. While you may have access to a professional conference facility, it may not be available. For many it is more convenient to rent hotel space. Unfortunately, not all hotels have the resources to provide space conducive to quiet thoughtful debate. While a hotel may offer a work place with tables and visual equipment arranged to the plan shown on the Typical Room Arrangement chart, you should see what they provide before making an agreement. You should beware of being offered "the best room" which is probably more suitable for a social reception than a business meeting. With sincere intentions for customer service, you might be given a beautifully decorated room with a view to please the most discerning holiday maker.

Visions of loveliness, noisy areas, and relaxing fireplaces can be avoided if you know such things exist. Prudent questions concern hotel features, room plans, numbers, and types of walls and fixtures. It is important to keep the same location for a meeting and know your surroundings. Hotel sales staff treat you as number one until another business priority turns up. You should ask about other bookings and avoid political, sports, sales meetings, and school graduations. You would benefit by knowing about planned maintenance on buildings and grounds. Once you have the facilities you should ignore any suggestion for a team to dine in a restaurant. Food and beverages should be brought in to keep your agenda free of catering announcements. Generally, you should keep people away from waiters who live up to their job title through the practice of cunning techniques to match your pace with that of a chef.

Food brought in can solve many logistical problems, but you should still take care, especially in small places. Setting up creature comforts in a convenient nearby area provides a welcome break in new surroundings, but you may have to protect your territory from scavengers. Catering is often a noisy affair and may be provided with little care for people in conversation. People setting up a table can be ignored until it becomes alarming. Lunch may be announced as someone switches on an electric coffee heater or food warmer which reduces or cuts the power to workshop equipment on the same circuit. Without menu arrangements, your meeting will be interrupted by someone needing to know what people want to eat. The arrival of food need not be a call for a break, but it does change the atmosphere to encourage one. Food can be left a while, but fruit, salad, and cold meats are best cleared away before they become unpleasant or attract hungry things. Noises and odors of electric or kerosene heaters can be avoided if you keep hot drinks in a thermos flask. In this you have a bonus in more frequent fresh brews. To be sure of arrangements, visit or phone the hotel and confirm your requirements in writing.

PRESENTATIONS TO START

While the checklist itemizes things to prepare for a workshop meeting, you also need to consider how people want to contribute to the agenda and provide workshop support. One checklist item refers to supporting presentations and you should discuss the merits of this activity.

Presentations can be useful but it follows procedure to include some presentation remarks at the beginning or end of a meeting. Merged topics must be relevant and brief to optimize agenda time for debate. Ensure that presentation content promotes the theme of the meeting. While oganized debate requires introduction, try to avoid opportunistic speakers with a pitch or selling emphasis. On the other hand, people might have the role or want to present ideas rather than participate in debate.

A decision to include a presentation is usually settled by a project manager or project leader for the personal emphasis they bring to an assignment. Appropriate topics would focus on background and business direction or cause effects and changes to be considered. An introductory presentation might outline project plans or implementation methods involved. Technology presentations might be useful if people need to know about an application for their situation. Different topics might be more appropriate for a separate meeting or briefing before a workshop. Thirty minutes should be sufficient for a presentation item. While people decide what to include, they also think of who should do it—those discussing an idea usually volunteer. In any event, you should see the material and review the agenda with the speakers so they are aware of the need of time for debate. As you review presentation topics, determine if a separate handout is required. Alternatively, you can include pages after a background or solution guidelines or appendices divider. Your choice to position presentation pages to workbook dividers also suggests the timing and whether the speaker is a guest, a participant, or session leader.

PRESENTATIONS TO FINISH

Near the end of a workshop, people usually ask "How Much?" and "How Soon?" and someone needs to be ready to answer these questions in terms of design results and action plans. Reasonable projections will be needed to sustain enthusiasm for workshop results. People usually look to a project leader or project manager to describe what happens next. At this point in the checklist, you should identify and prepare the appointed person to provide a summary and closing remarks. Assuming a session leader is not also a project leader, this is not a session leader role. While you may have found support to provide an introductory presentation, you now find people cautious about the prospect of summarizing commitments and action plans. It need not be difficult. For the typical questions you can select and update appropriate workbook pages in time for the closing remarks. Charts usually include revised solution guideline illustrations and lists of key design features and significant changes.

ILLUSTRATED JAD

Preparing an agenda and involving the assistance of others has a number of benefits for the sake of politics and good involvement. Apart from establishing a better environment for teamwork, it can raise pleasant surprises. In a workshop for an electronics company in Dallas, we spent three days designing a system to track new purchases. Items were processed through initial inspection stage with test results recorded before going to manufacturing inventory. In the usual workshop preparation, we discussed the assignment with area personnel during a site visit to Lubbock. After meeting people in an area walkabout, we reviewed the draft analysis structure. The area supervisor saw and contributed to the business logic in the verb and noun task sequence for the design scenario. Business representatives continued to support the development of draft materials for the workshop. Later, the team got together and examined the design scenario to redesign it for business realities. The design was creative and several people were recongized for their contributions to the overall success. During the workshop, the area supervisor was selected to provide the summary presentation. Using selected workshop materials, he gave an excellent presentation and closing remarks. This unexpected event was appreciated by many for being a remarkably clear and complete description of team decisions for new business plans and procedure design.

CHECKLIST FOR A WORKSHOP

In the checklist, *STEP 3* itemizes the key processes already started for a chosen analysis technique for an appropriate level of detail. Workshop logistics are detailed in *STEP 4*. While you may have considered most eventualities, these items mention the physical things required in place for a meeting. An important item for this stage is to review scribe responsibilities and provide the resources needed to create notes at a pace which supports and documents thoughtful debate. In the nature of workshop discussion, this varies from being slow at first to quite rapid as ideas flow and relevant details emerge. Clerical support is no more and no less complicated than providing good typing skills for the notes generated by a session leader and other appointed notekeepers. The tools needed to support this activity would be found in a text processing environment with special file management facilities for rapid text capture and printing of individual pages to deliver documents suitable for the workshop mechanics shown on the Typical Room Arrangement chart.

At this point, confusion might occur regarding what is required during and after the workshop as documented output. System developers generally want technological results in terms of designing and implementing technology. Along with providing summaries to executive sponsors, system developers are the ultimate consumers of design decisions. They provide reference inputs and become the users of workshop outputs. You may have to remind people that you need interim documents and notekeeping support for the bridging analysis. The best way for you to do this is to develop your own draft workshop documents in your own files and coach a secretary to be ready to work on these materials and produce timely updates. You can achieve this with manageable attention because the usual work load is represented in a range of 30 to 40 percent in revisions. In other words, about two-thirds of the resulting document is already done. This may not be true for other documents of a specialist nature which cannot start or provide little value until the analysis is more complete.

WORKSHOP DOCUMENTS WITHOUT DELAY

Ideas will not and need not wait for record keeping. Indeed, progressive design notes and diagrams should be updated to the pace of uninterrupted thoughts and conversations for well-informed decision making. With the right equipment, workbook pages can be changed along with the progress and dynamics of business discussion. Business design information and technical design decisions in a workbook are mostly text. In this form, this text presents the inputs to future development processes. Depending on the types of material and complexity, additional development outputs might be reviewed during the workshop or delivered after the meeting without breaking the discussion flow.

Progressive notes for workbook documents should not be considered as regular text for general document processing. Neither should they be considered sufficiently detailed for direct input to the structures required for typical development tools. The detail is mixed and fragmented. A regular text editor or document processor will generally limit the organization and production speed needed for dynamic material and rapidly changing notes. Recording design decisions into a systems development tool also limits pace and production. A tool which translates various inputs to another format, loses, or changes the original analysis organization should be avoided. Any of these will result in limited understanding, and agreement only to those able to comprehend the new output. The workshop pages and required documentation tools work better for group dynamics when they are designed to manage the character of short transient notes, rather like a stenographer's notebook.

The general appearance of a workbook is that of a few notes with lots of spaces for ideas on each page. It might look wasteful until people begin to add discussion notes and fill out the blanks. When a draft workbook is developed for a meeting, an electronic document should also be created in the same structure as the Analysis Guidelines. Documentation support is best provided by a person with a vested interest in accurate transcription. Such people would probably like copy typing and not mind reworking previously typed notes. A systems analyst may not do this. Those with training and a disposition for analysis tend to interpret and adjust both the notes and structure of a workbook towards methodical structures generally used in technological design. Employing an experienced secretary provides some protection from people wanting to reorganize documents. While a session leader starts accurate documentation, a secretary might also find seemingly unusual organization due for reorganization according to past training. Indeed, helpful people may think you as a session leader ignorant of required document standards and provide instructions on your behalf to change the appearance of team results. These difficulties can be avoided if you prepare a workbook yourself and explain the responsibilities for completion. Coaching in this regard should set the expectation that a secretary would work diligently on page revisions and not become involved or pause to listen to an interesting conversation or watch the dynamics of the process.

A WORKBOOK ON OVERHEAD TRANSPARENCIES

In the remaining checklist items, the session leader or assistant prepares the discussion document as a workbook binder and prints all the pages on overhead transparencies. Be careful to use transparencies compatible with particular printing and copying equipment. Laser printers provide good quality and work well for rapid, quiet output in a meeting. Clear foils may not travel through all printers—if a white edge on a foil is needed for printing, it should be removed for presentation. Check also that your marking pens actually write on overhead materials. An inkjet printer is convenient for a workshop, but compatible transparencies are needed. Several have a wax base which tends to coagulate water-soluble inks and smears or smudges printed text when you want to erase an error with a damp cloth.

WORKSHOP ARRANGEMENTS

Before the meeting is started, you as session leader should check the room arrangements and equipment. You may have to adjust a few things. Rearrange tables and chairs if they are not positioned as a square horseshoe. If the greater length of an oblong table plan is down the room you may distance team members from the viewing area. If the length is across the room, you create an oblique viewing angle for people at the front. If you expect intermittent attendance, plan to accommodate the full compliment in close proximity rather than allowing gaping spaces as people come and go. Your overhead screens should be placed for the shortest distance to the furthest participant. Small screens, silver screens, or shiny white boards are not really suitable as a working medium; you might want to orient the team and equipment to a clear wall which often works very well. While you expect projectors to be similar, you should check display patterns to position and focus each one. You should reserve the brightest and clearest for your best hand or most frequently used image. When you test a projector you should also check for a working spare bulb. Your management skills improve if you sort your overhead transparencies and organize divider sections to certain table areas. To recognize or read a transparency on dark table tops, take a few minutes to spread white paper over the work area. Test flip chart pens and overhead markers, and place a tumbler of water and cloths ready to clean off errors and make corrections. Finally, place a workbook or new insert pages with a pen and name card in front of each chair for the participants.

There is a checklist topic for the equipment you need. To feel confident about computers and printers, take your own with a supply of paper and transparencies. You should also carry a spare power bar with an extension cord and a roll of 2-inch duct tape to tidy up various items and fasten down loose cables. Setting up requires time; it is less worrying if you arrange the room the evening before the meeting. If you only have access to a room in the morning, arrange that equipment suppliers meet you early. If you are early enough, you might keep the doors closed until you are ready and free to greet people and tend to social needs as team members arrive.

READY TO THINK ABOUT BUSINESS

Now that you have managed the physical arrangements you can join team members in the coffee area and enjoy a drink and a snack before the beginning. When that time comes, people will be ready to turn the workbook dividers for the discussion topics they want to talk about. The team will be ready to cooperate and eager to think about practical business solutions. In following recommended procedures you will be ready with overhead transparencies at hand to conduct the meeting and document team decisions. You will have overcome the typical reactions against involving future system users in design. You will have prepared system developers for the differences the *Classic* JAD book building process brings to business engineering and technology design and systems development. You will know how to respond to team members to facilitate business like discussions for people to debate the issues and engineer creative design for the prospects of change.

At this point you would recall the job description for a successful business engineer as you continue to assist the composition of ideas and arrange the tactful involvement of people to harvest design messages. Your workshop setting and results might be similar to the sample documents in the following pages. From real situations, these demonstrate the basic analysis structures applied to discuss business engineering as Vision and Goals, Solution Requirement Expressions and procedure redesign as Procedure Design Specifications.

CHAPTER SEVENTEEN

JAD—Hold Development in Case You Want to Think

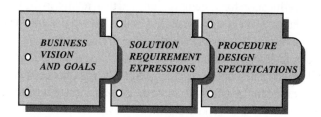

ILLUSTRATED JAD

On a flight to visit a client I had a few moments to look at a true stories magazine for light reading about life's funny situations. In one account, a man in prison learned communication skills, including how to read and write, in a prison education program. Having acquired the skills, he set about writing to people. In this way, he received an additional sentence for writing threatening letters to his trial judge.

IMPORTANT SKILLS

Following management skills to implement the process and mastering the art of workbook mechanics, a session leader also needs presentation and communication skills to make a productive workshop a more successful and enjoyable experience. In the normal course of a meeting, the session leader's confidence in leading group discussion primarily depends on an ability to apply the workshop process and create results. In this you, as session leader, must have an intuitive sense of timing to apply JAD structures to sequence conversations and relate solution ideas to analyze business context and add design content to development documents. Communication skills are important to manage workshop activities and group dynamics.

In conversational debate, conflicts are bound to arise and the job of facilitation may depend on a session leader's ability to handle people. In reality, the prospect of risk is reduced in the very nature of the process and method of producing results. There are times when temperatures rise and people become compelled to join in anxious debate. Should you become tempted to join in kind, you, or someone, will have to resort to extraordinary tact and diplomacy to restore relative calm. This setback can be avoided. Instead of adding to difficulty, you should always remember the documentation process to channel the energies of debate. In this you manage the discussion loop to keep people focused on decisions for results. Wanted results might still be argued, but even in a small step, a demonstration of progressive solutions will defuse most conflicts.

Usually, people are more concerned about being involved in a workshop than how they should participate in a process. Indeed, the use of structure and workshop mechanics should be so fluid as to be transparent. Your skills should promote this image in the easy style and comfort of a results-oriented environment. To a casual observer it might appear that a session leader only needs good communication skills. What many fail to realize is that without a supporting process, a session leader's composure would be the first to vanish in a heated moment.

PEOPLE IN THE LOOP

The following chart illustrates a discussion loop, starting with business perspectives to reach consensus and document business concepts and functions. The loop continues to document technical perspectives and provide concurrence in terms of verification for systems design, and then returns in the validation of business perspectives for expected change. The idea that interpersonal skills and communication techniques are inextricably linked to a workshop document escapes some. It might not occur to someone involved in a different agenda that a progressively updated workbook would be so valued by people who nurtured it through preparation and refined it in workshop participation. The importance of people in the documentation loop is shown in several examples which illustrate the combination of business and technical languages to advance business concepts in a workshop setting.

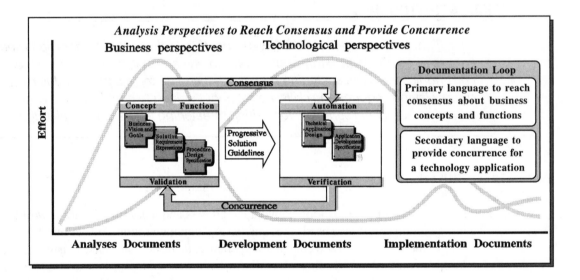

ILLUSTRATED JAD

The following brochure provides a recap as an executive overview and the workbook samples demonstrate the application of Classic JAD as a book building process. The results show the benefits of involving people with different skills and backgrounds in a discussion loop. The pages do not show complete design results. Instead, selected workbook pages demonstrate analysis structures in the sequences and relationships of real agendas and timeframes. The book building process is shown in the basic similarity of format and content of genuine narratives and diagrams from the discussion pages of actual workbooks. The flexibility of the approach is shown in the application of basic analysis structures adapted to the circumstance of each situation. The language of team documents varies for the types of decisions needed for particular stages of systems development. In some cases, a combination of workbooks record design solutions as business plans and concept analyses through requirement expressions and procedure design specifications for manual and automated processes. Other examples stand alone in providing sufficient detail to implement results for an immediate benefit.

Advancing Business Concepts in a JAD Workshop Setting

Anthony Crawford in praise of happy guesses, an empirical approach for quality messages in business engineering and procedure design

RECAP

ᛃᛃ Executive Overview

Joint Application Design an Executive Overview to Business Planning and Procedure Design

ᛃᛃ *Classic JAD* a Workshop Approach for Success

JAD is an interactive communication technique for business people to participate in *business planning* and *procedure design* in a workshop setting. It is a process to be implemented when people need to explore ideas and exchange knowledge to solve problems. This workshop approach is for people with business plans and system solutions in mind. You can use the approach to document various levels of system detail starting with *business vision and concepts analysis* and *business requirements* through *business procedure design* and *automation design*. You can discuss a wide range of subject materials concerning business practices and people activities.

Classic JAD a Process for Business Involvement and Team Work

Future system users and system developers use a business analysis structure for discussion and define the changes and actions needed to improve business. The process involves preparation and a workshop.

≠**Business Managers and System Developers define the assignment**
≠**JAD Session Leader recommends and adapts a workshop agenda**
≠**Workshop sponsor selects business and technical representatives**
≠**Team reviews draft materials and agenda at an** *Orientation* **meeting**
≠**Analysis materials prepared in a** *Workbook* **discussion sequence**
≠**Workshop meeting to debate the issues and reach team consensus**

Classic JAD a Process for Results

JAD results in a responsive business plan with an informative design in which you can be more confident and ultimately implement more successful system solutions. The benefits include:

≠**Future business direction for vision and goals**
≠**Shared responsibility for introducing change**
≠**Consensus about the issues and action plans**
≠**Appropriate technical or non-technical design**
≠**Practical business oriented systems solution**
≠**Design quality from user stated requirements**
≠**Economic and creative technology application**
≠**Reduced development and maintenance costs**
≠**More acceptable and reliable implementation**

ADVANCING BUSINESS CONCEPTS IN A JAD WORKSHOP SETTING
Classic JAD - Analysis Structures Demonstrated in Sample Workbook Pages

WORKBOOK 1

Re-engineering Systems Development Life Cycle

BUSINESS VISION AND GOALS

FEBRUARY 26, 1993

MEETING WORKBOOK

Page 1

WORKSHOP AGENDA FOR BUSINESS ANALYSIS

* Executive Sponsor Opening Remarks

* Introductions and Administration

* Overview/Background

* Workshop Process

* Management Guidelines

* Solution Guidelines

* Analysis Forms

* Action Items / Issues Log

* Summary and Closing Remarks

Page 3

WORKSHOP TEAM MEMBERS

Executive Sponsor
Phil E

Systems Team	Client Area
Tom F	Laurie B
Esther K	Rick D
Doreen H	Marie J
John S	Gail H
Ralph P	Carol S
Brenda W	Anna N
John R	Donna L
Jack M	Joy A
Gary D	Nancy D
Dave B	
Bob P	
John C	

Workshop Facilitator
Tony C

Documentation
Roman S

Page 4

PURPOSE OF THE REVIEW

Review opportunities for improvement and recommend system delivery alternatives and organizational structures to use appropriate procedures and supporting tools and techniques which respond to client and user requirements for timely and quality business systems and enhancements.

PURPOSE OF THE WORKSHOP

Involve client representatives and system developers in a structured workshop to review system development processes and responsibilities and propose refinements to the existing system delivery life cycle.

LEVEL OF DETAIL

- Statement of plan purpose and goals.
- Definition of scope.
- Identify key assumptions and influencing factors.
- Illustrate current environment and new ideal delivery process.
- Identify key stages in systems development and issues and concerns.
- Identify opportunities for change and recommend delivery approach.
- Assessment of opportunity requirements and priority.

The workshop document will provide team recommendation for a revised systems delivery process review and action for management.

SPONSORING EXECUTIVE: Phil E
TITLE: Director Technical Services.
DATE: February 2 5, 1993

Management Guidelines

Page 8

SCOPE (PHASE I)

INVOLVED PARTIES
1. Systems Operations
2. Project Management
3. Clients / System Users
4. Information and Technology

SYSTEMS DELIVERY
All business and technical requirements and enhancements:
-Batch Processing, On-line Application, Data Base

DEVELOPMENT ACTIVITIES - PROCESS FLOW
-Problem Definition/Change Controls   -Application System Testing
-Business Concepts Analysis   -Client Testing
-Business Requirements   -System Integrated Testing
-System External Specifications   -Documentation
-System (Architect) Design   -Training
-System Internal Specifications   -Production
-System Development   -Support
-Application Unit Testing   -Post Implementation Review

EXCLUDED FROM THIS REVIEW
-Sub-Support Groups (Migration/Technical Support)
-Ultimate End User (Originator of Request)
-Micro Applications (Phase II)
-Equipment Acquisition and Installation
-Help Center
-Project Management (SDM 70 / Navigator)
-Definition of Service Level Agreement

Page 9

OBJECTIVES AND EXPECTATIONS

- Timely and quality systems delivery
- Continuity of knowledge
- Optimize resource allocation
- Improve client relationship
- Manage project development process
- Avoid overlapped activities
- Improve communication
- Avoid misunderstanding
- Reduce overall development costs
- Appropriate automation for development activities
- Eliminate redundant steps
- Faster team spirit
- Consistent approach to systems delivery process
- Improve change management procedures
- Well defined hierarchical roles and responsibilities
- Better understanding of related functionality
- Speed up the overall delivery process
- Better product quality before delivery to clients
- Reduce stress through better awareness of each others processes and involvement
- Reduce occurrence of overtime.
- Reduce contention for system time.

Page 10

LIFE CYCLE ANALYSIS TOPICS

DEVELOPMENT PROCESS

REF	OPPORTUNITY AREA
1.	Vision and Goals
2.	Requirement Definition
3.	External Design
4.	Internal Design
5.	Development
6.	System Test
7.	Client Test
8.	Integrated Testing
9.	Production

Analysis Forms

Page 13

ISSUES AND CONCERNS WORKSHEET   FORM A1

Guidelines: List the general issues and concerns about the current development process.

-Some difficulty to differentiate problem definition versus change
-Documentation problems and subject to interpretation.
-Lack of understanding of business in support areas.
-No reference business model.
-Affects all development processes documentation.
-Existing documents focus on transactions.
-Current tools focus on development transactions.
-Difficult to understand how current systems work from available documentation.
-Some documents include manual business processes; other documents do not.
-Some standards adopted for documentation.
-Every center is responsible for their own program (some initiatives have addressed this problem)
-Changes originate from many areas and coordinated through one area.
-Problems are split out and supported by different people who may end up working on similar solutions.
-Resources allocated to project scope/size.
-Some ripple effect of changes implemented may not be recognized.
-Some experience/success in application of structure and better communication.
-Currently test plans are developed during systems development.
-Successful project team should work together (in same work area).
-Always seems to be more involved than first thought.
-Inconsistent use of automated tools.

Continued...   *Page 14*

PLAN ANALYSIS   FORM B1

Guidelines: Consider the issues and sate opportunities with reference to development process, provide recommendations with rank for (S)hort, (M)edium or (L)ong term implementation . Illustrate your decisions on a revised process chart.

Ref./Opportunities	Recommendations	R
1-Understand the business problem.	**Requirements Analysis & Design**	L
1-Save time in the process	-Develop and utilize business models.	L
1-Consultative Processes	-Assign responsibilities and resources to maintain business models.	S
1-Establish measurements	-Interviews and workshop techniques for requirements and specifications.	M
2-Coordinate test plans	-Identify and gather statistics by change category *through the entire process.*	S
2-Team approach throughout delivery process	-Early test strategy objectives development	S
	-Dedicated project teams (Ops/Systems) on major project/enhancements.	S
3-Reduce number of change controls.	-Allocate teams to common area with appropriate resources (workstations etc.)	S
3-Improve quality of requirements and specification documents	-Formalization of more *consultative processes* (team efforts/ walk throughs)	S
	-Update documents *through entire process*	L
	-Determine methodology to develop requirements and specifications	S
4-Improve impact analysis	-Identify appropriate tools	S
	-Consistent/structured approach to use impact analysis tool	

Continued...   *Page 15*

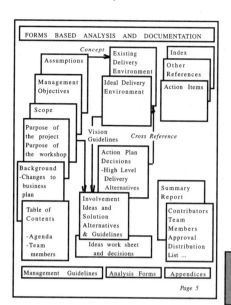

FORMS BASED ANALYSIS AND DOCUMENTATION

Concept

- Assumptions
- Existing Delivery Environment
- Management Objectives
- Ideal Delivery Environment
- Scope
- Purpose of the project
- Purpose of the workshop
- Vision Guidelines
- Background - Changes to business plan
- Action Plan Decisions - High Level Delivery Alternatives
- Table of Contents
  - Agenda
  - Team members
- Index
- Other References
- Action Items

Cross Reference

- Involvement Ideas and Solution Alternatives & Guidelines
- Ideas work sheet and decisions
- Summary Report
- Contributors Team Members Approval Distribution List ...

Management Guidelines	Analysis Forms	Appendices

Page 5

BACKGROUND

REDEFINED SYSTEMS DELIVERY PROCESS

Systems development support groups include systems and operations. Project initiatives start in a series of activities for requirements definition and design phases, or problem reports for maintenance phases. Recently, a review of systems development for a large project highlighted a number of areas for potential improvement. Key areas of concern include the following:

AREAS OF CONCERN

- Communication between all involved parties
- Separate resources applied to similar activities
- Standards for system documentation
- Consistent approach to development activity and system delivery
- Team spirit and cooperative involvement
- Efficiency and effectiveness of existing procedures
- Definition of roles and responsibilities

ACTION PLAN

A team review meeting is planned to consider better methods and process improvements to the entire systems delivery life cycle. While you will have to consider constraints and business influences, you should treat this review as your opportunity to discuss change and redefine the process.

YOUR ROLE IN THIS REVIEW

- Be unencumbered by day to day constraints.
- Think creatively for appropriate & practical solutions
- Fairly evaluate alternatives.

Background

Page 6

CURRENT SYSTEMS DEVELOPMENT PROCESS

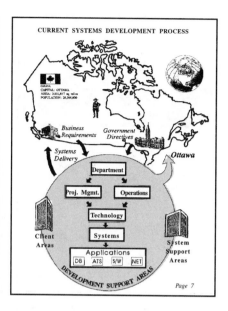

Page 7

ASSUMPTIONS AND INFLUENCING FACTORS

New Service Level agreement will reflect new process including standard receipt and approval process.

Batch processes are, and will continue to be, essential to transaction processing.

Government priorities and legislative requirements direct system development activities.

Continue to use and evolve current technology base.

Business demands for change / response to additional complexity.

Systems operations resources have operational responsibilities and delivery responsibilities whereas other areas focus resources on delivery objectives.

Staffing policy includes internal and consulting resources.

Integrity for batch and financial controls must always be considered.

Move to operating budgets will require that system development involves more controls.

Page 11

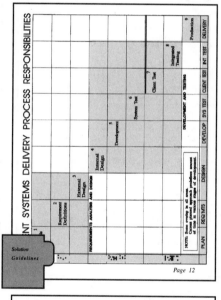

Solution Guidelines

Page 12

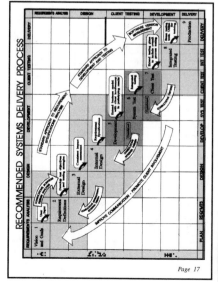

Page 17

ACTION ITEMS

ISSUES LOG	NAMES
1. Assign resources to clean up current specification documents.	OPS & Systems
2. Review recommendations and ranking S/M/L	TonyC
3. Publish and distribute workshop document.	Team
4. Management review	TBA
5. Meet to review action items already started and to be done.	Team

Appendices

Page 18

Index

WORKBOOK 2

*Management vision and goals
to plan new processes with supporting technology*

BUSINESS VISION AND GOALS

June 5, 1991

MEETING   WORKBOOK

Page 1

WORKSHOP AGENDA FOR BUSINESS ANALYSIS

* Executive Sponsor Opening Remarks
* Introductions and Administration
* Background Materials
  - Background
  - "PROJECT" Framework
* Workshop Process
  - JAD Process Model for Success
  - Communication Model
  - Documentation Level
* Management Guidelines
  - Purpose
  - Scope
  - Management Objectives & Expectations
  - Business Assumptions
* Business Requirements Analysis
  - Business Model
* Action Plan
* Summary and Closing Remarks

Page 3

WORKSHOP TEAM MEMBERS

EXECUTIVE SPONSOR
Art D

TEAM CONTRIBUTORS
Dennis B
Hope C
Terry C
Peter H
Barry H
Mark H
Rudy G. K
Ilan L
Jon K
Bob M
Harold L
Kevin M
N. (Randy) N
Tariq S
Marnix G
Pat W
Ed W

WORKSHOP FACILITATOR
Tony C

DOCUMENTATION
Roman S

Page 4

PURPOSE OF "PROJECT"

Develop a plan to improve customer service while optimigin asset management through integrated operations and management processes involved from forecasting and customer order to product delivery.

PURPOSE OF THE WORKSHOP

To involve managers and business representatives from 1al units in a structured workshop to define the guidelines for a plan which has joint agreement and commitment to further project activities.

The level of detail will be:

- Define purpose and scope
- Define objectives and assumptions
- Define a business model overview
- Key statements of direction for action plan

The workshop document will represent team consensus and provide the direction to evaluate business concepts and more detailed business requirements analysis.

SPONSORING EXECUTIVE: Art D
TITLE : President,
    ABC Canada Ltd.
DATE: June 5, 1991

Management Guidelines

Page 13

SCOPE OF "PROJECT"

LOCATIONS (CANADA)
-National Headquarters
-All Sales Branches
-All Distribution and Warehouse Locations
-All Retail Stores and Inventory Locations
-Parts and Service Locations
-Independents Interface

PRODUCTS
-Consumer Electronics, Magnetic, Communications, Non-ABC, Service Products (parts, labor, ESP)

BUSINESS FUNCTIONS

Customer Order Management Cycle
1. Future Orders
2. Create Demand
3. Allocate Stock
4. Order Processing
4.1 Current Order
4.2 Qualify Order
4.3.1 Check Inventory
4.3.2 Back Order
4.3.3 Price
4.4 Commit Stock/Inventory

Logistics Cycle
1. Receive
2. Putaway
3. Stock Management
4. Cycle count
5. Pick Plan
6. Release to Floor
7. Pick
8. Pack
9. Ship
10. Order Tracking/Status

EXCLUDING
-Accounts Receivable
-Procurement
-Pricing and agreements

Page 14

MANAGEMENT OBJECTIVES/EXPECTATIONS OF THE PLAN TO IMPLEMENT "PROJECT"

OBJECTIVES	MEASUREMENT CRITERIA
Manage inventory effectively.	Months supply on hand, aging, Back Orders
Manage stock effectively.	Stockouts, order fill rates
Improve business planning & sales forecast	Budget variances, inventory levels, gross margins
Market/customer driven targets, quality	Customer expectations, tracking, commitment to business & delivery
Reliability and efficiency of allocation services	Number of IT's, number of changes to allocation, # of B/O's, lost sales
Reliability and efficiency of distribution services	Time, cost, accuracy - returns breakage, shrinkage
Fulfillment of customer expectations	Zero fault, appointment, timeliness, accuracy, value added
Responsiveness - Ease of doing business with ABC	Tracking, timely information
Service level agreement	Accuracy, timeliness, fulfillment
Performance, compared to internal goals	Area specific logistical statistics, integrated standards
Performance, compared to external standards	Surveys, Best of breed, Competitive statistics
Develop partner relationship with customer	Future requirements, Market share, Integrate business plan, Percentage of business
Improve understanding of business areas	Morale, knowledge, cooperation

Page 15

SOLUTION ALTERNATIVES WORKSHEET

Guidelines: Consider the corporate purpose and objectives for the Project. List areas for improvement within the scope of design and note your ideas with alternatives for implementation. Team decisions will be shown as revisions to the Project Framework woth action items for the plan.

DEMAND Recognize demand at time of order entry on each local system and coordinate all demand for central allocations

FORECASTS Implement central forecasting algorithms based on local demands and internartional supply and order backlog

FINANCIAL Common accounting methods using same chart of accoiunts in all locations with EDI transactions triggered by order processing status

INTEGRATION All locations use common systems and shared access to data

Analysis Forms

Page 20

"PROJECT" FRAMEWORK

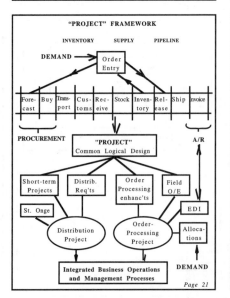

Page 21

ACTION ITEMS FOR THE PLAN	DATE	NAME
Constitute a project board.	6/7	TC
Develop a project proposal - includes 2 or more progress review meetings	7/31	IL/RK
Benefits analysis - measure impact of not going ahead	7/31	MVG
Review previous work effort for appropriate materials in the plan	7/31	IL/RK
Review operations and procedures in business units affected by these systems.		
Define functional requirements.		
Develop a project plan with a prioritized, phased implementation activities for incremental functionality.		
Compare viability of the plan with business imperatives		
Identify level of commitment and availability of dedicated resources.		
Identify internal and external resources, costs and time frames.		
Review alternative sources for systems solution.		

Page 22

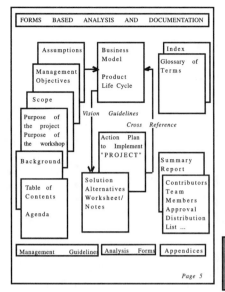

FORMS BASED ANALYSIS AND DOCUMENTATION

- Assumptions
- Management Objectives
- Scope
- Purpose of the project / Purpose of the workshop
- Background
- Table of Contents
- Agenda
- Business Model / Product Life Cycle
- Vision Guidelines / Cross Reference
- Action Plan to Implement "PROJECT"
- Solution Alternatives Worksheet/ Notes
- Index
- Glossary of Terms
- Summary Report
- Contributors Team Members Approval Distribution List ...

Management Guidelines | Analysis Forms | Appendices

Page 5

BACKGROUND

Following previous project analyses, general discussions and external reports, a consensus emerged about how to proceed.

To assure the success of a complex project such as is the Distribution and Warehouse Management project, we must take an integrated view of the key relevant processes, functions and interfaces, utilizing the expertise and contribution of appropriate departments and individuals within our company.

The integrated approach for goods order-processing and logistics system is illustrated in the following chart under the heading **"PROJECT"**.

It has been noted that success also depends on business direction and user stated requirements. In order to proceed, this document will be developed in a structured workshop from the involvement and contributions of appropriate ABC Canada departments and individuals.

The team of business managers and future systems users will review the current situation and decide on the issues concerning change and develop an action plan for implementation.

Background

Page 10

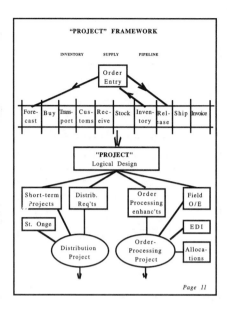

"PROJECT" FRAMEWORK

Page 11

ASSUMPTIONS FOR PLAN TO IMPLEMENT "PROJECT"
- Systems belong to Business Units - Not to IS.
- New systems will only work if business processes are reviewed and re-engineered as a front end to systems development.
- Policies, procedures, operations and service level standards need to be reviewed and/or established.
- Understanding the issues affecting these areas is critical to competitiveness of the business.
- Operational analysis is a crucial predecessor to systems analysis.
- Integration of info. and systems is a key corporate strategy.
- Integrating order processing & logistics is essential to design.
- Integrated system information will support other key business processes (eg.sales analysis, inventory mgmt., invoicing etc.)
- Combination of short and long term development activities.
- Additional business and IS resources will be needed to enhance the expertise and support the scope of this project.
- High quality, effective and practical solution is more important than fast implementation - balance Time/Quality/Function/Cost.
- Balanced approach for business function versus business automation (eg. Back Order handling).
- Business (change) trend is towards longer term customer oriented marketing programs versus order driven selling.
- EDI interfaces will be used
- Method to interface non-ABC products demand to suppliers.

WORKSHOP ASSUMPTIONS
- Business involvement is key to success.
- This workshop document will be used as a guideline for subsequent more detailed business analysis and documentation.

Page 16

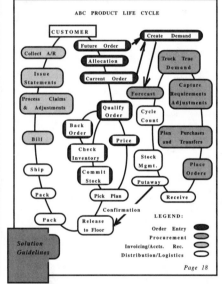

ABC PRODUCT LIFE CYCLE

Solution Guidelines

Page 18

GLOSSARY OF TERMS

INVENTORY - Logical; can be committed

STOCK - Physical itmes on hand

Appendices

Page 24

Index

Page 26

WORKBOOK 3

Review of business requirements and technological design for rapid development

"PROJECT" COMPRESSION PLAN

Project Management

Compression Options - January 18-19, 1993
Action Plan - January 20-21, 1993

MEETING WORKBOOK

Page 1

WORKSHOP AGENDA FOR BUSINESS ANALYSIS

* Executive Sponsor Opening Remarks

* Introductions and Administration

* Overview/Background

* Workshop Process

* Management Guidelines

* "PROJECT" Development Plan

* Analysis Forms   - Compression Options
                 - Action Plan

* Action Items / Issues Log

* Summary and Closing Remarks

Page 3

WORKSHOP TEAM MEMBERS

EXECUTIVE SPONSOR
Ron M. J

BUSINESS PLANNING TEAM
Pete H
Mary C
Diane R
Jen T
Larry O
Russ C
Sue P
Lauren C
Wade P
Fred S

TECHNICAL CONTRIBUTORS
John B   Supplier Consulting Support
Cindy M   Supplier Consulting Support

WORKSHOP FACILITATOR
Anthony C

DOCUMENTATION
Jill C

Page 4

PURPOSE OF THE COMPRESSION
Sequence appropriate system development activities and coordinate internal and external resources to provide the best available delivery date agreed upon by the team.

PURPOSE OF THE WORKSHOP
Involve system user representatives and developers in a structured workshop to review development activities and responsibilities for the earliest possible date "PROJECT" deliverables.

LEVEL OF DETAIL
- Statement of system development purpose and goals.
- Identify key assumptions and influencing factors.
- List phases of development and key activities.
- Identify prerequisite and required resources and skills.
- Identify opportunities to achieve earliest completion.
- Define delivery date and project actions.

The workshop document will represent consensus for a revised project development plan and will be used to acquire appropriate resources and funds for system delivery.

Sponsoring Executive: Ron M. J   **Date:** Jan. 18, 1993
Title: Customer Service Operations V.P.

Management Guidelines

Page 8

SCOPE OF EFFORT

LOCATIONS
-ABC project management
  -business managers
  -system developers
-External project management
  -out-sourced responsibilities

PROJECT MANAGEMENT ITEMS
-All business and technical requirements defined in January 8, 1993 document attachment 1. (Subset based on JAD Plans/Design).

DEVELOPMENT ACTIVITIES
-Start-up phase
-Systems engineering phase
-System implementation phase
-System readiness phase
-Field deployment activity

EXCLUDED FROM THIS PROJECT DEVELOPMENT
-Refer to January 8, 1993 document, attachment 2.
-Conducting the Beta test site.
-Field test and user accept is part of Beta site.
-Field delivery to Communications functionality.

Page 9

BUSINESS OBJECTIVES AND EXPECTATIONS

-Earliest system delivery.

-Appropriate use of internal and external resources.

-Management of project activities.

-Achieve roll out within time frame for delivery target.

-Note: Backwards Delivery Target :
    -Backing in from a normal 1993 implementation plan, the system delivery date target is May 31, 1993.

Page 10

DEVELOPMENT ANALYSIS TOPICS

-START-UP PHASE

Pages 20, 21 ....-SYSTEMS ENGINEERING PHASE 16-52

-SYSTEM IMPLEMENTATION PHASE

-SYSTEM READINESS PHASE

-SYSTEM DEPLOYMENT PHASE

Page 22

PLAN ANALYSIS   **FORM A**
TOPIC: SYSTEM ENGINEERING PHASE
Guidelines: Consider the above topic and provide a brief description. List the key development or activities involved and provide a brief description of any comments, issues and concerns. Identify responsibility: User (U), Developer (D), Analyst (A).

TOPIC: System engineering phase

Ref/Devlp't Activity	Week	Comments/Issues/Concerns
15 System Eng. Phs		Includes development activities 16-52
15 Requirm't Def'n	20.63	Includes the following:
17 Architecture	5	This is A time with 2 people each providing 2.5 weeks. Dependent on item 10. Depends on vendor responses involved in multiple activities/responses
18 Communications	16	Functional spec. Involves 2 A.
19 Review Comm.	5	Includes 2 A and 3 D.
20 Communications	8	Estimates for new OOA methodology.
Support Applic'n	15	Estimates for new OOA methodology.
21 Handheld		20.4 -Old methodology estimates shown. 21.9 -Old methodology estimates shown.
22 Review Req'mts Definitions	2	U involved. Several people needed to review all items in attachment 1 & 2. This drives many other steps as a prerequisite.
23 ID Prod. Sites & Administr. Staff	2	Assumes two different sites. Must determine sites and connectivity issues for certain configurations. Prerequisite to System design. Need to know equip and responsibilities, space, ops support etc. Need to consider staffing and other factors for best site.

Page 20

PLAN COMPRESSION ALTERNATIVES   **FORM B**
TOPIC: SYSTEM ENGINEERING PHASE
Guidelines: Consider the development activities associated with the above topic, determine development options, describe the best approach for a shorter interval for individual plan activities and indicate who is involved as User, Developer, Analyst, Production. Identify your alternative: 1.Parcelled out to external supplier 2.Eliminate function 3.Add more people to assist 4.Additional expertise 5.Parcelled activity

Ref/Devlp't. Options	Preds	Start	E/Time	U	D	A	P	1	2	3	4	5
15											X	X
16												
17	10		2/5			2						
18			8	2								
19	18		1	3	2							
20 Use new methodology			4			2						
21 Use new methodology			7.5			2						
22	18,19 20,21		1									
23	34		2				1					

Page 21

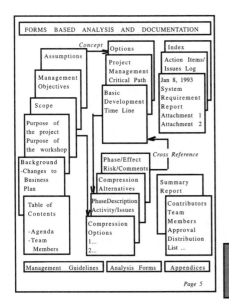

FORMS BASED ANALYSIS AND DOCUMENTATION

Concept — Options — Index

Assumptions

Management Objectives — Project Management Critical Path — Action Items/Issues Log

Scope — Basic Development Time Line — Jan 8, 1993 System Requirement Report / Attachment 1 / Attachment 2

Purpose of the project / Purpose of the workshop

Cross Reference

Background -Changes to Business Plan — Phase/Effect Risk/Comments — Summary Report

Compression Alternatives — Contributors / Team Members / Approval / Distribution List ...

Table of Contents — PhaseDescription Activity/Issues

-Agenda -Team Members — Compression Options 1... 2...

Management Guidelines | Analysis Forms | Appendices

Page 5

BACKGROUND - "PROJECT"

A STRATEGIC BUSINESS IMPERATIVE FOR 1993

ABC has completed a number of business planning and design workshops for the "PROJECT". A review meeting has taken place to orientize requirements. These have been published January 8, 1993 attachment 1 and 2.

Based on these results a development plan has been proposed with an overall delivery date for December 1993. This date was provided as preliminary assessment before detailed analysis of time lines. Due to the urgency of the business imperative we need to review and apply all possible alternatives for an earlier deliverable.

"PROJECT" Compression Plan - Review the project plan in a meeting and determine what activities can be shortened with additional resources, parallel work, outside agencies and extra work time.

YOUR ROLE IN THIS REVIEW:
- Be unencumbered by day to day constraints.
- Think "out of the box".
- Fairly evaluate alternatives.
- Think as if this is the only project to be worked this year and needs to be delivered in the shortest interval possible. (Cannot sacrifice quality for interval!).

Background

Page 6

BUSINESS ASSUMPTIONS

-External Resources can be provided as needed.
-Financial Process for business case approval.
  - Allocation of Funds: - Capital.
    - Expenses budgets transfer.
  - Benefits: - Anticipated benefits booked.
    - Cost reductions subtracted from budgets.
    - Additional revenues included in business plan.
-Key benefit for 1993 is obtained in reassigning clerical resources.
-Handheld technology is fundamental to implementing change and achieving the business benefit.
-Other projects depend on the implementation of the "PROJECT".
-Other longer range plans for technician productivity also depend on the "PROJECT".
-The original plan was estimated to show staff weeks required.
-Estimates do not include any requirements for Serialization.
-Estimates were "best guess" at this point in the project with the amount of information available currently. After the completion of System Requirements, the estimates will be re-examined.
-Schedules assume that no other new work will be done on Communications Support.
-Standard Package for all Communications / Handhelds.

EXISTING STAFF LEVELS
Communications Support — Architecture
- 5 developers. — - 2 developers.
- 2 analysts — - 2 analysts.

Page 11

PROJECT MANAGEMENT CRITICAL PATH ANALYSIS

BASIC DEVELOPMENT TIME LINE

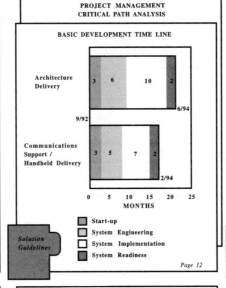

Architecture Delivery: 3 6 10 2 — 6/94 — 9/92

Communications Support / Handheld Delivery: 3 5 7 2 — 2/94

MONTHS 0 5 10 15 20 25

■ Start-up
▨ System Engineering
□ System Implementation
■ System Readiness

Solution Guidelines

Page 12

SUMMARY COMPRESSION OPTIONS

Guidelines: Review the Compression analysis on Form C and list the alternatives.

1. Add 2 developers to Communications.
2. Add 4 developers to Communications.
3. Eliminate standalone Architecture with existing staff.

Page 33... **4. Eliminate standalone Architecture with 2 additional developers.**

5. Eliminate standalone Architecture with 4 additional developers.
6. Parcel out whole/portion of communications with existing staff.
7. Parcel out whole/portion of communications with 2 additional developers.
8. Parcel out whole/portion of communications with 4 additional developers.
9. Add 2 developers to HH/Communications Support.
10. Add 4 developers to HH/Communications Support.
11. Outsource entire Architecture.
12. Outsource portions of deployment.
13. Move off messaging Architecture / Simplify messaging
14. Defer Compression/Decompression to 1st Anniversary
15. Defer Architecture Auto-recovery to 2nd release

Analysis Forms Part 1

Page 17

COMPRESSION OPTION: FORM C

Eliminate standalone Architecture with 2 additional developers

Guidelines: Refer to the project development activities and alternatives to consider the effect on the overall plan. List the risks involved and estimate the time saved.

PHASE / EFFECT	SAVES	REF.
1. START UP		
2. SYSTEM ENGINEERING		
-Speed up the implementation of development environment.	- 4 e.w.	34
-Saves on PO administration.	not critical	others
-Saves 1 week design time	-1 e.w.	
3. SYSTEM IMPLEMENTATION	in critical	
-Eliminate development of System interfaces.	-50 s.w.	70,109
4. SYSTEM READINESS		
5. SYSTEM DEPLOYMENT		

RISK/COMMENTS
-Overhead of additional processing on Communications Support.
-Capacity requirement of Communications Support Systems.
-Benefits in fewer points of failure.
-More links into Wireless Network and requirement for administration support/training.
-Less hours availability in communication.
-This design is contrary to primary design recommendation.
  -Additional network/connectivity costs.

Analysis Forms Part 2

TOTAL -11 Elapsed weeks.
CUMULATIVE TOTAL -27 Elapsed weeks

Page 33

Index

WORKSHOP 4

Change cause and effect analysis for business opportunities and process redesign

Subcommittee on Business Opportunity Assessment
Payment, Procurement and Asset Management

REQUIREMENTS ANALYSIS

AUGUST 26, 1991
SEPTEMBER 12-13, 1991

MEETING WORKBOOK

Page 1

WORKSHOP AGENDA FOR BUSINESS ANALYSIS

1. **Workshop**

1.1 **Workshop Introduction Agenda-Aug 26, 9:00 am-12:00 pm**
Executive Sponsor Opening Remarks-Andy M / Art S
Introductions and Administration
Overview of the Workshop Process
Background and Principles
Purpose
Scope
Business Objectives
Business Assumptions
Hand out the draft JAD workbooks

Workshop Business Analysis Agenda - September 12-13, 1991
Executive Sponsor Opening Remarks - Bernie G
Introductions and Administration
Review Management Guidelines
Business Concept Analysis
Action Items
Summary and Closing Remarks

Page 3

WORKSHOP TEAM MEMBERS

1.2 **Payment, Purchasing & Inventory Management Team**

Executive Sponsors
Focus Group - Chair: Art S
Department ABC: Andy M
Financial Information Systems: Bernie G

Business Participants
Paul E	Theresa M
Andy S	Tim L
Bill F	Diane S
Frank S	Ken C
Pat S	Jason C
Gerry V	Wayne S
Beverly G	Saul F
Dennis de J	Colin S
Terry C	

Project Team
Donna P - Project Coordinator
Howard C - Project Manager, Systems Development Contractor
Bruce R - Functional Manager, Systems Development Contractor
Marlene S - Finance Department
Oliver K - Systems Development Contractor

Workshop Facilitation - Tony C

Documentation - Roman S

Page 4

---

3. MANAGEMENT GUIDELINES

3.1 **Payment, Procurement & Inventory/Asset Mgmt. Purpose**
The purpose of the workshop is to generate opportunities which will radically improve the efficiency and effectiveness of payment, procurement, inventory services and related financial and administration practices.

3.2 **Analysis Guidelines -** To involve functional experts and managers from line deptartments and central agencies in a structured workshop to define the concepts of managing the business of payment, procurement and inventory.

The level of detail discussed in the pre-JAD workshop will be:
-Definition of purpose and scope
-Statement of objectives and assumptions
-Confirmation of business activities and solution guidelines

The level of detail discussed in the JAD workshop will be:
-Definition of business and change drivers
-Identification of business opportunity and benefit potential
-Review of business activities, comments, and issues
-Practical guidelines to enable success; measure risk/impact
-Rank the importance of implementing the opportunity

The workshop document will represent a consensus on business opportunities for business initiatives for payment, procurement and inventory. The workshop results will be used to influence decision making on policy areas through a report to be presented at the Financial Conference October . 15-17, 1991.

Management Guidelines

Page 8

3.3 SCOPE

BUSINESS UNITS
-all departments, central and common service agencies
-significant entities within department
-related special operating agencies, boards, commissions
-business partners
-financial institutions
-contracted outsourcing - Vendors and Suppliers

BUSINESS
Support all client areas
 - Payment for goods and services
 - Procurement of goods and services
 - Inventory and Assets and Real Property
 - Administration and Financial Management
 - Expenditures, Benefits and Transfer Payments

BUSINESS INVOLVEMENT
Procurement	Requisitioning
Contracting	Recording and Reporting
Generating payment	Accounting
Management of Assets	Planning
Integration Suppliers	Financial Institutions
Information Management	Cash Management

EXCLUDING
Payroll
Human Resource Management
Budget Allocations

Page 9

3.4 BUSINESS OBJECTIVES AND EXPECTATIONS

Streamline administration overhead, by:

-Refocusing management energy and direction
-Development of corporate approach to doing business
-Orientation to radical change
-Free up resources from administration to improve service and program delivery
-Responsive and better service
-Realize economies of scale
-Improve perception of departments
-Consistent with long term plan for integration
-Job enrichment
-Entrepreneurial and competitive approach to business
-Better internal communications and business interactions

Page 10

---

5. OPPORTUNITY ANALYSIS TOPICS

5.1 STRUCTURE AND CULTURE

5.2 POLICY AND PROCESS

5.3 IMPLEMENT SUPPORTING SYSTEMS

5.4 ELECTRONIC   COMMERCE

Page 21, 22 ... 5.5 INVENTORY AND ASSETS MGMT

Analysis Forms

Page 14

CHANGE ANALYSIS   **FORM A**
5.5 **Opportunity Topic :** Manage Inventory/Assets

Guidelines: Consider the above topic and provide a brief description. Based on the list of change drivers for radical improvement, provide any comments, issues or concerns.

Description : This concept refers to the activities related to the storage of goods and the retrieval of those goods for use.

Change Drivers	Comments/Issues/Concerns
1.Affordability Crisis	-largest consumption in one department
2.Quality Service Expectations	-trend to use self-serve stores -people prefer ordering from catalogue
3.Technology Initiatives	-some people don't know that self serve stores exist
4.Demand for Speed	-warehousing services are not
5.Accountability	perceived as cost item
6.Empowerment	-ultimate user is responsible for all
7.Risk Management	costs of warehousing
8.Value Added	-people are good administrators but
9.Philosophy and Culture and Market	they are not good managers because they have not been incented to be
10.Program Delivery Mechanisms	managers over the process -cost allocation and monopoly
11.Political Initiatives	ultimately cost the user more -plan to come off cost allocation
12.Credibility and Visibility	-traditional use of inventory -salary $ included in operating budget

Page 21

CHANGE ANALYSIS   **FORM B**
5.5 **Opportunity Topic :** Manage Inventory/Assets
RADICAL CHANGE OPPORTUNITY
Eliminate all warehousing other than first line depots.
THIS MEANS:
a.) Elimination of: stockpiling at second level, stock item supply, self serve units.
b.) Private sector provides government needs.
c.) Vendor holds stock and provides just as needed.
d.) Standardization of assets and commodity management.
e.) Joint business ventures.
SUPPORTED BY A NEW BUSINESS APPROACH
-Work on principles of direct ship to user.
-Geographic clustering of (shared) first line depots.
-Accountable for warehousing space, inventory & asset levels.
-Attribute full costs to resp. business unit budget and reporting.
-Formula driven cost allocation.
-Responsive to requirement of inventory.
-Full cost depreciation accounting.
-Planning includes all levels (including bench stock)
DEPENDENCIES
-Standardization of assets, commodities & supplies and codes.
-Sense of corporateness / cultural change / credibility to deliver
-Approach client satisfaction from identification needs rather than inventory management.
-Inventory life cycle management.
-Cost effective cost allocation (applied as an incentive).
-Do not replace central services by departmental services.
Time Frame to Implement: Short term
Rank: Must do   *Page 22*

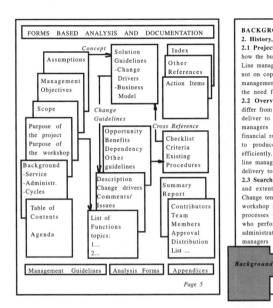

Page 5 — FORMS BASED ANALYSIS AND DOCUMENTATION
Concept — Assumptions; Management Objectives; Scope; Purpose of the project / Purpose of the workshop; Background -Service -Administr. -Cycles; Table of Contents; Agenda
Solution Guidelines -Change Drivers -Business Model
Index; Other References; Action Items
Change Guidelines — Opportunity Benefits Dependency Other guidelines; Description Change drivers Comments/ Issues; List of Functions topics: 1... 2...
Cross Reference — Checklist Criteria Existing Procedures; Summary Report; Contributors Team Members Approval Distribution List ...
Management Guidelines | Analysis Forms | Appendices

BACKGROUND
2. History, Overview, Opportunities, Principles
2.1 Project History- The time has come for radical changes in how the business is conducted. The public expects quality service. Line managers want to focus on providing cost-effective service, not on coping with internal administrative impediments. Senior management, both at the centre and in departments recognizes the need for closer cooperation and fundamental reforms.
2.2 Overview of the Administrative Processes- Departments differ from one another in the nature of the unique services they deliver to their internal and external client base. From a line managers perspective, human, material, information and financial resources are "requisitioned" and combined in concert to produce program outputs economically, effectively and efficiently. Clearly, the administrative burden imposed on the line manager should be minimized so they can focus on service delivery to their clients.
2.3 Search for Business Opportunities- The nature, organization and extent of administrative processes reflects their history. Change tends to be incremental, not radical. The purpose of this workshop is to question the very nature of the administrative processes which are performed, how they are performed, and who performs them. The goal is to fundamentally redesign administrative processes to be cost effective, to support line managers in the delivery of programs, and to support government-wide management of its resources.
Background — *Page 6*

2.4 SERVICE / PROGRAM DELIVERY
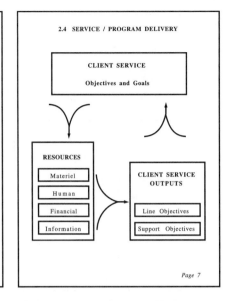
CLIENT SERVICE — Objectives and Goals
RESOURCES: Materiel, Human, Financial, Information
CLIENT SERVICE OUTPUTS: Line Objectives, Support Objectives
Page 7

3.5 BUSINESS ASSUMPTIONS
Central agencies and departments' senior management are willing to accept radical changes to optimize administration
Current systems under development may be changed to support new opportunities
Modes of delivery may change to support new opportunities
Willingness to train and/or acquire the skill sets required to support new opportunities
Roles and responsibilities for current business process may be changed to support new opportunities
Willingness to accept more business risk for opportunities
Willingness to invest resources to support new opportunities
Service delivery methods are changing and will continue to do so
Net cost will not increase
Central Policy making and Departmental level policy making will follow common guidelines while being flexible to allow for individual differences
Political decisions influence or change program delivery
Trend for greater alliance with private sector & other gov't levels
Workshop Assumptions
The recommendation from the workshop will be reviewed to develop an action plan
Page 11

4.1 CHANGE DRIVERS
1. Affordability Crisis
2. Quality Service Expectations
3. Technology Initiatives
4. Demand for Speed
5. Accountability
6. Empowerment
7. Risk Management
8. Value Added
9. Philosophy and Culture and Market
10. Program Delivery Mechanisms
11. Political Initiatives
12. Credibility and Visibility
Solution Guidelines — *Page 12*

4.2 BUSINESS MODEL
Focus for Discussion — PLAN, MANAGE, PROCURE, RECORD AND REPORT (diagram)
Page 13

ACTION ITEMS
ISSUES LOG
1. Identify observers and roles for special interest attendees in JAD workshop
2. Department to include material to ensure non-financial participation at upcoming conference
3. Method to communicate workshop results to the sub-committee to ensure an approach is developed to communicate with people/departments strategy.
4. Redefine business expectation to correct level and match to illustrative example
Appendices — *Page 25*

PROGRAM/SERVICE DELIVERY BENEFITS
-Goals and objectives driven
-Respond to client needs.
-Client decides service level.
-Paperless approach.
-Minimize delivery time.
-Optimize access to suppliers.
-Focus on the program.
-Best value negotiation/least cost administration.
-Proactive
-Reduced overhead.
-More appropriate choices for price and quality.
-Centralized warehouses.
-Increased standardization of parts.
-Warehouse cost savings passed onto program delivery.
-Reduced cost of holding inventory.
-Easier training.
-Promotes corporate behavior.
-Share business practices and programs.
-Common use of facilities.
-Common infrastructure.
-No binge buying.
-Avoid "re-inventing the wheel"
-Accrual Accounting
Page 26

Index

WORKBOOK 5

Business concept analysis for a common approach to work management

BUSINESS VISION AND GOALS

JANUARY 27-28, 1992

MEETING WORKBOOK

Page 1

WORKSHOP AGENDA FOR BUSINESS ANALYSIS

* Executive Sponsor Opening Remarks

* Introductions and Administration

* Overview/Background

* Workshop Process

* Management Guidelines
 -Purpose
 -Scope
 -Objectives & Expectations
 -Assumptions

* Solution Guidelines
 -One-Stop Shopping Concept
 -Key Definitions

* Business Analysis Forms
 -Concept Requirements
 -Functions Requirements

* Action Items / Issues Log

* Summary and Closing Remarks

Page 3

WORKSHOP TEAM MEMBERS

BUSINESS CONTRIBUTORS
Bob G
Marty M
Gary P
Jim S
Tony S
Wayne T
Rich W
John K
Perry C
Anthony V
Pete R

TECHNICAL CONTRIBUTORS
Wendy T
Joan H
Ken L

OBSERVERS
Doug C

WORKSHOP FACILITATOR - Tony C

DOCUMENTATION - Roman S

Page 4

PURPOSE OF THE PROJECT

Provide unparalleled service to our customers by implementing an automated planning and scheduling tool for the departments that will assist them in job scheduling, minimizing costs, meeting job commitment dates and fostering improved communication with our customers.

BASIC PRINCIPLE
The new system will be able to provide "one-stop shopping" airline reservation like service to customers.

PURPOSE OF THE WORKSHOP
To involve System users and Systems Development Personnel in a structured workshop to define the requirements for planning and scheduling and determine the environment which will support the above.

The level of detail will be:
 - Define purpose and scope
 - Define objectives and assumptions
 - Describe the Planning and Scheduling concept, and issues or concerns about related topics.
 - Statement of business opportunity and system requirements
 - Definition of guidelines involved

The workshop document will represent consensus for system development and implementation activities.

Management Guidelines

SPONSOR: Steering Committee
DATE : January 14, 1992

Page 8

SCOPE OF PROJECT
LOCATIONS : -All . Offices, Customer Design Services, Operating, Maintenance, Engineering, & Constructing Organization
BUSINESS UNITS: - Electric, Gas, Conservation
RELATED AREAS: -Administration, Customer Relations
CLIENTS : -Internal and External Including Government and Regulatory Agencies.
KEY COMPONENTS OF PLANNING & SCHEDULING
- Crew Capability Planning
- Integrated Job Scheduling Organizations
RESOURCES INVOLVED:
- Individuals, Crews, Materials, Equipment, Vehicles, Budget
CONCEPTS ANALYSIS TOPICS:
Reservation, Request for Service, Immediate Response, Planning, Preliminary Schedule, Final Schedule, Work Priorities, Work Completion, Inquiries & Reporting Resources, Interfaces
KEY INFORMATION
External and Internal Customer, Materials Availability, Job Definition/Job Progress/Job Requirements, Project, Budget Information, Personnel/Skills Availability, Equipment/Type Availability, Forecast/Preliminary Job, Corporate Guidelines, (Corporate Systems)
EXCLUDING FROM DESIGN
Inventory Management and Accounting, Skills Development, Time Reporting and Payroll, Cost Estimates, Project Management Process, Budgeting Process, Daily Dispatched Work, Corporate Management Information

Page 9

MANAGEMENT OBJECTIVES AND EXPECTATIONS
-Optimize costs
-Support unparalleled customer service
-Corporate approach to planning and scheduling of resources
-Automated planning
-Effective resource utilization
-Improved controls
-Meet or exceed mandatory deadlines
-Improved communications with internal organization and external customers
-Improved customer perception
-Improved coordination and follow up amongst internal organizations
-Automated reporting
-Respond to customer inquiries
-Daily reallocation of crews
-Flexibility to respond to operating conditions
-Respond to unplanned work
-Avoid resource and cost overcommitment
-Optimize paper content
-Optimize schedule based on business rules
-Manage priorities
-Customer service measurements
-Coordination of related information and systems
-Event driven system
-Access to information for user defined analyses
-Optimize use of overtime
-Exception reporting generated by user defined flags and codes

Page 10

VISION ANALYSIS   **FORM A1**
CONCEPT TOPIC: Planning and Scheduling System

Guidelines : Review the key items listed to ensure they accurately portray the concept. Provide comments on the processes by describing a known business problem or future concerns. Identify additional items as required and identify information needs.

Key Items	Information	Comments / Issues / Concerns
Reservation	-Customer Service -Internal/ external customer	-Service system will work with and interface with Planning and Scheduling system (reservation component)
Request for Service	-phone call -letter -MIS system -radio -tickets -diagrams -map	-External - most to be handled by SPOC -some will go directly to operating department or design department -Internal will always go directly to operating department or design dept. -Service system will generate job
Immediate Response	-customer job (in 5 days) -emergency	-operating & design is/will generate non-service job -customer work in 5 working days or less will be handled in the reservation portion of the system (this excludes emergency work); multi-week plan
Planning	-multi-week planning	updated daily and recorded weekly -currently field updates handled manually

Analysis Forms

Continued ...   *Page 15*

VISION ANALYSIS   **FORM A2**
CONCEPT TOPIC: Planning and Scheduling System

Key Items	Information	Comments / Issues / Concerns
Planning	-Project	-jobs are scheduled to critical path -Project does not have all job #'s
Preliminary Schedule	-tentative plan -resources identified tentatively committed	-domino effect caused by change- non-stock items do not show -must be available on demand -involves many options and changes -required for weekly review meetings -includes: crews, matls and equipment -skills info. currently not available -estimating systems include skills data
Final Schedule	-plan -approvals -resources committed	-does not cover all personnel -notify material req'mt manually -resources are mapped to final plan -final schedule matls must be locked in
Work Priorities	-commitment date -customer need date	-customer work remains a high priority -internal work does not use priority across business lines; sometimes priority used to decide tie breaker
Work Completion	-guidelines -personnel -inspectors	-guidelines not as clear as they should be -personnel report work load which is verified and status updated daily
Inquiries and Reporting	-all types of information from all sources	-on line access to information -report listing; notification & letters -currency of information -historical data/audit trail

Page 16

VISION ANALYSIS   **FORM B1**
CONCEPT TOPIC: Planning and Scheduling System

Guidelines: Consider the items associated with the above topic, identify any business opportunities and provide requirements for the new system design. If needed, provide a description of management policies needed to operate the business system and provide other guidelines which may assist the design.

BUSINESS OPPORTUNITIES:
-All departments use common approach to receive and handle request for service
-All work will be on one system.
-Work stand alone.
-Identify corporate-wide resources pool to accomplish task.
-Automate scheduling and resource assignment.
-Improve customer communications.
-Enhance visibility and utilization of corporate resources.
-Manage effect of changes to schedule.
-Better management of crews
-Reduce clerical effort.
-More complete identification of job requirements.
-Enhance Material and Equipment Management.
-Schedule, prioritize to established corporate guidelines.
-Meet and exceed customer expectations.
-Flexible reporting.
-Current schedule.
-Respond to dynamic changes.
-Measure effectiveness.

Continued...   *Page 17*

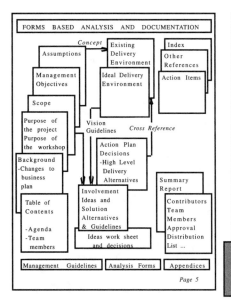

FORMS BASED ANALYSIS AND DOCUMENTATION

Concept

- Assumptions
- Existing Delivery Environment
- Ideal Delivery Environment
- Index
- Other References
- Action Items
- Management Objectives
- Scope
- Vision Guidelines
- *Cross Reference*
- Purpose of the project
- Purpose of the workshop
- Action Plan Decisions -High Level Delivery Alternatives
- Background -Changes to business plan
- Involvement Ideas and Solution Alternatives & Guidelines
- Summary Report
- Contributors Team Members Approval Distribution List ...
- Table of Contents
  -Agenda
  -Team members
- Ideas work sheet and decisions

| Management Guidelines | Analysis Forms | Appendices |

Page 5

BACKGROUND

Date: January 20, 1992
Title: Planning and Scheduling Subsystem Scope
Prepared: Planning and Scheduling Working Committee
Goal: Improve the level of service to our customers by providing an automated planning and scheduling tool for all departments that will assist them in job scheduling, minimizing costs, meeting job commitment dates and fostering improved communication with our customers. This initiative will support the concept of Single Point Of Contact or
Description: The Planning and Scheduling Subsystem will provide an automated mechanism for weekly (with the ability for multiple weeks) resource capability planning and job scheduling. Crews and jobs will be scheduled on a daily basis, in weekly blocks.
System Interfaces: The Planning and Scheduling tool will function as a real time subsystem. As jobs are scheduled, the schedule dates will be automatically sent to system. The system will interface with the job cost file,, the automated estimating system, and if feasible, Project 2, for appropriate information.
Key Assumptions: The Planning and Scheduling subsystem will be an interactive, real time system. It will provide resource leveling capabilities and assist other departments in establishing customer commitment dates.

Background

Page 6

KEY DEFINITIONS

PROJECT is a package of jobs covering one or all organizations to get something done for a customer.

JOB is a package of work activities for an organization.

PLANNING is analysis and preparation of an outline of activities which can, or have to, take place in order to create an optimum schedule in a multi-week period.

PROJECT SCHEDULE is a series of time phased activities and resource allocations aligned to achieve a specific objective or set of objectives.

JOB SCHEDULE is a list of time phased job assignments to crews available to an organization (in support of a project schedule when applicable).

PRELIMINARY SCHEDULE is all work due and tentatively scheduled for a given work period.

FINAL SCHEDULE is a schedule in which all resources deficiencies and other conflicts have been resolved to be formally approved and adopted by the appropriate parties.

Page 14

BUSINESS ASSUMPTIONS
-Continue to use Project for long term planning.
-All resources must be considered to schedule work.
-ABC Utility Co. organization is evolving.
-Interactive, Real-time system.
-Work planned weekly and adjusted daily to meet changing conditions.
-Daily job progress reports will be needed to support the concept.
-Field information available/reported on daily basis.
-Crew members may be loaned to different areas or supervisors within the same organization.
-Comply with corporate guidelines for customer service.
-Firm customer date will depend on resources available to be committed.
-All jobs candidates for planning; scheduling requires material availability.
-Candidates for scheduling: jobs that have met customer prerequisites, have been authorized, permits obtained, notifications made as required
-"One-stop shopping" work load will be supported using a dynamic portion of the ABC Co. resource pool available to respond to changing demand on internal and external customer jobs.
-ABC Co. resource pool includes own personnel & outside contractors.
-All jobs in Project will be handled by this system.
-Emergency jobs will be handled by crews allocated to low priority work.
-Reservation concept will not eliminate single point of contact/one-stop shopping concept, rather it supports it.
-System will be used by non-technical personnel.
-Planning and Scheduling system will be stand a lone system.
-interfaces with Planning and Scheduling system.
-Internal customers continue to use interfaces.
-Critical path planning will continue to be processed on Project.
-Crews work to 40 hour base work week.

Page 11

TECHNICAL ASSUMPTIONS

-Implemented on mainframe.
-Interface and feeds with various mainframe systems.
-Real-time system.
-Cost effective, user friendly system solution.
-Use advanced technology as applicable.
-Hardware requirements will be included in cost analysis.
-Hardware will be available.

IMPLEMENTATION ASSUMPTIONS
-Includes training and user documentation.
-Implementation and support should not require additional personnel.

WORKSHOP ASSUMPTIONS
-Decision to build or buy system will be based on this document.

Page 12

PLANNING AND SCHEDULING SYSTEM CONCEPT

- External Customer — Request / Confirm — **CUSTOMER SERVICE** Reservation
- **FUNCTIONS** — Request / Confirm — Commitments
- Internal/ External Customers — Preliminary Plan Confirm Availability
- Service Rules Single Job
- Service Rules Multi-job
- SCOPE
- Planning Crews,Pwr Equip Matls,Vehicles
- Job Scheduling Crew, Materials, Power Equip, Vehicles — Adjustments
- Crew Capabilities
- Schedule Multi-week Work Plan / Plan Actual
- Adjustments
- Crew Structure
- Crew Compliment
- Crew Skills
- Availability
- Crew Info
- Go to work

Job Definition/Requirement/Progress
Resources: Materials, Power Equipment, Crews, Vehicles
Project, Budget, Personnel/Skills, Forecast, System

Solution Guidelines

Page 13

VISION ANALYSIS FORM B2

SYSTEM DESIGN REQUIREMENT:
-Implement Planning and Scheduling for all work.
-Method to define work classification and processing rules for Service and non-servicejobs.
-access/interrogate available dates from planning and scheduling
-Electronic scheduling for dates selected by operator.
-Method to support Single Job Scheduling and multi-job scheduling).
-Easy path for department access to all scheduling functions.
-Link to selected mainframe systems containing knowledge of available (human/ material/equipment) resources.
-Identify status of all resources - availability for current and future
-Status generated reports and notifications (Including plan reports)
-Update plan and schedule daily adjustments in the field.
-Track and access to job status.
-Interface Project to pass resource commitments & duration to jobs.
-Method to advise/inquire job backlog by start date.
-Customized report using adhoc query language.
-**Automated scheduling of work and resources:**
-**Jobs**: -question/map request requirements to identify job detail
-**Crews**:-map skills available to skills required for each job.
   -link between job and skills requirement
-**Materials**: -map material available to material required for each job.
   -method to trigger resource allocations to materials mgmt. system
   -method to receive confirmation/status for materials allocated.
   -method to notify due date for material due to material mgmt. sys
-**Equipment**: -map type of power operated equipment available to types of equipment required for each job.

Continued ....

Page 18

VISION ANALYSIS FORM B3

   -method to trigger equipment allocation to equip. mgmt. system
   -method to receive confirmation/status for equipment allocated.
-**Final**: -method to update selected job status.
   -security to ensure authorized people update job status.
   -track schedule to job completion.
-Method to set job priority to classification level (eg. major/minor)
-Method to track jobs by priority.
-Customer notification when job bumped or schedule is changed.
-Feedback completion status to Project
-On-line access to schedule detail; Adhoc reporting.
-Automatic generation of notification letters.
-Method for supervisor to revise schedule as needed to reflect dynamic local plan and actual work.
-Comparative analysis to measure actual to scheduled work.
-Method to structure crew compliment.

OTHER GUIDELINES:
-Work classification and processing rules provided by Planning and Scheduling system.
-used to schedule Immediate Response for customer work.
-Resource Management system must be capable of allocating and identifying resources to Planning and Scheduling system based on due date requirements.
-Enhance Project to identify job numbers.
-Ensure reference to all materials including non-stock items.
-Enhance system to include skills required for job categories.
-Trend to use "Just In Time" concept

Page 19

Index

WORKSHOP 6

Risk assessment and change analysis
for insurance policy administration

STRATEGY & REQUIREMENTS ANALYSIS

SEPTEMBER 29, 1989

MEETING WORKBOOK

Page 1

WORKSHOP AGENDA FOR BUSINESS ANALYSIS

* Executive Sponsor Opening Remarks - Richard F

* Introductions and Administration

* Workshop Process

* Management Guidelines
  -Purpose
  -Scope
  -Management Objectives & Expectations
  -Business Assumptions

* Business Regulations Analysis
  -Analysis Forms

* Action Items

* Summary and Closing Remarks

Page 3

WORKSHOP TEAM MEMBERS

MANAGEMENT SPONSOR
Richard F .... Individual Operations V.P.

PROJECT MANAGER
Wayne W.................. Manager, Product Implementation

PRODUCT MANAGEMENT
John O .... Traditional Life Insurance Policies
Sharon T .... Interest Sensitive Life Insurance
Bill C .... Investment Products
John R .... Investment Products Actuary

LEGAL SUPPORT
Steve R .... Lawyer

PRODUCT ADMINISTRATION
Dawn L...................... Interest Sensitive Policy Issues
Anne B .... Traditional Policy Issue
Maureen B .... Traditional Administration
Elaine W .... Interest Sensitive Administration
Maria F .... Investments Administration

WORKSHOP SUPPORT
Anthony C .... Facilitator, Crawford & Associates
Roman S .... Documentation, Crawford & Associates

Page 4

PURPOSE OF THE PROJECT
Interpret the regulations to develop a workplan to comply with new regulations which will support different products consistently. This will also consider future business and provide a model for ABC Co. to use to respond to other changes as they occur.

PURPOSE OF THE WORKSHOP
Involve business representatives in a structured workshop to discuss the regulatory environment and the impact on ABC Co. product lines.

The level of detail will be:
1. List regulations topics.
2. List products and components affected.
3. Define risk assessment and degree of compliance.
4. Common interpretation of material changes.
5. Statement of direction for compliance.
6. Time frame for the workplan.

The workshop result will be used to develop a common approach for ABC Co. to implement the strategy across product lines.

Management Guidelines

Page 7

SCOPE OF THE PROJECT

REGULATIONS:
-Massachusetts Regulations - 211 CMR 35
-Future Regulations as they occur from other states

LOCATIONS:
-Home office
-All other branch offices

PRODUCTS/GROUPS:

INSURANCE
-Traditional
-Interest Sensitive

INVESTMENT
-Annuities
-Single Premium

BUSINESS AREAS
NEW BUSINESS
-New sales of existing products
-New sales of new products

IN-FORCE BUSINESS
-Client originated material changes
-ABC Life Insurance Co. originated material changes

Page 8

MGMT. OBJECTIVES/EXPECTATIONS

-Compliance with Unisex regulation.

-Maintain license to do business.

-Maintain / Increase market position.

-Respond to other changes concerning Unisex regulations.

-Simplify the new product development for Unisex business.

-Provide a common interpretation and source of reference for the strategic direction.

-Managed costs and timeframe for implementation.

-Provide a statement of direction to respond to the regulatory intent.

-Design a systems and administration solution which responds to Massachusetts regulations and any other source of state regulations.

Page 9

REGULATION TOPICS

Page 12... 1. Dividends
2. Contractually Guaranteed Maximums/Minimums
Page 16... 3. Mortality Tables - Life
4. Mortality Tables - Interest Sensitive
5. Mortality Tables - Annuity
6. Residency
7. Riders
8. Changes Predetermined by Policy
9. Reinstatements / Settlement Options
10. Material Changes / Renewal by Agreement
    (i) Increases in Coverage & Premium
    (ii) Additional Purchase Benefit
    (iii) Attained Age Conversions
    (iv) Change of Insured / Exchange of Life
    (v) Dividend (see topic 1)
    (vi) Death Benefit Option Change
    (vii) Addition of Riders
    (viii) Smoking Status Change
    (ix) Plan Change
    (x) Policy Split/Policy Combination
    (xi) Policy Exchange

Analysis Forms

Page 11

BUSINESS ANALYSIS   **FORM A**
ISSUE TOPIC: Dividends

Guidelines Consider the above topic and list product components or features affected. In addition for each define the risk of NON compliance in terms of High, Medium or Low. Describe the degree of compliance ABC Co should implement in terms of Full, Partial or None.

ISSUE: (i) Dividends constitutes a change in payment. This does not unisex the whole policy, but rather only the dividend paid. **(ii)** The determination of dividends paid is partly a function of amount premium paid, constraints, interest rates, cash values etc. some of which are now sex distinct. Can we argue that since the premiums on In-force is different, we are in effect crediting back dividends to reflect this premium?

Products/Components/Features Affected	Risk	Compliance
NEW BUSINESS	High	Full
All Traditional Par		
-EWL		1990
-TMS		1990
-New Premier		1990
-CEO		1990
-LPR		1990
INFORCE:	Low	Partial
All Traditional Par Business		

Page 12

BUSINESS ANALYSIS   **FORM B**
ISSUE / TOPIC: Dividends
Guidelines: consider the above topic and define the questions/ changes. In addition identify the product lines affected and the degree of complexity in terms of High, Medium or Low. Provide a statement of direction in terms of what ABC Co has to implement and identify if a decision review is needed in terms of person responsible and date. Indicate the schedule in terms of the date's 1/1/90, 1/6/90 or 1/1/91. Cross reference your answers using the number column.

Interpretation / Questions	Product Line	Complexity
1 Justify current practice of paying dividend sex distinct mortality.	In Force, Life, Par	Medium
2 Method to handle 58CSO policy		
3 Pricing changed riders	C E O	

No. Statement of Direction for Compliance	Review	Schedule
NEW BUSINESS We will be pricing for a "Unisex dividend" on the new Business that we sell in 1990 on trad., namely EWL and TMS. New Premier will be Unisexed when introduced in 1990. Old Premier will be withdrawn from Massachusetts.	Kevin	Nov 30
INFORCE LIFE PAR Implement a simple adjustment to dividend formula based on mortality (eg. male+$.10 female-$.10)	John	1st Q/90
Formula to price for smokers vs. non-smokers Use/Assume male only 58CSO tables will comply with the law for NSP's No change to guarantee or current COI Change Inforce Business for 80/20 rule	Sharon	Oct 30/90

Page 13

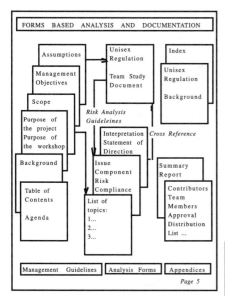

BACKGROUND

In late 1987, the Commissioner of Insurance for the State of Massachusetts issued a regulation barring discrimination on the basis of sex in all forms of insurance. Further clarification of the regulation revealed that not only insurance, but also annuities, were affected. Interpretation is not clear-cut, but it primarily affects rates and values.

From September 1, 1988, to January 1, 1990, the State of Massachusetts has accepted the use of male insurance rates and values, and female annuity rates and values.

However, starting on January 1, 1989, the State of Massachusetts has indicated that they will fully enforce non-discrimination, which we interpret to mean that we will be expected to use true unisex rates and values.

As a result of lobbying efforts by the insurance community, the Commissioner is considering delaying the final implementation date. An information bulletin is expected soon, which should indicate whether the date will or will not be put off.

ACTION PLAN - Utilize a structured workshop to involve business managers and system representatives to define a common strategy to respond to the business needs.

Page 6

BUSINESS ASSUMPTIONS

-Significant degree of compliance by January 1990.

-Will continue to do business in Unisex market.

-Regulatory changes will occur.

-Some business decisions may consider risk.

-Other states may implement some form of Unisex regulations.

-Solutions must be generic to accommodate variations across states.

-Eventual compliance and good faith effort is a requirement.

-Compliance will be cost justified in terms of risk.

-There will be a change in product pricing

-Assume 80/20 blend Male/Female ratio

TECHNICAL ASSUMPTIONS

-Implementation of the strategic plan can be accomplished within reasonable costs and available time frame.

Page 10

BUSINESS ANALYSIS   **FORM A**

ISSUE TOPIC: Mortality Table and Rates - Life

ISSUE: (i) Must use single proportional table to determine the standard non-forfeiture values under a life insurance policy.
(ii) Starting in 1990 must use NEW Regulations.
(iii) Use of one mortality table for all insurance and annuity products (doesn't make any sense for annuities to use the same table as in life insurance)
(iv) The male to female mix must be consistent across product lines.
(v) The gross premium rate for male and females must be the same. (can we charge whatever we want?)

Products/Components/Features Affected	Risk	Compliance
NEW BUSINESS: E W L	High	Full
T M S		
New Premier		
V U L		
M P P		
New UL		
F P		
Immediate Annuities		
SPDA II		
CSA's		
Centennial Term		
IN-FORCE: P2V2	High	Full
P2000		
Old SV's		
Old Premier		
58 CSO Products ??		

Page 16

BUSINESS ANALYSIS   **FORM B**

ISSUE / TOPIC: Mortality Table and Rates - Life

Interpretation / Questions	Product Line	Complexity
1. Law refers to cash value.	Life	
2. Refer to min. or actual cash values	Life	
3. Impact of NEW Regs. referring to using any table variables	Life	Medium to High
4. Use two different tables on a survivorship policy.	Life	

No. Statement of Direction for Compliance	Review	Schedule
1. Use a proportional table.	Steve	Oct 10/89
2. Must use a defined blend of males and females to create a product (80/20)	Steve	Oct 10/89
Scenario 1 - Based on actual cash value and NEW Regulations apply:	Steve	
- Then develop Single Life Products based on 80/20.	John	Nov30/89
Scenario 2 - Does not base on actual cash, NEW Regulations do not apply:	Steve	
- Then no need for Change		
Scenario 3 - Must use some table for both lives under survivor policy:	Develop new prod.	Nov 30/89
- Then change product	John	
Scenario 4 - Use different tables:	John	
- Then no action is required on policy	(memo)	

Page 17

Index

WORKBOOK 7

Non-technical opoerations design
to support franchised business partners

ABC AVIATION ASSOCIATES MEETING

WESTERN REGION - NOVEMBER 28-29, 1988

CENTRAL REGION - DECEMBER 1-2, 1988

EASTERN REGION - DECEMBER 7-8, 1988

MEETING WORKBOOK

Page 1

WORKSHOP AGENDA FOR BUSINESS ANALYSIS

* Executive Sponsor Opening Remarks

* Introductions and Administration

* Workshop Process

* Management Guidelines
  - Purpose
  - Scope
  - Management Objectives & Expectations
  - Business Assumptions

* Business Requirements Analysis
  - Analysis Forms

* Summary and Closing Remarks

Page 3

WORKSHOP TEAM MEMBERS

EXECUTIVE SPONSOR
Jim N   A B C

WORKSHOP TEAM
Lyle A   ABC Associate
Brian H   ABC Associate
Gordon H   ABC Associate
Dave K   ABC Associate
Charles P   ABC Associate
Roland W   ABC Associate
Dick W   ABC Associate
Mike P   A B C
Bernard F   A B C
Ernie H   A B C.

WORKSHOP FACILITATOR
Tony C

Page 4

PURPOSE OF THE PROJECT

Implement ABC Oil Company sponsored service and Image Marketing Programs which will maximize ABC dealer and agents profitability and establish ABC as the premier marketer in the general aviation business.

PURPOSE OF THE WORKSHOP

Involve progressively thinking dealers and agents in a structured meeting to discuss ideas for aviation programs and provide guidelines to implement standards and marketing programs.

The level of detail will be:
1. Description of today's situation and recommendations.
2. Identification of opportunities and ideas for improvements.
3. Description of benefits to your business.

The workshop output will be used by ABC to develop standards and implement marketing programs..

Executive Sponsor : Jim N
Title: Product Advisor
Date: November 8, 1988

Management Guidelines

Page 6

SCOPE OF THE ABC SPONSORED PROGRAM

LOCATIONS :

- All Aviation Dealers and Agents.
- All ABC Aviation Fuel Stations

BUSINESS :

- Marketing Programs for the General Aviation Business.

MARKETING PROGRAM FOCUS :

- Image
- Services and Offering
- Merchandising
- Networking
- Sales

EXCLUDING

- Pricing and Commissions.
- Organization.
- Technical and Financial Aspects.

Page 7

MANAGEMENT OBJECTIVES AND EXPECTATIONS

Promote a first class image that advertises itself.

Improve customer perception.

Increase market share.

Increase customer loyalty.

Develop consistent offering across locations.

Attract a brand value.

Effective merchandise package.

Page 8

MARKETING SEGMENTS

Sample Pages 12,13,14   1. Image - Uniforms
                                  - Facilities
                                  - Services
                                  - Program

2. Offering - Service
                - Financial Services

3. Network - Promotions

4. Sales   - Objectives

5. Merchandising - Promotions

Analysis Forms

Page 11

BUSINESS ANALYSIS   **FORM A**
Current Situation and Recommendations
Marketing Segment - Image   **Topic** - Uniforms
Guidelines : Considering this marketing segment and the list of discussion topics, describe the current situation with comments on customer reactions and make recommendations for change.

Topic .	Todays Situation	Comments
Uniforms	Same standards as automotive	Not well advertised
- Colors	Red shirt, Grey pants, Grey coat	Identified with ABC automotive (not aviation)
- Type	Pants, Coveralls	Coveralls look sloppy
Reception	No Standard	Need for some standard
- Winter	Parka, Coveralls	Color/Type need discussion
- Logo	ABC oval or badge	Not aviation related
- Supplier	Several retailers/ suppliers	Confusion with standards Long wait for supply, Mail order
Footwear	No standard	
- Safety	Not clearly defined	Should meet safety standards
- Policy	Policy varies	Policies not clearly stated

Page 12

BUSINESS ANALYSIS   **FORM B**
Statement for Future Direction
Marketing Segment - Image   **Topic** - Uniforms
Guidelines : Considering this marketing segment, recommend possible changes and assign responsibility for appropriate follow up. Qualify suggestions using the following codes:
A=Customer wants this,   **B**=Increase profit,   **C**=Attracts customers,   **D**=Differentiates ABC from competition

Subject .	Statement for Direction	Qual	Area
- Style	Uniform standard for Aviation	C,D	A B C
- Color	Recommend navy blue uniform with white shirt and red tie	C,D	
- Type	Do not allow coveralls to be used by line crew.	C,D	
- Reception	Blue skirt, white blouse, accent scarf	C,D	
- Winter	Blue parka with hood	C,D	
- Logo	Incorporate aviation wings	C,D	A B C
- Supplier	More local supplier	C,D	A B C

Page 13

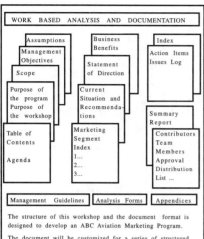

WORK BASED ANALYSIS AND DOCUMENTATION

Assumptions	Business Benefits	Index
Management Objectives		Action Items Issues Log
Scope	Statement of Direction	
Purpose of the program Purpose of the workshop	Current Situation and Recommendations	Summary Report
Table of Contents	Marketing Segment Index 1... 2... 3...	Contributors Team Members Approval Distribution List ...
Agenda		

| Management Guidelines | Analysis Forms | Appendices |

The structure of this workshop and the document format is designed to develop an ABC Aviation Marketing Program.

The document will be customized for a series of structured workshops to provide a business forum for ABC Aviation Associates.

Page 5

BACKGROUND

Executive Sponsor's opening remarks and business situation handouts.
(Separate Document)

Background

BUSINESS ASSUMPTIONS FOR THE ABC PROGRAM

English and French.

Programs directed at entrepreneurial dealers and agents.

Programs will benefit those who participate most.

Geared towards competitive environment.

Page 9

| BUSINESS ANALYSIS | FORM C |

What it will do for your Business

Marketing Segment - Image   **Topic** - Uniforms

Guidelines: Consider the above marketing segment and topic and describe the changes in terms of how it will benefit your business. Qualify your comments with the appropriate code(s).

Subject.	Qual	What it will do for your Business
Uniform		
-Style	C,D	Improves Image
-Color		Standard is consistent with aviation image Promotes first class image Not a gas jockey
-Type		In keeping with professional image
-Reception		In keeping with professional image
-Logo		Identifiable, Professional, Motivational
-Supplier		Easy to conform to standard

Page 14

Index

WORKBOOK 8

Customized accounting processes
for invoice payments

REQUIREMENTS ANALYSIS

NOVEMBER 1-3, 1989

Page 1

WORKSHOP AGENDA FOR BUSINESS ANALYSIS

* Executive Sponsor Opening Remarks

* Introductions and Administration

* Workshop Process

* Background Materials
  -Background

* Management Guidelines
  -Purpose
  -Scope
  -Management Objectives & Expectations
  -Business Assumptions

* Business Requirements Analysis
  -Analysis Forms

* Summary and Closing Remarks

Page 3

WORKSHOP TEAM MEMBERS

EXECUTIVE SPONSOR
Kevin M   Assistant V.P. Comptroller

BUSINESS CONTRIBUTORS
Karen F   Accts. Payable Supervisor
Ed W   Assistant Comptroller
Bruce L   General Accounts Manager
Mark H   Internal Audit Manager
Terry C   Corporate Planning Manager

TECHNICAL CONTRIBUTORS
Vinod D   Project Manager
Thomas S   Applications Programming Manager

OBSERVERS
Randy N

WORKSHOP FACILITATOR
Tony C

DOCUMENTATION
Roman S

Page 4

PURPOSE OF THE PROJECT
Develop an accounts payable system for recording, tracking, payment and distribution of liabilities and to provide timely information for improved operations and control.

ANALYSIS GUIDELINES
To involve business and technical representatives in a structured workshop to discuss the accounts payable environment and the technical requirements to implement a system to handle accounts payable.

The level of detail will be:
-define purpose and scope
-define objectives and assumptions
-key operational processes and information used
-descriptions and concerns
-opportunities for improvement and system requirements
-identification of other considerations for implementation

The workshop document will be used for further analysis for external design and system development. This will involve a second workshop to define screen and report features.

Sponsoring Executive: Kevin M
Title: Assistant Vice President Comptroller

Management Guidelines

Page 9

SCOPE OF THE PROJECT

LOCATIONS
-Head office, Distribution centres (excluding branch offices)
PRODUCTS
-All purchases, Advertising, Supplies, Services, Capital assets
BUSINESS FUNCTIONS
-Entry of Vendor Invoices
-Tracking for Approval
-Preparation of Cheques
-Cheque Reconciliation
-Vendor and Table File Maintenance
-Period-end Processing
-Periodic Reporting, Exception Reporting, G.S.T. Reporting
-Tracking Accruals
-On-line Inquiry
-Distribution to General Ledger
-Supplies/Vendor Analysis
-Provincial Sales Tax Allocation
-Expense Analysis
-System Operations
INTERFACES
-Cash Payment
-General Ledger (Accts. Payable, Distribution and Payments)
EXCLUSIONS
-Matching Invoice to P.O.
-Claims Settlement Processing
-Accounts Receivable

Page 10

MGMT. OBJECTIVES/EXPECTATIONS

-manage liabilities and expenses
-accurate and timely information
-on-time payment
-managed cash flows and future needs
-accurate distribution to G/L
-improved controls
-simplified operations
-security and access controls
-system flexibility for growth and enhancements
-automated reporting and information sources
-automate regular and recurring payments
-support/reports for cancellations/corrections/reprinting
-on-line enquiry to accounts payable transactions
-optimize payment schedule and discounts available
-capture purchase history/info. with payment process
-credit/debit adjustments
-manage hold-back amounts
-process manual cheques as required
-file maintenance for vendor information
-automate audit trail
-reporting G.S.T. credits and payments
-vendor analysis
-expense analysis

Page 11

FUNCTIONAL TOPICS

Sample Pages 15,16 1. Entry of Vendor Invoices
                    2. Vendor and Table File Maintenance
                    3. Preparation of Cheques
Sample Pages 22,23 4. Cheque Reconciliation
                    5. Reissue Cheques
                    6. Period End Processing
                    7. Periodic Reporting / On-line Inquiry
                    8. System Setup

Analysis Forms

Page 14

BUSINESS ANALYSIS   FORM A
FUNCTION: Entry of Vendor Invoices

Guidelines: Review the list of steps below to ensure they accurately portray the above function completely. Add additional comments and information as required.

Key Process	Info.	Comments
1.On-line Entry of Vendor invoices	Invoices	-2000-3000 per month manually
-Entry -Corrections	Expense Reports	-each invoice approved by manager
		-manual or automated entry
	Credit Note	of recurring invoices
2.Edit Controls		-data type verification
		-reasonableness verification
	Debit Memo	-detection of duplicates
		-account number includes
3.Build Pending Payment Record	Purchase Order	Acct# + Centre + sub ID
		-Payment record is used for scheduling payments
		-fields on the vendor record
4.Build Pending Approval Record	Terms	must be updated
		-calculate payment data and
	Due dates	discount mode
		- use user defined dummy
5.File Documents		invoice # if appropriate
	Discounts	-use system assigned seq. #

Page 15

BUSINESS ANALYSIS   FORM B
FUNCTION: Entry of Vendor Invoices

Guidelines: Consider the processes associated with the above function. List the opportunities and requirements for the new system. State any management policies.

BUSINESS OPPORTUNITIES:
-Improved accuracy of information.
-Manage pending payments/approvals.
-Use process for partial/repeat payments.
-Track invoices and corrections.

SYSTEM DESIGN REQUIREMENTS:
-Extended edits: Valid codes/dates: entered/inv. due/approved
-Validate account code to table.
-Search for duplicates to vendor / invoice detail level.
-Assign sequential internal file control number per invoice.
-Capture unique number: vendor & invoice
-Add remarks/comments to invoice record.
-Access controls for corrective process.
-Flag currency indicator.
-List daily/operator totals for end of day balancing.

MANAGEMENT POLICIES:
-File paper documents by number: internal file number.
-No batch control totals on input.
-Errors corrected by comparing daily batch totals.
-Compare daily totals for approval by adding machine totals.

Page 16

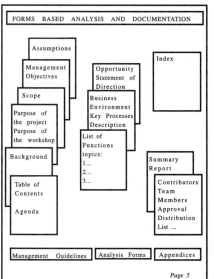

FORMS BASED ANALYSIS AND DOCUMENTATION

Assumptions

Management Objectives

Scope

Purpose of the project
Purpose of the workshop

Background

Table of Contents

Agenda

Opportunity Statement of Direction

Business Environment Key Processes Description

List of Functions topics:
1...
2...
3...

Index

Summary Report

Contributors
Team
Members
Approval
Distribution
List ...

| Management Guidelines | Analysis Forms | Appendices |

Page 5

BACKGROUND

The accounts payable system monitors all unpaid vendor invoices. It keeps management aware of which invoices:

-Should be paid in order to take advantage of discounts

-Are near their due date

-Are overdue

ACTION PLAN - Utilize structured workshops to involve administrative services representatives to further define their business requirements.

Background

Page 7

BUSINESS ASSUMPTIONS

-The system will be interfaced to the General Ledger system.
-Managers require additional detail for business analysis.
-All A/P transactions will be transferred to G/L for posting.
-Invoices will be processed at Head Office & designated locations.
-All cheques will be printed at Head Office.
-Invoice has been approved by an authorized manager.
-The invoice can be entered prior to approval.
-Purchase order may or may not have been prepared.
-Claims processed manually for credit memo to acct. if required.
-Audit trails/report is required.
-Tracking is assumed to be available from key entry.
-Full benefit of control and reporting requires P.O info. mgmt.
-System development is for April 1990 delivery.
-Trend is toward EDI communicated invoices.
-User training will be provided from systems documentation and user maintained procedure manuals.
-On-line transaction history for 3 months after cheque reconciled.
-Account code edits will be processed to extent possible using a validation process against a user maintained table.
-G/L posts invalid transactions to suspense account for exception handling.
-Utilize system backup procedures.

TECHNICAL ASSUMPTIONS

-Existing system contains pre-defined procedures for invoice authorization.

Page 12

BUSINESS ANALYSIS   FORM A

FUNCTION: Cheque Reconciliation

Guidelines: Review the list of steps below to ensure they accurately portray the above function completely. Add additional comments and information as required.

Key Process	Info.	Comments
1.Input Cashed Cheque Details	Bank Tape (Acct. Stmt.)	-assumes that bank can provide tape -requires predefined format.
2.Reconciling Cashed Cheques	Bank Tape Cheque Register	-cashed cheques are matched against outstanding cheque file -outputs include reconciliation report and list of:-outstanding cheques

Page 22

BUSINESS ANALYSIS   FORM B

FUNCTION: Entry of Vendor Invoices

Guidelines: Consider the processes associated with the above function. List the opportunities and requirements for the new system. State any management policies.

BUSINESS OPPORTUNITIES:
-Identify unprocessed/outstanding cheques.

SYSTEM DESIGN REQUIREMENT:
-Read tape. Identify amount variance by cheque number.
-Compare amount and number.
-Identify unprocessed/outstanding cheques.
-Update cheque register (flag) record as reconciled for all matched cheque numbers.

MANAGEMENT POLICIES:
-General Accounting will handle exceptions.

Page 23

Index

WORKBOOK 9

Business Design for automated work forse schedulingand reporting

REQUIREMENTS ANALYSIS

Page 1

WORKSHOP AGENDA FOR BUSINESS ANALYSIS

* Executive Sponsor Opening Remarks
* Introductions and Administration
* Overview/Background
* Workshop Process
* Management Guidelines
  - Purpose
  - Scope
  - Objectives & Expectations
  - Assumptions
* Solution Guidelines
  - One-Stop Shopping Concept
  - Key Definitions
* Business Analysis Forms
  - Concept Requirements
  - Functions Requirements
* Action Items / Issues Log
* Summary and Closing Remarks

Page 3

WORKSHOP TEAM MEMBERS

BUSINESS CONTRIBUTORS
Wayne B
Perry C
Bob G
John K
Marty M
Gary P
Jim S
Tony S
Wayne T
Anthony V
Rich W

TECHNICAL CONTRIBUTORS
Gil L
Craig S
Wendy T

OBSERVERS
Doug C

WORKSHOP FACILITATOR -Tony C

DOCUMENTATION - Roman S

Page 4

PURPOSE OF THE PROJECT

Provide unparalleled service to our customers by implementing an automated planning and scheduling tool for the departments that will assist them in job scheduling, minimizing costs, meeting job commitment dates and fostering improved communication with our customers.

BASIC PRINCIPLE

The new system will be able to provide "one-stop shopping" single point of contact system to provide airline reservation like service to customers.

PURPOSE OF THE WORKSHOP

To involve System users and Systems Development Personnel in a structured workshop to define the requirements for planning and scheduling and determine the environment which will support the above.

The level of detail will be:
- Define purpose and scope
- Define objectives and assumptions
- Describe the Planning and Scheduling concept, and issues or concerns about related topics.
- Statement of business opportunity and system requirements
- Definition of guidelines involved

The workshop document will represent consensus for system development and implementation activities.

Management Guidelines

SPONSOR: Steering Committee
DATE : January 14, 1992

Page 8

SCOPE OF PROJECT

LOCATIONS (Involved in Planning & Scheduling Functions)

-All ABC Offices, Customer Design Services, Sales and Marketing, Operating, Maintenance, Engineering and Constructing Organization
BUSINESS UNITS: All energy departments
CLIENTS: -Internal and External Including Government and Regulatory Agencies.
KEY COMPONENTS (Of Planning & Scheduling)
Crew Capability Planning, Integrated Job Scheduling among Organizations, Customer Reservation System, Field Working Schedule (Ref. SOLUTION GUIDELINES)
BUSINESS FUNCTIONS
Crew Capability, Automated Preliminary Plan, Job Schedule, Working Schedule, Reservations, Inquiries and Reports
RESOURCES INVOLVED (In Planning & Scheduling System)
Individuals, Crews, Materials, Equipment/Vehicles
KEY INFORMATION AND COMMUNICATIONS
Corporate Systems, External & Internal Customer, Materials Availability, Equipment Availability, Job Definition/Job Progress/ Job Requirements, Project, Budget Information, Personnel/Skills Availability, Forecast/Preliminary Job, Non Automated Equipment Material/Type/Availability, Customer Relations
MANAGEMENT POLICY INVOLVED: Corporate Guidelines
EXCLUDING FROM DESIGN: Inventory Management and Accounting, Skills Development, Time Reporting and Payroll, Cost Estimates, Project Management Process, Budgeting Process, Daily Dispatched Work, Change Design, Corporate Management Information, Emergency Work

Page 9

MANAGEMENT OBJECTIVES AND EXPECTATIONS

-Optimize costs
-Support unparalleled customer service
-Corporate approach to planning and scheduling of resources
-Automated planning
-Effective resource utilization
-Improved controls
-Meet or exceed mandatory deadlines
-Improved communications with internal organization and external customers
-Improved customer perception
-Improved coordination and follow up amongst internal organizations
-Automated reporting
-Respond to customer inquiries
-Daily reallocation of crews
-Flexibility to respond to operating conditions
-Respond to unplanned work
-Avoid resource and cost overcommitment
-Optimize paper content
-Optimize schedule based on business rules
-Manage priorities
-Customer service measurements
-Coordination of related information and systems
-Event driven system
-Access to information for user defined analyses
-Optimize use of overtime
-Exception reporting generated by user defined flags and codes
-All information will be through one system

Page 10

BUSINESS FUNCTIONS

Sample Pages 16-19... 1. Work Force Capability

2. Automated Preliminary Schedule

Sample Pages 24-25... 3. Final Job Schedule

4. Working Schedule

Sample Pages 29-30... 5. Reservations

6. Inquiries and Reports

Analysis Forms

Page 15

PLAN DESIGN   **FORM A1**
BUSINESS FUNCTION: Final Job Schedule

Guidelines: Consider the above function and provide a brief description. Review the activities listed and provide comments on each activity from the point of view of describing a known business problem or concerns with the current system. Identify additional processes as required and list information used during the process.

Description: a schedule in which all resource deficiencies and other conflicts have been resolved; it is formally approved and adopted by the appropriate parties in advance of the working period.

Key Items	Information	Comments / Issues / Concerns
-Review preliminary plan to select jobs for schedule	-preliminary plan -selected reports	-some meeting activity -reports used as working document
-Resolve resource deficiencies	-flagged sources -materials availability	-reservation of material -reservation of vehicles -currently a manual process -add resources, if necessary
-Select jobs for final schedule	-vehicle availability -plan	-resources are mapped to final plan -final schedule matls. must be locked in
-Approval Final Schedule	-approvals -resources committed -operating manager	-this schedule should list only the work identified during the planning process as being completely available to be done -should be listed by input of schedule date' in system

Page 24

PLAN DESIGN   **FORM A2**
BUSINESS FUNCTION: Final Job Schedule (Cont'd)

Key Items	Information	Comments / Issues / Concerns
-Approval Final Schedule	-requestor -field supervisor	-the final schedule should be available to requesting departments and executing departments -an addendum of unscheduled but 'due' jobs should be feedback to requestor with explanation of constraint
-Personnel Availability	-in-house contractor -corporate policy	-planning and scheduling supervisor to manual review of workload/ -options reviewed with manager if problems encountered -corrective action taken by supvsr./ mgr. to address problem (shift work, O.T., deferrals)
Commitments	-locked in times	-this action crosses divisional boundaries -are resources available ?
Schedule adjustments	-manpower reordering -of jobs	-should employees be upgraded ? -identify manpower available in other areas
Reports	-schedule	-available by each Thurs. A.M. -approvals -dispatch and notification of personnel (FAX and/or phone) -same elements of preliminary schedule -system-wide information available

Continued...   *...Page 25*

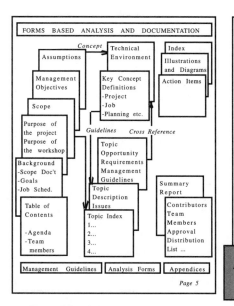

FORMS BASED ANALYSIS AND DOCUMENTATION

Concept
- Assumptions
- Technical Environment
- Index
  - Illustrations and Diagrams
  - Action Items
- Management Objectives
- Key Concept Definitions
  - -Project
  - -Job
  - -Planning etc.
- Scope
- Purpose of the project
- Purpose of the workshop

Guidelines   *Cross Reference*
- Topic Opportunity Requirements Management Guidelines
- Background
  - -Scope Doc't
  - -Goals
  - -Job Sched.
- Topic Description Issues
- Summary Report
- Table of Contents
  - -Agenda
  - -Team members
- Topic Index
  - 1...
  - 2...
  - 3...
  - 4...
- Contributors Team Members Approval Distribution List ...

Management Guidelines	Analysis Forms	Appendices

Page 5

BACKGROUND

Date: January 20, 1992
Title: Planning and Scheduling Subsystem Scope
Prepared: Planning and Scheduling Working Committee
Goal: Improve the level of service to our customers by providing an automated planning and scheduling tool for all departments that will assist them in job scheduling, minimizing costs, meeting job commitment dates and fostering improved communication with our customers. This will support the concept of Single Point Of Contact or.
Description: The Planning and Scheduling Subsystem will provide an automated mechanism for weekly (with the ability for multiple weeks) resource capability planning and job scheduling. Crews and jobs will be scheduled on a daily basis, in weekly blocks.
System Interfaces: The Planning and Scheduling tool will function as a real time subsystem of system . As jobs are scheduled, the schedule dates will be automatically sent to system. The system will interface with the job cost file, , the automated estimating system, and if feasible, Project, for appropriate information.
Key Assumptions: The Planning and Scheduling subsystem will be an interactive, real time system. It will provide resource leveling capabilities and assist other departments in establishing customer commitment dates.

Background

Page 6

KEY DEFINITIONS

JOB is a package of work activities.
PROJECT is a package of jobs.
PLANNING is analysis and preparation of an outline of activities which must take place in order to create an optimum schedule in a multi-week period.
PROJECT SCHEDULE is a series of time phased activities and resource allocations aligned to achieve a specific objective or set of objectives.
JOB SCHEDULE is a list of time phased job assignments to crews/personnel available to an organization (in support of a project schedule when applicable).
WORK FORCE CAPABILITIES : method to establish a data base definition of a rolling projection for personnel, skills, availability and location assignments to establish resource complement available for work.
AUTOMATED PRELIMINARY SCHEDULE is all work due and tentatively scheduled for a given work period.
FINAL JOB SCHEDULE is a schedule in which all resource deficiencies and other conflicts have been resolved and formally approved and adopted by the appropriate parties in advance of the working period.
WORKING SCHEDULE is the operational schedule of work requirements with allowance for periodic adjustments to respond to work situations and actual conditions.
RESERVATION is the component of the planning and scheduling system which interfaces with single point of contact to provide a view of all the time available for customer work.

Page 14

BUSINESS ASSUMPTIONS

-System depends on standardized mechanism to identify jobs and skills required for jobs.
-Ensure system is used to identify skills required for job categories.
-System has to have skills identification for
-All resources must be considered to schedule work.
-Organization is evolving.
-Interactive, Real-time system.
-Work Planned weekly and adjusted daily to meet changing conditions.
-Daily job progress reports will be needed to support the concept.
-Field information available/reported on daily basis.
-Crew members may be loaned to different areas or supervisors within the same organization.
-Comply with corporate guidelines for customer service.
-Crews work to 40 hour base work week.
-Firm customer date will depend on resources available to be committed.
-All jobs are candidates for planning.
-Jobs which have met customer prerequisites or have been authorized, or permits obtained, or notifications made as required are candidates for scheduling.
-Scheduling requires material availability.
-"One-stop shopping" work load will be supported using a dynamic portion of the resource pool available to respond to changing demand on internal and external customer jobs.
-Resource pool includes own personnel and outside contractors.
-All jobs in Project will be handled by this system.
-Emergency jobs will, in most cases, be handled by crews allocated to low priority work.   **(Continued...)**

Page 11

-Reservation concept will not eliminate single point of contact/ one-stop shopping concept, rather it supports it.
-System will be used by non-technical personnel.
-Planning and Scheduling system will be independent
-Interfaces with Planning and Scheduling.
-Internal customers continue to use interfaces.
-Continue to use Project, Critical path planning will continue to be processed on Project; Feedback status to Project; Enhance Project identify job numbers.
-Trend to use JIT (Just In Time) concept.
-Continue to use status code/update method for work completion.
-Continue to use existing Crew/Personnel training programmes.
-Material req'mts (stock & non-stock) will originate through system.
-Material requests will be handled by enhanced inventory system which will support stock and non-stock items.

TECHNICAL ASSUMPTIONS
-Implemented on mainframe.
-Interface and feeds with various mainframe systems.
-Real-time system.
-Cost effective, user friendly system solution.
-Use advanced technology as applicable.
-Hardware requirements will be included in cost analysis.
-Hardware will be available.

WORKSHOP ASSUMPTIONS
-Decision to build or buy system will be based on this document.

IMPLEMENTATION ASSUMPTIONS
-Includes training and user documentation.
-Implementation and support should not require additional operating department personnel.

Page 12

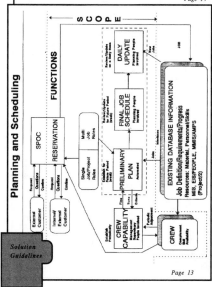

Planning and Scheduling

SCOPE

FUNCTIONS

- SPOC
- RESERVATION
- DAILY UPDATE
- FINAL JOB SCHEDULE
- PRELIMINARY PLAN
- CREW CAPABILITY
- CREW

EXISTING DATABASE INFORMATION
Job Definition/Requirements/Progress
Resources: Material, Personnel/Skills
MIS, EIS/PEOPLE, MMIS/AMPS
(Project/2)

Solution Guidelines

Page 13

PLAN DESIGN   FORM B

BUSINESS FUNCTION: Final Job Schedule
BUSINESS OPPORTUNITIES:
-Manage effect of changes to schedule; Potential for fewer changes
-Reduce clerical effort.
-More complete identification of job requirements.
-Meet and exceed customer expectations.

SYSTEM DESIGN REQUIREMENT:
-Easy path for department access to all scheduling functions.
-Track and access to job status in system.
-Interface to Project to pass resource commitments to jobs.
-Final Scheduling of work and resources: -on-line access to schedule detail, -method to select jobs to be worked, -security features to ensure authorized people update schedule.
-Method to reallocate crew resources to jobs.
-Electronic notification when commitment made, job bumped or schedule is changed etc.
-On demand printout of final schedule.
-Method to compare final schedule to actual for one week schedule.
-Schedule changes for coordinated interdept. job interface
-Interface job schedule changes to system.

OTHER GUIDELINES:
-All jobs on the schedule be in system ; Changes to be coordinated interdepartmental jobs schedule must be done
-Some work may be completed without ever being on the schedule.
-Final job sched. info. and actual is used for performance evaluation.
-Continue to revise time estimates using input to system .
-Continue to revise schedule by selecting jobs to be done taking into account current situation.

Page 26

ACTION ITEMS / ISSUES LOG	NAME
Follow up with steering committee that expectations for scope of Planning and Scheduling are met (Presentation)	Wendy T Doug C.
Design mechanism to flag jobs not budgeted	Bob G.
Consider JIT, Reserving Materials to job as part of scope (integral part of proposed system). Develop method to: -trigger resource allocations to materials mgmt. system -notify due date for matls. due to materials mgmt. system	Inventory System Support Group
Evaluate system event codes/mechanism. Automatic generation of notification letters based on event codes/date not met etc.	
Update assemblies and labor system with skills data.	Doug C.
Determine design to accept input data from schedule changes in a Planning & Scheduling system	Steering Committee
Develop a detailed estimate for Planning and Scheduling system design effort.	
All materials availability including P.O.'s -map type of power operated equipment available to types of equipment required for each job. -method to trigger equipment allocation to equipment mgmt. system -method to receive confirmation/status for equipment allocated.	Equipment
Include list of 32 unavailable criteria. Define table variables for all user groups	Wendy T

Appendices

Page 32

TOPIC	page #

Index

Page 32

WORKBOOK 10

Mobile truck inventory management
and sales activity reporting

REQUIREMENTS DOCUMENT

SEPTEMBER 29, 1989

Page 1

WORKSHOP AGENDA FOR BUSINESS ANALYSIS

* Executive Sponsor Opening Remarks

* Introductions and Administration

* Workshop Process

* Management Guidelines
  - Purpose
  - Scope
  - Management Objectives & Expectations
  - Business Assumptions

* Business Requirements Analysis
  - Analysis Forms

* Action Items

* Summary and Closing Remarks

Page 3

WORKSHOP TEAM MEMBERS

EXECUTIVE SPONSORS
Jack D
Fred J

BUSINESS CONTRIBUTORS

Besem B	Bernie M
Terry B	Harry N
Jeff E	John N
Jeff F	Takis P
Brian F	Ken P
Tom G	Sylvain P
Liz G	Tom P
Marc G	Paul P
Paul G	Dave P
Alain L	Gerassimos V
Thor M	Pierre V

OBSERVERS

Jack D	Sue K
Steve D	George K
Jeff F	Dave P
Fred J	

WORKSHOP FACILITATOR - Tony C

DOCUMENTATION - Roman S

Page 4

PURPOSE OF THE PROJECT

To replace the handheld and distribution centre systems in order to support ABC's strategic business goals.

PURPOSE OF THE WORKSHOP

To involve business representatives and systems developers in a structured workshop to define the system requirements.

The level of detail will be:
- Define purpose and scope
- Define objectives and assumptions
- Identify functions involved and issues or concerns about related topics
- Statement of opportunity and system requirements
- Definition of other guidelines to assist the project

The workshop document will represent consensus of ABC system requirements. The document will be used to approach vendors in search of appropriate system solutions and software applications.

SPONSORING EXECUTIVES:
Jack D   Executive Vice-President of Sales
Fred J   Chief Financial Officer

Management Guidelines

Page 7

SCOPE OF THE PROJECT

LOCATIONS :
ABC's Sales Zones: **1**-Atlantic, **2**-Quebec, **3**-Ontario, **4**-West

PRODUCTS:
All ABC Co products: POS Material, Racks

BUSINESS ACTIVITIES:
Sales, Distribution Center, Truck (Basic Information)

ALL CUSTOMER SEGMENTS

BUSINESS FUNCTIONS
Selling: Down The Street (DTS), Pre-Sell, Telemarketing, Direct Sales, Distributors and Brokers, Invoicing/Delivery Documents, Route Book, Survey and Operational Statistics
Control: Handheld Orders and Inventory, DC Inventory, End of Day
Reporting: Communication, Sales, Compliance

COMMUNICATIONS LEVELS:
Handheld terminals, Distribution Center, Sales Office, Accounting Office

EXCLUDING
-Plant Production and Plant Warehouse Operations
-Accounts Receivable and Sales Audit Functions
-Key Account Reporting

Page 8

MANAGEMENT OBJECTIVES/EXPECTATIONS

-Flexibility to respond quickly to changing business environment
-Alignment of Sales Representatives and company objectives
-Alignment of Retailer and company objectives
-Alignment of Sales Representatives and Sales Management
-Focus sales and management activity
-Effective use of salesperson time
-Smooth migration plan
-Security and access controls
-Common hardware and software platform
-Support all sales methods
-Support financial information objectives
-Accurate audit and reporting capability
-On-line access to timely and accurate information
-Respond to customer needs
-Support existing tracking and control system
-Competitive advantage
-Assist sales to meet volume and profitability targets
-Access to history
-Potential for direct communication with customer
-Increase productivity for sales representative
-Less break down time
-Ability to monitor sales time management
-Facilitate data gathering for adhoc and exception reporting
-Improve methods to measure sales expenses
-Capture (basic) truck information
-Method to measure competitive market activity
-Method to roll up and compile reporting detail

Page 9

ANALYSIS TOPICS

SELLING
1. Down The Street (DTS)
2. Pre-Sell
3. Telemarketing
4. Direct Sales
5. Distributors and Brokers
6. Invoicing/Delivery Documents
7. Route Book
Pages 32-33 ... 8. Survey & Operational Statistics

CONTROL
Pages 34-35 .... 9. Handheld Inventory
10. DC Inventory
11. End of Day (EOD)

REPORTING
Pages 40-41 .... 12. Communication
Page 42 .... 13. Sales Reporting
14. Compliance Reporting

Ranking Legend : H = High   - Essential
M = Medium - Productivity Gain
L = Low   - Nice to Have

Analysis Forms

Page 13

BUSINESS ANALYSIS   FORM A

TOPIC: Survey and Operational Statistics
Guidelines: Consider the above topic and provide a brief description. Then list the key topic issues to ensure complete analysis. In addition, provide a brief description of key topics under comments, issues and concerns.

DESCRIPTION: Use of handheld tool to collect point of sale information and basic truck operations.

Topic/Activity	Comments/Issues/Concerns
Collect Survey Information	-Potential collection of competitor activity/ information -Store details (size, channel, isles, stock, etc.) -Manual process -Currently uses a Database System to provide customer information
Operating Expenses	-Fuel consumption and costs -Mileage (fleet management) -Service costs -Currently this information is kept in a separate system -Other expenses include costs for general supplies, travel, postage, road tolls (refer to expense report)

Page 32

BUSINESS ANALYSIS   FORM B

TOPIC: Survey and Operational Statistics
Guidelines: Consider the items associated with the above topic and identify business opportunities and provide requirements for the design. Identify the requirements as Handheld **(H)** or DC **(D)** and rank them as High, Medium or Low. List any other guidelines you think will assist the implementation.

BUSINESS OPPORTUNITIES:
-Streamline the survey process
-Add value to information
-Productivity gain for sales representatives time
-Better understanding and identify areas of opportunity
-Improve compliance with survey

DESIGN REQUIREMENT:	H/D	HML
-Question based data gathering using simple Y/N and numbers	H	H
-Interface survey information to DC and Host systems	H	M
-Analysis and adhoc inquiry, survey eg. by customer, by customer group, channel etc.	H	M
-Simple data gathering for basic truck information eg. fuel costs, repairs, mileage (km), basic expenses	H	M
-Additional Y/N question relating to safety responsibility	H	M
-Summary totals of operating expenses	H	M

OTHER GUIDELINES:
-Ensure that truck/fleet expense tracking and data gathering does not duplicate effort - refer to fleet maintenance
-Basic truck operational costs assists the goal for truck P & L
-Detail analysis data processing will be provided on a timely basis using DC or Host systems which have the data and processing power

Page 33

Page 5

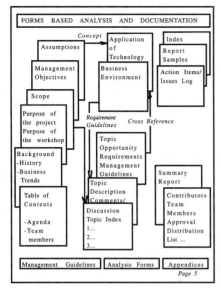

FORMS BASED ANALYSIS AND DOCUMENTATION

Page 5

Page 6

BACKGROUND

The current business environment is one of growth and rapid change which has resulted in the evolution of new sales techniques in dealing with the customer.

Sales representatives, being entrepreneurial, are beginning to operate their routes as business units and require appropriate support tools. While the current technological and business environment does not fully support these changing business requirements, emerging technology can be utilized to create an operational structure that will better support the sales representative in his entrepreneurial efforts.

ACTION PLAN - Utilize a structured workshop to gather requirements for a handheld sales support system.

Background

Page 6

Page 10

BUSINESS ASSUMPTIONS

-ABC Co's business continues to grow and change.
-Most of the key systems will need replacing within two years.
-A common hardware and software platform will be implemented.
-Operational cost must be reasonable.
-Ability to respond to system change requests is paramount.
-System design focused to support core business functions which uphold good business process versus control to enforce business process.
-Salesman computer will be selected for portability and functionality features.
-Future system will allow consolidation of financial information to support Route P & L.
-All hardware and software must comply with industry standards.
-Cost justification at key feature level will be required.
-The new system will be implemented in one zone as a pilot and rolled out to the new 3 zones as appropriate. The timing for the first zone is 1993.
-Finished goods in the plant may be treated as another distribution center.
-Trend for customers/industry to use EDI.

TECHNICAL ASSUMPTIONS

-All existing handhelds and DC computers will be upgraded or replaced to support requirements.
-Frequent access to network may be necessary.

Page 10

Page 11

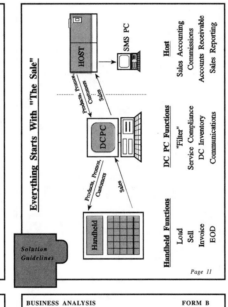

Everything Starts With "The Sale"

Solution Guidelines

Page 11

Page 12

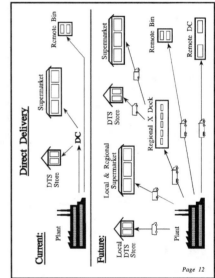

Direct Delivery — Current: / Future:

Page 12

Page 34

BUSINESS ANALYSIS   **FORM A**

TOPIC: Handheld Inventory

DESCRIPTION: Management of truck and bin inventory on handheld system.

Topic/Activity	Comments/Issues/Concerns
Truck Inventory	-Must be maintained for fresh goods, stales, damages, manufacturing defects, etc.
	-Other categories of inventory may be required in the future; Each category of inventory should be maintained separately
	-There must be an audit capability on the handheld to allow sales mgmt. to verify inventory quantities
	-HH Audit functions must be secured by password
	-Build-ups for loads
	-Inventory includes non-product items
	-Generate standard order for route
	-Should be able to sell only those products actually in inventory
	-The invoice reflects actual delivery
	-Stales are written off
Loads	-From DC
	-From plant
	-Some transfer of product
	-Returns
	-Compliance
Audit	-To physical inventory
	-Information/Transactions to sales audit

Page 34

Page 35

BUSINESS ANALYSIS   **FORM B**

TOPIC: Handheld Inventory

BUSINESS OPPORTUNITIES:
-Balance inventory by item; Balance inventory build up to sell off
-Accurate invoicing for the customer
-Manage inventory levels to customer needs
-100 % delivery is compliance with minimum inventory
-Separate inventories for truck and bin; Maintain shelf life
-Correct build up by day
-Facilitate transfer of inventory between sales reps

DESIGN REQUIREMENT:	HML
-Prevent override	H
-Identify error situations/force inventory update by DSM certification	H
-Identify inventory items to truck/bin level separately	H
-Automated build-up to item level for truck /bin taking into account in-transit items	H
-Combine truck and bin inventory for initial order for weekly need	H
-Capture/record physical count of inventory	H
-Summarize daily account sales to create daily truck build-up	H
-Generate recommended truck order taking into account remaining inventory and historical trends	H
-Adjust order for promotions	H
-Include all product and non-product items eg. equipment, cartons	H
-Combined write-off all stales, damages, manufacturing defects	H
-Track stales, damages, manufacturing defects separately	H
-Generate compliance report for loads requested versus actual loads received to line item/all levels including stores, bins, DC, plant	H
-Allow multiple sales representatives per route	H

OTHER GUIDELINES:
-Use new approach to transfer inventory between sales reps
-A load request is mandatory before loading

Page 35

Index

Index

WORKBOOK 11

Manufactured inventory management
and vehicle loading

SPECIFICATIONS ANALYSIS

SEPTEMBER 12-14, 1989

MEETING WORKBOOK

Page 1

WORKSHOP AGENDA FOR BUSINESS ANALYSIS

* **Executive Sponsor Opening Remarks**

* **Introductions and Administration**

* **Workshop Process**

* **Management Guidelines**
  -Purpose
  -Scope
  -Management Objectives & Expectations
  -Business Assumptions

* **Solution Guidelines**
  -Vehicle Loading User Concept Diagram
  -A to H Business Model

* **Business Requirements Analysis**
  -Screen and Report Exhibits

* **Action Plan**

* **Summary and Closing Remarks**

Page 3

WORKSHOP TEAM MEMBERS

EXECUTIVE SPONSOR
Mo L   Director, Materials Management

PARTICIPANTS
Roger A   Industrial Engineering
Al B   Tubing
George B   Shipping
Roger D   Cold Strip Dept.
Dynzel H   Prod. Sched. Coil Paint & Tubing
Charlie L   Shipping,
Paul M   Prod. Sched.
Ernie P   Industrial Engineering
Liz R   IRM, Applications Dev.
Jack R   Prod., Sched.,
Jim R   Shipping
David T   IRM, Applications Dev.
Don W   Coil Paint

EXPERT WITNESSES
Kevin C   I R M
Bob M

WORKSHOP FACILITATOR
Tony C

DOCUMENTATION
Frank K   John L

Page 4

PURPOSE OF THE SYSTEM
The Vehicle Loading system is intended to replace the current shipping systems two locations with a divisional - single business unit concept - system to meet current processing requirements and respond quickly to future customer needs.

PURPOSE OF THE PROJECT
The Vehicle Loading project is intended to provide the component of the system that improves the accuracy of loading materials on/into transportation vehicles, the timely reporting of completed loads, and production incentive reporting.

PURPOSE OF THE WORKSHOP
The purpose of the workshop is to involve business representatives from Vehicle Loading in a structured workshop to describe business activities and procedures for a new system.

The level of detail will be:
-Procedure Descriptions
-Screen and Report Definitions
-Data Interface Definitions
-Security and Contingency Features Descriptions

System developers will use the workshop output to continue analysis and internal design for systems development.

Management Guidelines

Page 15

SCOPE OF THE PROJECT
The scope of Vehicle Loading begins when a shop floor user requests load information and ends when the user reports that loading is complete.

LOCATIONS SUPPORTED BY SYSTEM
Location1 Works: Shipping, Coil Paint, Tubing, Hot Roll Processing, East Processing, Reclamation, Green Coil Storage, After Pickle Bldg (646), Slab Yard, Hot Strip.
Location2 Works: Custom Steel, Shipping, Bldg 115 (interplants), Ironton, Caster Bldg.

MATERIAL TYPES : Coils, Sheets/Plates, Pup Coils, 2"x2" Material, Tubing, Offal Bars, Ingots and Slabs.

MODE OF TRANSPORTATION: Truck, Rail Barge

FUNCTIONS
Loads per building/door (truck, rail, barge), Loads per vehicle, Report loading complete, Production reporting, Verification of correct tags and material

OTHER SUPPORT FUNCTIONS
Substitute, material/update load, Print load tags, Reprint ship tags, Reject vehicle (truck, rail), Return vehicle (truck)

INTERFACES: Order Status
EXCLUSIONS: By-product shipments, Misc. shipments

Page 16

MGMT. OBJECTIVES/EXPECTATIONS

Develop a common approach and procedures for Vehicle Loading consistent with a **Single Business Concept** (SBC).

Provide current/accurate loading requirement information.

Improve control/planning of loading operations.

Improve control of the tagging/re-tagging process to ensure that for each load the correct customer information is on the tag.

Timely posting of complete loading times on the shop floor.

Report loading production to be used for incentive.

Reduce paperwork content and handling.

Design and implement the system using both handheld terminals and CRT's.

Provide a contingency plan that will effectively allow loading of vehicles for shipment to continue during system outage.

Provide security features for authorized system users.

Improve timeliness and accuracy of information for users and other system interfaces.

Page 17

DATABASE

When the Vehicle Loading function begins, the database will contain all of the lift and load information, including loading and packaging codes, necessary to load vehicles.

The material preparation system has updated lift packaging information and set the lift status to "ready", meaning packaged and located.

The material movement system has tracked movements and provides a valid ship location for locating the lifts.

The Load Building System has built the lifts into loads, and the Route and Scheduling system has finalized the load(s).

LIFT TYPES

The Work's material processing units have satisfied customer requirements by producing lifts of different types. Lift types include: Coils, Sheets, Pup Coils, 2" x 2" (Location2), Sheet/Plate, Tubing, Offal bars.

Operational Controls

Design Scenario

Page 23

Page 24

HANDHELD TERMINALS
Log on/off procedures will emulate CRT procedures.
Their primary function is to verify correct lift(s) and to post loading complete from the loading area.
Handheld terminals will be supplied to support material movements, but application programs will not.

PRELOCATE/LOCATE
Prelocate indicates that user is locating lifts without a gate pass.
Locate indicates that user is locating lifts from the gate pass.

PRINT STATUS CODES
Codes associated with the printing of documents will adhere to the standards set up by the Documents and Notifications system. The following words appear after the PRINT SEQUENCE NUMBER field:
-**Blank**   =first print of the document
-**Updated**   =updated print of the document
-**Copy**   =copy of the first print of the document
-**Replacement** =only displayed when the document is reprinted
                 by sequence number

LOADING STATUS CODES
The following codes appear after displayed/printed load numbers indicate the status of the load: (**C**)ompleted load, (**U**)pdated or changed to load, (**R**)ejected load at gate, (**D**)eleted or cancelled load, (**P**)artially completed load.

Page 26

DISPLAY TRUCK LOADING LAYOUT

```
ESxx    TRUCK LOADING LAYOUT  Date:xx/xx/xx

Enter Selection : xx           Bldg/Door : x xxxx
Enter Request : x (D/P)        Station : xxxxxxxxx
Enter Date : xx/xx/xx          From xx:xxP to xx:xxP
Bldg/Door : xxxx               All Bldgs : x


Time Load              # of  Cust                    New
Due  No.  Carrier Weight Pkgs Name City State Tags
xx:xxp xxxx xxxxx  xxxxxxx  xx xxxxxx xxxx xxxx   x
xx:xxp xxxx xxxxx  xxxxxxx  xx xxxxxx xxxx xxxx   x
xx:xxp xxxx xxxxx  xxxxxxx  xx xxxxxx xxxx xxxx   x


Loads due at door _____
Loads completed at door _____

****************** Error Message **************
```

Purpose- The function of this process is to display all of the loads scheduled for shipment by truck to assist in vehicle loading.

Monitor and Assign Work

Page 41

Page 42....

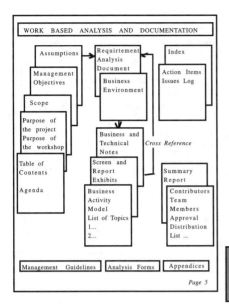

WORK BASED ANALYSIS AND DOCUMENTATION

Assumptions — Requirement Analysis Document — Index

Management Objectives — Business Environment — Action Items Issues Log

Scope

Purpose of the project Purpose of the workshop — Business and Technical Notes — Cross Reference

Table of Contents — Screen and Report Exhibits — Summary Report

Agenda — Business Activity Model List of Topics 1... 2... — Contributors Team Members Approval Distribution List ...

Management Guidelines | Analysis Forms | Appendices

Page 5

BACKGROUND - SYSTEM OVERVIEW

The Shipping, Traffic, and Carrier Management system supports shipments of steel for the ABC Co.. This covers shipments of finished material and semi-finished material, including ingots and slabs, shipments from Works to Works, from Works to outside processors, and from Works to final customers. Limited support for shipments from processors to final customers is also provided.

The entire scope of Project is too large to be developed and installed in a single project. So, the system has been broken down into nine projects for implementation. The nine projects are:
1. Shop Floor (Material Preparation & Tracking) 2. Load Building, 3. Automatic Load Building 4. Route and Schedule 5. Download Freight Rates 6. Arrival/Departure 7. Documents/Notifications, 8. Shop Floor Loading 9. Transportation Support

Underlying all of these projects are the "bridges", by which messages are sent between database and other systems that support the order cycle. These systems include: Order Status, Rolling, North and South Plant Data Collection, Mill Order Entry, Hot Mill Release, Data Collection, Invoicing, Traffic Cop, Outside Processor Inventory Control System, Freight Rate System, Shipping System.

Background

Page 7

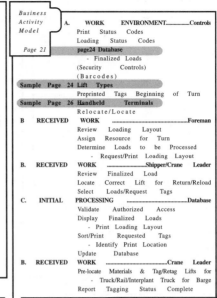

Business Activity Model

Page 21

A. **WORK ENVIRONMENT**.............Controls
Print Status Codes
Loading Status Codes
page24 Database
- Finalized Loads
(Security Controls)
(Barcodes)
Sample Page 24 Lift Types
Preprinted Tags Beginning of Turn
Sample Page 26 Handheld Terminals
Relocate/Locate

B RECEIVED WORK ....Foreman
Review Loading Layout
Assign Resource for Turn
Determine Loads to be Processed
- Request/Print Loading Layout

B. RECEIVED WORK ....Shipper/Crane Leader
Review Finalized Load
Locate Correct Lift for Return/Reload
Select Loads/Request Tags

C. INITIAL PROCESSING ....Database
Validate Authorized Access
Display Finalized Loads
- Print Loading Layout
Sort/Print Requested Tags
- Identify Print Location
Update Database

B. RECEIVED WORK ....Crane Leader
Pre-locate Materials & Tag/Retag Lifts for
- Truck/Rail/Interplant Truck for Barge
Report Tagging Status Complete

D. MONITOR AND ASSIGN ....General Inquiry
Sample Page 42..... Loading Layout: a)Truck b)Rail c)Barge
Load Display (Truck/Rail/Barge)
E. WORK IN PROGRESS.............................Changes
Customer/Office Originated Change
(Substitute Materials Process)
E. WORK IN PROGRESS....................Crane Leader
Approve/Reject Vehicle Equipment
Identify Report (Reject Vehicle Process)
E. WORK IN PROGRESS...........................Shipper
Review Current Load Display
Request Tags for Changed Lift
Sample Page 56..... Report Completed Load
E. WORK IN PROGRESS....................Crane Leader
Replace existing Tags
Get Material/Load Vehicle
Unload Returned Lift/Reload Vehicle
Notify Completed Load
F. RECORDING RESULTS..........................System
Validate Authorized Access
Retrieve Load Display by Load Number
Sample Page 56 < Identify/Print Requested Tags
Update Database
Interface with Order Status
Log Event (Hand Held)
G. SENDING WORK..................................Gate
(Weigh/Inspect Departing Vehicles)
Direct Driver for Return/Reload
H. MANAGEMENT REPORTS
Sample Page 60..... Production Report   *Page 21, 22*

BUSINESS ASSUMPTIONS

Single business concept applies to all development activity. The system will be defined to be the same for Location1 and Location2, to the extent possible.

The user functionals will provide training before, during, and after implementation of the system.

User and system manuals will be delivered with the system.

The system will conform to DATA standards for design and security.

Correct weights are critical to business. The driver will leave with the correct tag and correct information.

This project is part of the system and is dependent on the completion and integration of other projects activities including: Arrival/Departure, Load Building

The material Tracking Project will be operational for Location2 Works, but not Location1Works.

Handheld terminals and bar codes will be used in the loading of vehicles.

The procedures to get the proper vehicle to the loading area are defined in other related projects.

Page 18

VEHICLE LOADING USER CONCEPT DIAGRAM
(boxed processes are not part of Vehicle Loading)

14. Request Production Report
Prod. Report

Route & Schedule
0. Finalize Load for Shipment

2. Request Truck Loading Layout (plan & control foreman)
Loading Layout

Arrival & Departure
13. Return Vehicle Processing (off weight)

1. Print Loads (auto generated)

3. Request Load (display)

12. Post Loading Complete
handheld terminal

Verify Correct Lifts
Post/Update Load Status

4. / 7. Pre-locate/Locate Lifts
Load Prints/Gate Pass
1A Damaged
Load #12345

Data Base

5. Receive Load Cancel or Change Notification

11. Inspect / Reject Loaded Vehicle

Load Building

10. Load Vehicle From Gate Pass

6. Request Substitute Material (damaged/lost)
substitute
Load #12345

Arrival & Departure
8. Reject Vehicle Processing (Wrong equip.)

Material Preparation
9. Reprint Ship Tags (flagged lifts)
tags

7. / 4. Arrive and Inspect Truck
Gate Pass Arrival

Solution Guidelines

Page 20

USER PROCEDURE

The user performs the following functions:
-Accepts or changes displayed information.
-Selects the Print/Display Truck Loading Layout option from the Vehicle Loading Menu.
-Enters the required fields and (D)isplays the Truck Loading Layout.
-Enters a date/turn, building/door combination, or requests all buildings. If nothing is entered, the screen defaults are used.

SYSTEM PROCESS

The system performs the following functions:
-Selects loads by date/from-to time, building, door, using entered fields or screen defaults
-Provide forward and backward paging
-Flags loads changed that require ship tags
-Provides the ability to look at multiple screens

.... Continued   *Page 42*

POST LOADING COMPLETE - HANDHELD TERMINAL

```
ESIRXXX        Post Load Complete      Bldg : X XXX
Enter Sel: XX    Load: XXXXXXX    Veh: XXXXXX
S.C. No: DASH
XXXXXXX-XXXXXXXXXXXX   Error  Message  Line
```

```
XXXXXXX-XXXXXXXXXXXX   Error  Message  Line
XXXXXXX-XXXXXXXXXXXX   Error  Message  Line
XXXXXXX-XXXXXXXXXXXX   Error  Message  Line
XXXXXXX-XXXXXXXXXXXX   Error  Message  Line
```

```
XXXXXXX-XXXXXXXXXXXX   Error  Message  Line
XXXXXXX-XXXXXXXXXXXX   Error  Message  Line
-- Program error message line --
-- System error message line --
```

NOTE: This diagram represents the twelve handheld terminal screens that you can scroll through (errors screen repeated 10 times) to make up one IBM 3278 screen (24 lines x 80 characters).

Purpose- This process posts loads complete and verifies correct lifts for the load being processed as they are being loaded. The handheld terminal displays four lines at a time and scrolls six times to provide twenty four lines.

Post Loading Complete

Page 54   *Page 56....*

USER PROCEDURE

The user performs the following functions:
-Scan load number
-Enter vehicle number
-Scan lift ID's

SYSTEM PROCESS

The system performs the following functions:
-Verifies that the load number and the lift ID's are correct for load being processed
-Updates the database with completed loading time
-Updates the database with the complete status
-Notifies the user when all lifts for a load are complete
-Returns successful (send/receive) message
-Returns error messages, if:
-invalid lift ID
-lift/load previously cancelled
-departed vehicle cannot be loaded
-vehicle has not arrived, and therefore cannot be loaded
-Generates loading incentive transaction
NOTES:
-Treat Location1 barge as truck, but must realize that mode is rail
-Response time with handheld terminal will determine method of verification
-Loading will not do any kind of material location verification
-Split door applies to Location1 only
-Handheld screen format is not known, exactly

.... Continued   *Page 56*

VEHICLE LOADING PRODUCTION REPORT

```
        VEHICLE   LOADING   PRODUCTION
                REPORT   REQUEST
ESIR                          Date: xx/xx/xx
ESSFXX                        Bldg/Door: x  xxxx
                              Station:  xxxxxxxx

Enter Selection: xx

Reporting Date: xx/xx/xx          Reporting Turn: x




**************** Error Message ****************
```

Purpose- The function of this report is to provide Shipping Management with loading activity information and to provide the necessary date required to calculate incentives.

Management Reports

Page 60....

USER PROCEDURE

The user performs the following functions:
-Selects the Vehicle Loading Production Report from the Shipping Office Menu
-Enters the date and turn

SYSTEM PROCESS

The system performs the following functions:
-Selects all shipped load activity for entered date, building and turn
-Sorts the information by date, building and turn
-Prints the production report

.... Continued   *Page 60*

VEHICLE LOADING PRODUCTION REPORT

```
Program ID: ESVLXXX               PAGE: XXX
Program Run: XX/XX/XX       Sequence No: XXXX

    VEHICLE LOADING PRODUCTION REPORT
              XXXXXXX WORKS

Building: XXXX     Turn: X     Date: XX/XX/XX
```

Veh. Mode	Veh. Type	Coils Sheets	Total Load Weight	No. Lifts	Singles	Assembly Comb
XXXXX	XXXXX	XXXXXX	XXXXXXX	XXXXXX	XXXXXX	XXXXXX
XXXXX	XXXXX	XXXXXX	XXXXXXX	XXXXXX	XXXXXX	XXXXXX
XXXXX	XXXXX	XXXXXX	XXXXXXX	XXXXXX	XXXXXX	XXXXXX
XXXXX	XXXXX	XXXXXX	XXXXXXX	XXXXXX	XXXXXX	XXXXXX

Loading Summary	Loads Processed	Lifts Loaded	Weight of Loads
Trucks	xxx	xxxx	xxxxxxx
Rail	xxx	xxxx	xxxxxxx
Barge	xxx	xxxx	xxxxxxx
Totals	xxxx	xxxxx	xxxxxxxx

GLOSSARY OF TERMS

Band - a flat strap used to secure lifts and loads

Building/Door - a unique building number at Location2 and a door number at Location1 used to locate material

Core - The eye or inside diameter of a coil

Duns/Dash - Nine digit number followed by a hyphen and a four digit number (dash) and sometimes a letter which identifies exclusively a customer's order (also referred to as Order no., Duns no., Account no., Mill order no., DDAI)

Floating Load - A rail load which is permitted to move in a longitudinal direction so that impact shocks are dissipated through movement of the load

Gate Pass - Printed document which contains load ID and other pertinent information and allows the truck to enter the gate

JAD - Joint Application Design (*Crafords Version*)

Lift - An individual weight on a stockcard. Amount of steel packaged together for one crane lift. Typically either a coil or stack of sheets. A single unsecured unit of material of a specified weight that can be handled as a unit by mechanical equipment.

Load Change - the change of a data element regarding a load (not including the substitution of lifts).

Load Number - identifier for the RMF/Shipping schedule to be used by the carrier (formerly schedule number at Location2).

Load Substitution - the substitution of one lift for another on a built load.

Appendices

Page 64....

ACTION ITEMS / ISSUES LOG	NAME
Coil paint (shipping office) needs access to printer to notify when a load is due.	DT/DW
Define functionality to be on the handheld for vehicle loading.	
Determine if project scope should be changed to include intra plant shipments to barge terminal.	LR/RT
Determine data element sizes.	D T
Follow up if copy of load tally with loads will be printed when vehicle loads are printed.	DT/SB
Follow up menu to include functions, print load tags.	D T
Approve the gate pass as a primary document for truck loading at Location2.	C L
Determine standards for handheld/scanner equipment for Location2 material tracking, Location1 material and DATA Base.	GH/ML
Define inquiry screen for truck loading recap summary.	DT/ RMcN
Review production report with system users. Define common use of data terminology.	DT/JR/ AB/LR
Review this project as it relates to tubing.	DT/JR
Develop a standard form for rail car and barge inspection/rejection.	CL/JR/ RMcN
Need for measuring last operation hot band weight.	GH/ML

SHIPPING MENU

```
ESIR       Shipping Menu      DATE: 10/06/88  TURN: 2
                                     BLDG: A 118
                                  STATION:  ARV37085

(1) Material Preparation/Material Movement Menu
(2) Vehicle Loading /Material Movement Menu
(3) Shipping Office Menu
(4) Change Reporting Date/Turn
(E) Exit
                ENTER SELECTION: X
```

SHIPPING OFFICE MENU

```
ESIR    Shipping Office Menu   DATE: 10/06/88  TURN: 2
                                     BLDG: A 118
                                  STATION:  ARV37085

(1) Status by Location Report
(2) Material Preparation Production Report
(3) Material Movement Production Report
(4) Change Building/Door
(5) Vehicle Loading Production Report
(M) Shipping Menu
(E) Vehicle Loading Production Report

                ENTER SELECTION: X
```

Index

WORKBOOK 12

Operational design for customer service requests and daily work assignments

SPECIFICATIONS ANALYSIS

JULY 28-30, 1992

MEETING WORKBOOK

Page 1

WORKSHOP AGENDA FOR BUSINESS ANALYSIS

* Executive Sponsor Opening Remarks
* Introductions and Administration
* Overview/Background
* Workshop Process
* Management Guidelines
  -Purpose
  -Scope
  -Objectives & Expectations
  -Assumptions
* Solution Guidelines
  -Business Model
  -Workflow Model
* Detailed Business Analysis
  -Screen Exhibits
  -Report Exhibits
* Action Items
* Summary and Closing Remarks

Page 3

WORKSHOP TEAM MEMBERS

BUSINESS CONTRIBUTORS
Wayne B
Doug C
Sean M
Jocelyn P
Gary P
Ed P
Jim S
Tony S
Anthony V
Rich W

TECHNICAL CONTRIBUTORS
Sharon A
Kevin B
Lupe N
Carol O
Craig S
Wendy T

OBSERVERS
Bernice A
Bob G

WORKSHOP FACILITATOR
Tony C
DOCUMENTATION
Roman S

Page 4

PURPOSE OF THE PROJECT

Provide unparalleled service to our customers by implementing an automated planning and scheduling tool for the departments that will assist them in job scheduling, minimizing costs, meeting job commitment dates and fostering improved communication with our customers.

BASIC PRINCIPLE

The Planning & Scheduling system will support the "one-stop shopping" Single Point Of Contact System to provide "airline reservation system"-like service to customers.

PURPOSE OF THE WORKSHOP

To involve System users and Systems Development Personnel in a structured workshop to define the requirements for planning and scheduling and determine the environment which will support the above.

The level of detail will be:
  - Define purpose and scope
  - Define objectives and assumptions
  - Describe the Planning and Scheduling system solution
  - Define screens and reports and user procedures
  - System design detail requirements

The workshop document will represent consensus for system development and implementation activities.

Management Guidelines

SPONSOR: Steering Committee
DATE : January 14, 1992

Page 8

SCOPE OF PROJECT

LOCATIONS : -All Offices, Cust. Design Services, Sales & Marketing, Operating, Maintenance, Engineering & Constructing Organization

BUSINESS UNITS: All energy departments

CLIENTS : -Internal and External Including Government and Regulatory Agencies.

KEY COMPONENTS OF PLANNING & SCHEDULING
- Crew Capability Planning
- Integrated Job Scheduling among Organizations (Prelim. & Final)
- Customer Reservation System; - Daily Schedule

BUSINESS FUNCTIONS: Crew Capability, Reservations, Automated Preliminary Plan, Final Job Schedule, Daily Updates, Inquiries&Reports

RESOURCES INVOLVED:
-Individuals, Crews, Materials Availability Inquiries

KEY INFORMATION AND COMMUNICATIONS
Corporate Systems, External and Internal Customer, Materials Availability, Job Definition/Job Progress/Job Requirements, Personnel/Skills Availability, Non-Automated Equipment/Material/Type/Availability, Customer Relations

MANAGEMENT POLICY INVOLVED: Corporate Guidelines
EXCLUDING FROM DESIGN: Inventory Management and Accounting, Skills Development, Time Reporting and Payroll, Cost Estimates, Project Management Process, Budgeting Process, Daily Dispatched Work, Change Design, Corporate Management Information, Emergency Work, Materials Reservation, Automated Equipment Availability
NOTE : Assess requirements for forecasting preliminary job

Page 9

MANAGEMENT OBJECTIVES AND EXPECTATIONS
-Optimize costs
-Support unparalleled customer service
-Corporate approach to planning and scheduling of resources
-Automated planning
-Effective resource utilization
-Improved controls
-Meet or exceed mandatory deadlines
-Improved communications with internal organization and external customers
-Improved customer perception
-Improved coordination and follow up amongst internal organizations
-Automated reporting
-Respond to customer inquiries
-Daily reallocation of crews
-Flexibility to respond to operating conditions
-Respond to unplanned work
-Avoid resource and cost overcommitment
-Optimize paper use
-Optimize schedule based on business rules
-Manage priorities
-Customer service measurements
-Coordination of related information and systems
-Event driven system
-Access to information for user defined analyses
-Optimize use of overtime
-Exception reporting generated by user defined flags and codes
-Identify and track jobs without prerequisites
-All jobs will be through one system *Page 10*

CODES
-Code determines Job Type and Job Duration taking into account all departments for external customer reservation.
 (**Note**: systemalso uses Codes for internal work; Non-customer work can use similar codes described as Major/Minor.)
-At reservation, questioning techniques establish Code and related assemblies (Code, work classification) which derives a goal time.
-Not showing individual job times, the following diagram illustrates an example for duration to start and complete a job.

DEPTS.	A	B	C	Other
Goal Time	3 Days Effort	9 Days Effort	4 Days Effort	
Duration Time	2 Weeks Window	3 Weeks Window	3 Weeks Window	

TIME LINE

-Ideally, window time and effort time will converge in the application of automated planning and scheduling and Codes point to narrower windows. **NOTE**: For non-customer jobs:

Workshop Exhibits *Page 18*

Page 19

WORK TYPE DEFINITIONS
-Work types are user defined groupings.
-Work types are specified at a detail level for scheduling and related to a summary level for reservations.
-Detail level work types define work categories to allow time allocation for weekly scheduling.
-Summary level work types define general classes of work to enable resource allocations for reservations.

SUMMARY LEVEL	DETAIL LEVEL
Customer	3 Week Customer Design Services
	5 Day OH New Services
	10 Day UG New Services
Project	Public Works Jobs
	Transmission Work
	Distribution System Improvements
Low Priority	Accident Jobs
	High Priority Maintenance

WORK TYPE

RESERVATION SUMMARY LEVEL USING CODES

PLANNING AND SCHEDULING

DETAIL LEVEL CODES

Page 21

PRELIMINARY PLAN RULES
-The criteria for planning work on a preliminary schedule include:
-**Jobs**: Criteria to put job into schedule period - Sorting rules:
  -date based on due dates calculated to table variables or Project
  -coordinate based on system events /mechanism to table criteria.
  -sequence work to optional priority criteria:
  -initially sort job backlog by Department/Division/Area, by job type in date order with option to sort by other user-defined criteria.
  -special job skills based on job type is included in work order estimate.
  -flag jobs not authorized in operating department schedule.
-**Crews**:-criteria to assign crews to the above work.
  -match skills available to skills required for each job type; assign based on priority/duration within due date (workload vs. manpower analysis)
  -allocate safety margin as per estimate.
  -adjust time for any given job by replacing estimated travel time with travel time based on the order of jobs assigned to a given crew
  -weekly input criteria for amount of resources dedicated to work job type (eg. low priority work, available for emergencies) in terms of percentage of work force or units of manpower.
  -capability to overschedule by percentage or units of manpower
  -estimate includes the time and skills required and job duration (ie. longest man-hours by operator)
  -method to adjust criteria for known contingency (eg. sick leave, priority, weather, etc.)
  -allocate crews to new business/work types in terms of percentage of work force or units of crews.
-**Materials**:-method to receive confirmation/status for materials.
  -flag material availability against material required for each job.
-**Equipment**: -method to indicate what equipment is required
Page 22

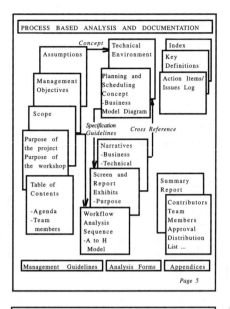

PROCESS BASED ANALYSIS AND DOCUMENTATION

- Concept
- Assumptions
- Technical Environment
- Index
- Key Definitions
- Management Objectives
- Planning and Scheduling Concept -Business Model Diagram
- Action Items/ Issues Log
- Scope
- Specification Guidelines / Cross Reference
- Purpose of the project / Purpose of the workshop
- Narratives -Business -Technical
- Screen and Report Exhibits -Purpose
- Summary Report
- Table of Contents -Agenda -Team members
- Workflow Analysis Sequence -A to H Model
- Contributors Team Members Approval Distribution List ...

Management Guidelines | Analysis Forms | Appendices

Page 5

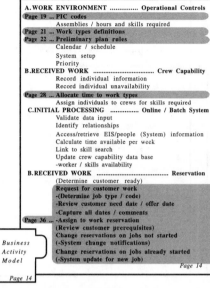

A. WORK ENVIRONMENT .... Operational Controls
Page 19 ... PIC codes
    Assemblies / hours and skills required
Page 21 ... Work types definitions
Page 22 ... Preliminary plan rules
    Calendar / schedule
    System setup
    Priority

B. RECEIVED WORK .... Crew Capability
    Record individual information
    Record individual unavailability
Page 28 ... Allocate time to work types
    Assign individuals to crews for skills required

C. INITIAL PROCESSING .... Online / Batch System
    Validate data input
    Identify relationships
    Access/retrieve EIS/people (System) information
    Calculate time available per week
    Link to skill search
    Update crew capability data base
    -worker / skills availability

B. RECEIVED WORK .... Reservation
    (Determine customer ready)
    Request for customer work
    -(Determine job type / code)
    -Review customer need date / offer date
    -Capture all dates / comments
Page 36 ... -Assign to work reservation
    (Review customer prerequisites)
    Change reservations on jobs not started
    (-System change notifications)
    Change reservations on jobs already started
    (-System update for new job)

Business Activity Model

Page 14

C. Initial Processing .... Online System
    (Update customer record)
    (Notify follow-up departments)
    Validate data entry
    Identify / display code(s) / assign job number
    Calculate availability
Page 36 ... Display offer and earliest dates
    Create customer job (System)
    Reverse schedule
    Create reservation record / update reference / status
    (Form letter generate customer confirmation)
    (Change notification)

C. Initial Processing .... Batch Processing
    Check work status / start / due date
    -Identify exceptions / jeopardized job / dates
    Notify to review reservation

D. Monitor and Assign .... Inquiry
    List / review jobs in schedule
    Jobs in jeopardy / detail
    Customer calls / request / jeopardy / detail

E. Work in Progress .... Preliminary Plan
    Determine preliminary work for upcoming time period
Page 40 ... Review / request print sorted preliminary schedule

E. Work in Progress .... Weekly Job Schedule
    Select / remove work for upcoming time period
    Assign hours / start time
Page 43 ... Assign single / multiple / temporary crews to jobs
    Review / request print sorted weekly schedule

E. Work in Progress .... Daily Update
    Check for new work / changed schedule
    Coordinate new work with existing schedule

Page 15

    Reallocate crews / temporary crews to work
    Review / request print daily schedule
    Print sorted daily activity reports

F. Recording Results .... Online System
    Access System / sort hierarchy jobs for period
    Check material / manpower availability
    Print / display preliminary schedule
    Identify dynamic headings / display type
Page 40 ... Update hours and start date
    Interface / update system dates
    Identify / flag jobs for schedule
    Identify crew for selected jobs
    -Calculate / display availability exceptions
    -Identify job / related jobs / delays / conflicts
    Print / display weekly schedule
    Print daily activity reports
    (Form letters - customer correspondence)

G. Sending Work ....
    Distribute weekly schedule / daily update
    Distribute daily activity reports

H. Management Reports .... Operational Reports
Page 50 ... 4GL report tool
    Customer commitment tracking
    Daily summaries
    Compliance report - actual to weekly schedule
    Customer notification report
    Resource requirements - manpower to availability

Solution Guidelines

Page 16

BUSINESS ASSUMPTIONS
-System depends on standardized mechanism to identify jobs and skills Job Codes for jobs.
-Ensure System is used to identify skills required for job categories.
-Data has to have skills identification for assemblies.
-All resources must be considered to schedule work.
-ABC Co. organization is evolving.
-Interactive, Real-time system.
-Work planned weekly and adjusted daily to meet changing conditions.
-Daily job progress reports will be needed to support the concept.
-Field information available/reported on daily basis.
-Crew members may be loaned to different areas or supervisors.
-Comply with corporate guidelines for customer service.
-Firm customer date will depend on resources available to be committed.
-All jobs must be in data base to be handled by this system.
-Jobs may be scheduled with/without customer pre-requisites, permits, authorizations, notifications, material availability, manpower, budget,etc.
-"One-stop shopping" work load will be supported using a dynamic portion of the ABC Co. resource pool available to respond to changing demand on internal and external customer jobs.
-ABC Co. resource pool includes own personnel and outside contractors.
-Emergency jobs will be handled by crews allocated to low priority work.
-Reservation concept will not eliminate single point of contact/ one-stop shopping concept, rather it supports it.
-Planning and Scheduling system will be independent of service
-Service interfaces with Planning and Scheduling.
-Internal customers continue to use System interfaces.
-Critical path planning will continue to be processed on Project

Continued ...   *Page 11*

-System will be used by non-technical personnel.
-Crews work to 40 hour base work week.
-Continue to use System status code/update method for work completion.
-Continue to use existing Crew/Personnel training programs.
-Material requirements (stock & non-stock) will originate through system.
-Material requests will be handled by enhanced materials system which will support stock and non-stock items.
-Material allocation is handled by System.
-Planning and scheduling system will not reserve material, but will check material availability.

TECHNICAL ASSUMPTIONS
-Implemented on mainframe.
-Interface and feeds with various mainframe systems.
-Real-time system.
-Cost effective, user friendly system solution.
-Use advanced technology as applicable.
-Hardware requirements will be included in cost analysis.
-Hardware will be available.
-DB2 (a relational database) will be used

IMPLEMENTATION ASSUMPTIONS
-Includes training and user documentation.
-Implementation and support should not require additional operating department personnel.

WORKSHOP ASSUMPTIONS
-Decision to build or buy system will be based on this document.

Page 12

ALLOCATE TIME TO WORK TYPES

ABC Co. Allocate Time to Work Types

Dept ..   Division .....   Area ..
Week   _/_/_   Total Hour Available ......

Work Type	Allocation Hours	Percent
	....	...%
	....	...%
	....	...%
	....	...%
	....	...%
Balance	....	100%

PF3 to Return

PURPOSE: Specify weekly time allocation to work types for reservations and scheduling.
BUSINESS NARRATIVE:
-Entering department, division, and area will display work types and allow time allocation to work types on a weekly basis.
TECHNICAL NARRATIVE:
-Time will be allocated weekly with the system calculating daily allocations.
-System will produce a scrollable week.
    -An edit check will be created to ensure calculations add up to 100%.
    -Historical data will be collected for reporting.

Crew Capability

Page 28

Page 27

JOB REQUEST - DATE ASSIGNMENT

ABC Co. Job Request - Date Assignment
CUSTOMER
Name ....   Customer Reference # ....
Code   Description   JOB #
—————— —————— ——————
—————— —————— ——————
—————— —————— ——————
—————— —————— ——————

Need Date 7/7/92   Time____   Available (Y/N) _ Status ____
Offer Dates Available: 7/12/92   7/15/92   7/23/92
Commitment Date: _/_/_
Earliest Date: _/_/_
Comments ....
    ....
Reschedule (Y/N) .   Reason ....
    ....
PF3 to Return

PURPOSE: Reserve time for customer work based on work type and availability of resources. Also used to revise a time for a customer or department originated changes for jobs not started. Also used to confirm a new commitment date for new or changed jobs.

Reservation

Page 36

Page 32

BUSINESS NARRATIVE:
-The type of work requested by a customer is characterized by a code which may be entered/derived from answering series of questions.
-The departments involved and the time required by each will be determined by the work type.
-If crew availability will not permit the customer's need date to be met, the customer will be offered a selection of viable dates.
-System verification of the need date or customer acceptance of a viable date will reserve crew time and create jobs.
TECHNICAL NARRATIVE:
-Locking mechanism will be built into system to reserve dates needed. Dates are held only during transaction.
-Dates are determined through table-driven information.
-If Customer Need Date is greater than Earliest Date Available, Job Request Date will be met.
-If Customer Need Date is unavailable, customer is given three alternative scrollable dates from which customer can select.
-There may be several groups involved in order to complete a job. Hours can be reserved for available groups even if all groups aren't available on a certain date.
-Job Request must be able to accommodate a max. of five Codes.
-**NOTE:** For Electric; Jobs must be examined on site in order to validate a commitment date. After job review, ABC Co. may need to negotiate new Customer Commitment Date.
-For Gas; Work done outside of system.
-After questions answered, Code(s) and Need Date are met, a Job Number is created.
-System will be auto-generated.
-Date used for Code(s) is last parallel date.
-Date selected is first parallel date.

Continued...   *...Page 36*

PRELIMINARY SCHEDULE

ABC Co. Preliminary Schedule
Enter Options:
Dept   ..   Division ....   Area ..
Report Period: From ......   To ......
Sort Criteria: Status   ..
Area   ..   Crew ID   ..
Need Date ..   Work Type   ..
Location ..   Code   ..
Town   ..   Last Day Worked ..
Grid   ..
Page Break   ..
Print?   ..   ....   Y = Yes, Printer ID
PF3 to Return

PURPOSE: Specify options to produce Preliminary Schedule.
BUSINESS NARRATIVE:
-Entering From Date and To Date for a dept, division, and area will generate a Preliminary Schedule which can be viewed or printed.
-The Preliminary Schedule will indicate crew availability for jobs in the area's backlog that are workable and have material available.
-Sort criteria can be selected dynamically.
TECHNICAL NARRATIVE: -User will have the ability to specify sorting precedence of the following fields: Need Date, Start Date, Location, Work Type, Town, Grid, Status, Work ID, Commit Date, Code, Customer.
-User will be able to display an abbreviated version on-line and also print a hard copy.   *Page 40*

Preliminary Plan

Page 39

ASSIGN CREWS

ABC Co. Assign Crews
Dept__   Div____   Area__   From__/__/__   To__/__/__
                    Total Available Hours   _____
                    Available Not Used   _____
                            Crew Crew
                    Assigned   Start   Start   Code/ Suggested
Job   Name   Hours   Date   Time   Status   Crew   Crew
____ _____   ....   _____   ____   ....
____ _____   ....   _____   ____   ....
____ _____   ....   _____   ____   ....
____ _____   ....   _____   ____   ....
PF3 to Return

PURPOSE: View jobs on Weekly Schedule and assign crews to jobs.
BUSINESS NARRATIVE: -Jobs may be assigned crews by entering Crew ID's, Crew Start Date, Time, and Hours Assigned.
-Jobs selected for the Weekly Schedule are displayed.
-A suggested crew is indicated if a Weekly Schedule was generated.
TECHNICAL NARRATIVE: -Assigned Hours may default to Remaining Hours if Assigned Hours are unspecified.
-Crew Start Time will be added to screen (field displayed/protected).
-Total Available Hours Remaining column will be added.
-Total Hours will be decremented based on real-time hours allocated to crews.
-Need ability to assign multiple crews to a job.
-Not Used Hours will be displayed. (Calculation: **Total Available Hours - Hours Assigned**).

Weekly Job Schedule

Page 41   *Page 43*

PRELIMINARY SCHEDULE - REPORT

o	7/22/92	**ABC Electric Utility Company**	Page 1 of 5	o
o		**Preliminary Schedule**		o

o Dept__ Division____ Area__ From 7/19/92 to 8/01/92
o **Job# Name/Descr**
o **Code Street Remain Earliest Latest**
o **Grid Town Job Hrs. Start Start Due Status Crew Skill**
o 9457 Cablevision 10 7/20/92 7/31/92 In Progress EL2301
o P46 Woodbury   Smith Class A
o 4-677   Jones Class B
o 8459 CDE Stores 42 7/29/92 7/31/92 *Delay UG Not Done
o P47 Westbury   Mech Class A
o 5-398   Mech Class B
o 6398 Fire Dept 173 7/30/92 7/31/92 Workable Matl Unavail.
o P48 Sea Cliff   Mech Class A
o 4-662   Control Tech

PURPOSE: A schedule of all potential work for the upcoming time period, indicating resource availability and best crew utilization based on the current backlog.
BUSINESS NARRATIVE: -The Preliminary Schedule will indicate resource availability for potential work.
-Resources are assigned to only workable jobs with available material.
TECHNICAL NARRATIVE: -If Start Date does not exist, it is calculated by the system as:
Due Date - (Estimated Hours / Crew Hours Per Day)
-Earliest Start Date is the system Schedule date field.   *Page 50*

Management Reports

Page 49

BUSINESS ENGINEERING CHANGES

* Increased ability to gather information
* Designed for different user views of data
* Provides a common approach for planning and scheduling
* Better use of managerial control over detail/responsibilities
* Meets need of corporate goals
* Linkage to One-Stop Shopping
* Improved customer relations
* Manage customer jobs together
* Fast access and more capability
* Streamlined process
* Reduction in multiple system interactions
* Automated crew boards
* Increased communication between support groups
* Automated preliminary schedule
* Easy to identify problem situations
* Managing to planned resource allocations
* Manage jobs to individual departments
* Reduce total number of jobs in jeopardy

Appendices

Page 56

ACTION ITEMS   (NAME)

Develop Matrix for Codes with time duration, crew capability for all departments.
Review presentation method for Single Point Of Contact (eg. graphics relating grid points to service, house, etc.).
Review usable skill codes and other employee/contractor information.
Provide list of unavailable codes / delay codes/ status codes / event codes, etc. (terminology).
Further define Priority.
Determine method to provide detail (distinguish for duplicate names, ie. several "Smiths").
Investigate relationship between customer information and job request/status/reservation.
How to remove job reservation if pre-check code is in system.
Enhance system to generate list of changed jobs with Customer Reference Number for revised reservation dates.
Define use of Compliance Report.
Develop standards for PF Keys and scroll capabilities (investigate other ABC Co. systems).
Review mandatory/optional data generated by System (eg. start date, Project date, etc.).
Define form letters to be used.
Obtain sample reports: -Commitment Tracking   **(Sharon A)**
Coordinate time reporting **(with Doug C's task group)**
Review crew member reassignment and reassignment of jobs between crews - like electronic board, including system setup.

Page 57

KEY DEFINITIONS

JOB is a package of work activities.
PROJECT is a package of jobs.
PLANNING is analysis and preparation of an outline of activities which must take place in order to create an optimum schedule in a multi-week period.
PROJECT SCHEDULE is a series of time phased activities and resource allocations aligned to achieve a specific objective or set of objectives.
JOB SCHEDULE is a list of time phased job assignments to crews/personnel available to an organization (in support of a project schedule when applicable).
WORK FORCE CAPABILITIES is a method to establish a database definition of a rolling projection for personnel, skills, availability, and location assignments to establish resource complement available for work.
AUTOMATED PRELIMINARY SCHEDULE is all work due and tentatively scheduled for a given work period.
FINAL JOB SCHEDULE is a schedule in which all resource deficiencies and other conflicts have been resolved to be formally approved and adopted by the appropriate parties in advance of the working period.
WORKING SCHEDULE is the operational schedule of work requirements with allowance for periodic adjustments to respond to work situations and actual conditions.
RESERVATION is the component of the Planning and Scheduling system which interfaces with Single Point of Contact to provide a view of time available for customer work.

Page 58

WORKBOOK 13

Detailed business design for invoice processing and check writing

SPECIFICATIONS ANALYSIS

NOVEMBER 22-24, 1989

MEETING WORKBOOK

Page 1

WORKSHOP AGENDA FOR BUSINESS ANALYSIS

* **Executive Sponsor Opening Remarks**

* **Introductions and Administration**

* **Workshop Process**

* **Management Guidelines**
  - Purpose
  - Scope
  - Management Objectives & Expectations
  - Business Assumptions

* **Solution Guidelines**
  - A to H Business Model

* **Business Requirements Analysis**
  - Screen and Report Exhibits

* **Action Plan**

* **Summary and Closing Remarks**

Page 3

WORKSHOP TEAM MEMBERS

EXECUTIVE SPONSOR
Kevin M   Assistant V.P. Comptroller

BUSINESS CONTRIBUTORS
Karen F   Accts Payable Supervisor
Ed W   Assistant Comptroller
Bruce L   General Accounts Manager
Mark H   Internal Audit Manager
Terry C   Corporate Planning Manager
Connie W   Sr. Accts Payable Clerk
Rita A   Intermediate Accts. Payable Clerk

TECHNICAL CONTRIBUTORS
Vinod D   Project Manager
Thomas S   Applications Programming Manager
Dip L   Programmer Analyst

OBSERVERS
Randy N   Systems Design Manager
Ilan L   General Manager, I.S.

FACILITATOR
Anthony C

DOCUMENTATION
Roman S

Page 4

PURPOSE OF THE PROJECT

Develop an accounts payable system for tracking payment and expense distribution of liabilities and to provide timely information for improved operations and control.

ANALYSIS GUIDELINES

To involve business and technical representatives in a structured workshop to discuss the accounts payable environment and the technical requirements to implement a system to handle accounts payable.

The level of detail will be:
- Define purpose and scope
- Define objectives and assumptions
- Key operational processes & information used
- Define screens and reports
- Identify data needs
- Define operational procedures

The workshop document will be used for further analysis for external design and system development.

Sponsoring Executive: Kevin M
Title: Assistant Vice President Comptroller

Management Guidelines

Page 7

SCOPE OF THE PROJECT

LOCATIONS
- Head office, Distribution centres (excluding branch offices)

PRODUCTS
- All purchases, Advertising, Supplies, Services, Capital assets

BUSINESS FUNCTIONS
- Entry of Vendor Invoices
- Tracking for Approval
- Preparation of Cheques
- Cheque Reconciliation
- Vendor and Table File Maintenance
- Period-end Processing
- Periodic Reporting, Exception Reporting, G.S.T. Reporting
- Tracking Accruals
- On-line Inquiry
- Distribution to General Ledger
- Supplies/Vendor Analysis
- Provincial Sales Tax Allocation
- Expense Analysis

INTERFACES
- General Ledger (Accts. Payable, Distribution and Payments)

EXCLUSIONS
- Matching Invoice to P.O.
- Claims Settlement Processing
- Fixed Assets
- Accrued Liabilities

Page 8

MGMT. OBJECTIVES/EXPECTATIONS

- manage liabilities and expenses
- accurate and timely information
- on-time payment
- managed cash flows and future needs
- accurate distribution to G/L
- improved controls
- simplified operations
- security and access controls
- system flexibility for growth and enhancements
- automated reporting and information sources
- automate regular and recurring payments
- on-line inquiry to accounts payable transactions
- optimize payment schedule and discounts available
- process manual cheques as required
- automate audit trail
- vendor analysis
- expense analysis
- credit/debit adjustments

Page 9

GENERAL LEDGER ACCOUNTS

12,000 Codes used as a chart of accounts, currently these are updated by MIS key entry through an update form. The codes are maintained on the G/L system and must be used to edit the data input. For the new system there are alternative methods to establish the codes.

Alternative 1 - Key in codes to a new table and user maintains the values. The implications of this are; high user involvement for initial load and update, prone to errors and lack of synchronization with G/L.

Alternative 2 - Load G/L codes periodically to the new system table to keep current codes available for edits on-line.

Alternative 3 - Edit codes through direct interface to G/L codes is preferred approach in the long run.

Alternative 4 - Limit edits to a defined subset of codes maintained in the new system table. The implications of this are that the interface to G/L must be more frequent (daily) to avoid build-up of errors.

Resolution - Alternatives assessed and decided to implement Alternative number three as best for most accurate and timely for the user. Reference page 30 Point #8.

NOTE : The system will validate the existence of G/L account codes excluding subledger number but including subledger ID using G/L master file and G/L control file. The subledger will not be a part of this. Subledger consists of ID and a code. The system will only validate the subledger ID, E as an exception.

Operational Controls

Design Scenario

Page 16

PERIOD END DATES

Year end : Roll over previous amounts to next period on last day of fiscal period end.
Fiscal End : Last day of fiscal month end.
Fiscal Period : Period 1-12 within fiscal year.
Dates maintained in table by MIS based on accounting info.
Cut Off Date : Date at which transactions are posted to G/L. It is a combination of fiscal period and user defined date.
Methods of Control - Posting to G/L must include transactions selected by : Date of entry, Period end date, Cut off date within period, Date entered by accts. pyble., at posting time MIS provide screen.
eg. Cutoff Date 89/02/15, G/L fiscal period number 89/01/29 Compare invoice date to fiscal period cut off date for posting to fiscal period end date specified as still open.

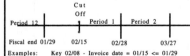

```
                        Cut
                        Off
Period 12  |            |    Period 1    |  Period 2  |
           |            |                |            |
Fiscal end 01/29   02/15      02/28         03/27
```

Examples: Key 02/08 - Invoice date = 01/15 <= 01/29

Page 18

QUICK INVOICE ADD SCREEN

```
23          QUICK  INVOICE  ADD  _____
Filing No => _____        Location Code=> ___
Vendor ID => _____        Invoice No=> _____
Name/Address=> _____   _____
Inv. Type=> _____       Invoice Date => ____
Invoice Amount . => _____
Disc. % Amt. => _____Days - Disc. => ___
Days - - Net => ____        Calc Due Date=>___
Reference No.=> _____
Approval Y/N. =>____  Appr. Rec. Date=>_____
Bank Code ... => _____
Pay Cntrl. Code=>_
Remarks=> _____

ACCNT  CENTRE   AMOUNT    SUB-LEDGER
_____  _____   _____   _____
_____  _____   _____   _____
_____  _____   _____   _____
```

Purpose- This screen is used to rapidly enter invoice information and easily update the vendor file.

Invoice Entry

Page 24

Page 28....

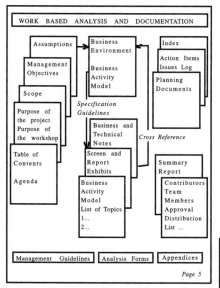

WORK BASED ANALYSIS AND DOCUMENTATION

- Assumptions
- Business Environment
- Index
- Management Objectives
- Business Activity Model
- Action Items Issues Log
- Scope
- Planning Documents
- *Specification Guidelines*
- Purpose of the project Purpose of the workshop
- Business and Technical Notes
- *Cross Reference*
- Table of Contents
- Screen and Report Exhibits
- Summary Report
- Agenda
- Business Activity Model List of Topics 1... 2...
- Contributors Team Members Approval Distribution List ...

Management Guidelines | Analysis Forms | Appendices

Page 5

BACKGROUND
Continuation of business plan previously documented.

Background

C. INITIAL PROCESSING ....On-Line Support

Sample Page 28 . . . . . .
- Validate Authorized Access
- Assign Filing Numbers
- Search/Display Vendors
- Identify Invoice Type/Edit Rules
- Cross Ref/Validate Vendor
- Search Invoice Duplicates
- Validate Account Codes/Totals

Sample Page 32 . . . . **Create/Flag Recurring Invoice**
- Update Cheque Register
- Update Invoice Record/Status

D. MONITOR AND ASSIGN ....**General Inquiry**
- List Invoice Status
- Purged Invoice Browse
- List Cheque Status

E. WORK IN PROGRESS ....**Payment Management**
- Select Invoice/Modify Distrib.
- Request Rpt./Review Payments
- Hold Invoice Status
- Void/Reprint Cheque
- Change Cheque Status

F. RECORDING RESULTS ....On-Line Support
- Search/Sort/Print Invoices Due
- Check G/L or Paid Status
- Print Cheque

Continued ...
- Update Invoice Record Status
- Update Vendor Audit Info.

BUSINESS ASSUMPTIONS

The system will be interfaced to the General Ledger system

All automated cheques will be printed at H/O

Trend is toward EDI communicated invoices.

Utilize system backup procedures.

Will use existing pre-defined procedures for invoice authorization.

Cheque stubs will be redesigned.

Invoices are processed at face value and adjustments/corrections done by credit/debit memo.

All accts payable transactions are transferred to G/L for posting.

Invoice has been approved by authorized mgr before payment.

The invoice can be entered prior to approval.

Utilize system backup procedures.

Page 10

A. WORK ENVIRONMENT................**Operational Controls**
Sample Page 16   **General Ledger Acct Codes**
- Vendor Info./Vendor Update
Sample Page 18   **Period End Dates**
- File Number Controls
- Recurring Invoice No. Controls
- Cheque Register Controls/Log
- Tax Liability
- Security/Access Controls
- Signature Approved Invoice

B. RECEIVED WORK ....**Invoice Entry**
- Menu Select
- Vendor Browse
Sample Page 28   **Invoice Type/Quick Add**
- User Originated Changes
- Manual Cheque
- Cancel/Reissue Cheques
- Corrections/Adjustments
Sample Page 32   **Recurring Invoice**
- Approve for Payment
- Outstanding Credit Balance
- Expense Distribution
- Identify Zero-Balance
- Compare/Balance Invoice Totals
- Stop/Hold/Reissue Chq Status

Business Activity Model

Solution Guidelines   *Page 12*

Continued ...   *Page 12*

F. RECORDING RESULTS ....**Batch Support**
- Interface/Update G/L
- Update Invoice Record Status
- Compare Bank Tapes/ Chq. Reg
- Print Cheques Cashed
- Print Outstanding Cheques
- Purge Cheque Register

G. SENDING WORK ....**Cheque Distribution**
- Quality Control/Visual Inspection
- Authorized Cheque Signature
- Mail Vendor Payments

H. MANAGEMENT REPORTS...........**Reconciliation Reports**
Sample Page 65 . . . . **Reconciliation Exceptions**
- Outstanding Cheques
- Cheques Cashed
- Cheques Cashed Exceptions
- Cheque Register Dated

H. MANAGEMENT REPORTS.......................**Periodic Reports**
- Invoice Summary/Aging Report
- Vendor Summary/Activity
- Audit Trail/Report Summary
- Outstanding Credit Report
- Archiving Invoices
- Outstanding Cheques Report
- Cash Requirement

Page 13, 14

USER PROCEDURE

1. Approved invoice / expense reports with up to 8 cost centers.
2. Enter vendor ID, consists of vendor number with prefix of **R** or **E** depending on vendor. Will bring all information from vendor file. File number - written on top of invoice document by clerk at time of entry.
3. When putting in vendor ID - if Vendor ID not known then you can flip to vendor browse and obtain correct vendor number.
4. If vendor ID not there you can exit from this function for vendor set up by an authorized person and re-enter. (you do lose your data entered, file number is not yet created).
5. Visual check by clerk to make sure vendor name/address matches vendor.
6. Codes used to identify invoice type: **VI** - Vendor Invoice, **EE** - Employee Expense, **DN** - Debit Note, **CN** - Credit Note, **DA** - Debit Adjustment, **CA** - Credit Adjustment
7. Date to be entered as **YYMMDD** (year month day).
8. Invoice amount - when entering credit must use negative sign.
9. Invoice number - for utilities, put statement date and location and put account number in Reference.
10. Days due - cursor will stop - can change (original terms comes from vendor file).
11. Discount % has default from vendor file - can be overridden by % number.
12. When entering account distribution, enter negative sign by amount to show credit.
13. Use SENT TO area to refer to where the documents may be sent for approval.

.... Continued   *Page 28*

---

14. Duplicate invoices:-Will be searched - rolling 12 months from date of invoice - vendor ID plus invoice number. (Incl. suffix)
- After validation of invoice, suffix used to allow processing.
- Positive action to clear screen, change entry error if necessary.
- G/L account code validation.
- Payables should visually check G/L codes, not ALWAYS take department G/L account code.
- System to validate totals against total amount of invoice when account distribution is present, whether approved or not.
- Any changes, system will re-balance.
- Appr. received date, date received back in A/P from approval.
- Pay control code - default to terms. **H** - Hold payment.
  F - Force, disregard due date, print cheque next cheque run.
  M - Manually paid (cheque will not generate).
- Terms may change - to accommodate invoice, print audit trail.
- Calculated due date will be based on the discount terms.
- Place hold on invoice when waiting for credit adjustment.
- In the case of blank invoice the user can enter the date and amount (with no blanks) to provide a reference for system use.

SYSTEM PROCESS
- Location code (system generated by operator ID)
- Vendor ID/invoice number
- Vendor name (picked up from Vendor file)
- Invoice type, Invoice date, Invoice amount
1. File number created only when entry completed successfully, edited and invoice record is created with appropriate status codes. Distribution may or may not have been entered.
2. The amounts will be processed with a negative sign.

Page 29

---

3. Enter vendor ID, hit enter, display vendor name, address, terms,(Disc% amts, days-disc, days net). Do not edit the rest of the entry fields. If vendor not found, access vendor master.
4. After entry of other fields, edit. If no errors, update record.
5. Manual cheques are not allowed on this screen.
6. Edit rules: **a**) For credit note, credit adjustment, the invoice amount must be less than zero. **b**) For employee expenses, the vendor # must be employee #. **c**) No discounts for employees.
7. Search invoice duplicates (vendor ID + invoice number) less suffix using online file and the purged invoice file. If duplicates are found, display error message.
8. Account code validation - the system will validate the existence of G/L account code excluding Sub-ledger No. and including Sub-ledger ID using G/L master file and G/L control file.
9. If distribution entered, validate distribution, total equal to inv. amount if the distribution entered. If distribution not entered, do not validate. Rebalance on any change in distribution.
10. Approval=default " **N** " Appr. received date<= today's date. If approval given, distribution must balance to invoice amt.
11. Log creation date of this invoice.
12. Bank code - system default from vendor master.
13. Payment code " **F** " force will print cheque in next cheque run.
14. Audit trail (batch) inv. terms, if different than vendor terms.
15. Print audit of payment code " **F** " force payments.
16. Keep a running total of number of invoices and invoice amount entered daily by operator and have it available on-line.
17. Calculate due date: The system will calculate the due date to qualify for the discount eg. Invoice due date + Discount days.

Page 30

RECURRING INVOICE SCREEN

```
24     MONTHLY RECURRING INVOICE ADD
Filing No :      _____      Location Code ___
*————————INVOICE INFO————————*
Vendor ID =>  _____   _  _____   Invoice No=> _____
Name/Address=> _____  _____
Inv. Start Date_____   No. of Invoices=> ____
Invoice Amount . => _____
Disc. % Amt. => _____Days - Disc. => ____
Days - - Net => ____
Reference No.=> _____
Approval Y/N. =>____  Appr. Rec. Date=>____
Bank Code ... =>  _____   __
Remarks=> _____
ACCNT  CENTRE   AMOUNT   SUB-LEDGER
_____  _____  _____  _____
_____  _____  _____  _____
_____  _____  _____  _____
_____  _____  _____  _____
_____
```

Purpose- This screen is used to enter invoice information for the automatic generation of monthly recurring invoices.

Invoice Entry

Page 32 ....

Page 24

RECURRING INVOICE NOTES

USER PROCEDURE

1. Use this screen to input invoice detail for recurring invoices.
2. Define the number of invoices and the start date.
3. Security to be determined - user.
4. Approval ID " **Y**" all approved. " **N**" each to be approved.
5. Manager to approve changes prior to entering on screen.
6. File number issued for each suffix OR invoice number.
7. At time of renewal of recurring invoice, new one to be entered with new invoice number.
8. To cancel, operator finds all pending recurring invoices and creates credits to cancel at the invoice level.
9. For rent invoice - invoice date must be the date the first cheque is to be printed eg. Rental starts from May 1, 1990. Enter the invoice date as 25th of April, 1990 and terms as zero. Then the cheque will be printed with the due date of 25th of April 1990 and 25th of every month thereafter.

SYSTEM PROCESS

1. Invoice suffix created from 01 to nn(nn is the # of Inv's).
2. Invoice date: in one month increments from the invoice start date. The day will be same as the start day. If the start day is greater than the last day of the invoice month, then the invoice day will be the last day of the month.
3. Invoice suffix = the next available invoice suffix.
4. Real invoices created when recurring invoice entry done.
5. Filing number to be created for each invoice number.
6. The vendor ID and invoice number cannot be modified.

.... Continued   Page 32

RECONCILIATION EXCEPTIONS REPORT

```
RECONCILIATION EXCEPTIONS    NOV. 22/89

Transit __ Account ___ Tape Creation Date_____

CHEQUE
ID    AMOUNT SERIAL   AMOUNT SERIAL




CUSTOMER              NO. OF
TOTALS               CHEQUES   AMOUNT

       Old Outstanding _____
       New Input       _____   _____
       Matched         _____   _____
       New Outstanding _____   _____
       Variance        _____   _____
```

Purpose- This report is used to monitor any exceptions when reconciling to accounts payable for adjustment.

Reconciliation

Page 65 .....

Page 64

RECONCILIATION EXCEPTIONS NOTES

USER PROCEDURE

1. Any change of status for cheques are to be done by A/P only.
2. General Accounting to let A/P know of adjustment to be made.
3. Weekly for inquiry.
4. If manual cheque has been cashed but not entered, then it will be entered and forced closed.
5. Bank Statement Amount = New Outstanding + Variance

SYSTEM PROCESS

1. Read bank tape.
2. Show negative sign if amount is negative.
3. Old outstanding - before the last reconciliation (the date that the bank created the tape).
4. New input - cheques printed since the above
5. Items matched - Matched cheques, count cheque amount.
6. Variance:Matched cheques - variance between cheque amount and cashed amount + cheques cashed that we did not issue.
7. New outstanding = Old outstanding + New input - Items matched

.... Continued   Page 65

Index

WORKBOOK 14

Document design replaces existing inefficient computer processes

SPECIFICATIONS ANALYSIS

SEPTEMBER 12-14, 1989

MEETING WORKBOOK

Page 1

WORKSHOP AGENDA FOR BUSINESS ANALYSIS

* Executive Sponsor Opening Remarks

* Introductions and Administration

* Workshop Process

* Management Guidelines
  - Purpose
  - Scope
  - Management Objectives & Expectations
  - Business Assumptions

* Solution Guidelines
  - Document Flow

* Business Requirements Analysis
  ECN Users Guide
  - Originating Phase
  - Business and Technical Analysis Phase
  - Implementation and Analysis Phase

* Action Plan

* Summary and Closing Remarks

Page 3

WORKSHOP TEAM MEMBERS

EXECUTIVE SPONSOR
Doug H

TEAM LIST
Bob B
Mike C
Ted C
Karl H
Anne L
John M
Gary N
Frank S
Kirk S
Angela S
Rahul V
Tokiro Y

FACILITATOR
Anthony C

DOCUMENTATION
Mary D

Page 5

PURPOSE OF THE PROJECT

To develop a paper forms based system to replace the current computerized Change process.

The purpose of this document is to develop a new guide to support the process through which changes are made to manufactured products after the product is in full production.

PURPOSE OF THE WORKSHOP

The purpose of the workshop is to involve business representatives in a structured workshop to describe business activities and procedures for an all manual forms system.

The level of detail will be:
  - Purpose and scope of the guide
  - Objectives and assumptions
  - Outline of functions and procedures involved
  - Detail steps and Change form design

The workshop document will provide the basis for a new Change user guide.

Management Guidelines

Page 8

SCOPE OF THE PROJECT

- This guide is to be used for changes to Telephone product design after PSR and all O.E.M. Products (both Post and Pre PSR)

Page 9

MANAGEMENT OBJECTIVES AND EXPECTATIONS

Implement an Change in a cost effective fashion.

Reduce the interval in which changes are implemented (goal 5 days).

Eliminate redundant steps, duplication of data and paper flow in order to simplify the Change Process.

Promote autonomy in the process so that minimal management intervention is required.

Minimize the number of people who process an Change from when the need for an Change to be written is identified to when the changed product is ready for delivery to end customer.

Ensure that all the necessary change information is provided.

Manage the timely distribution of the information efficiently.

Define appropriate approval levels on a per change basis.

Support the concept of one time data entry.

Eliminate advance Changes through fast Change implementation.

Page 10

PROCESS OVERVIEW

The following pages outline the use of a Process Guide which presents in detail the steps and information required at each stage of the new ECN process. In summary, the process, committees, and documents all work together to streamline the effort required to introduce a change on a product from design and technology to manufacture, and allow it to be done in a fast, cost-effective fashion. By doing so, the process allows the goals of simplification, speed and improved customer service to be met.

While the process involves six detailed stages (described on the next two pages) the entire process can be summarized into three basic phases: **1. Originating Phase**
  2. Business and Technical Analysis Phase
  3. Implementation Phase

These phases are explained through the A to H models within the *Solution Guidelines* section and identify where and when specific forms are to be used. These forms appear as exhibits within the *Design Scenario* section of this workbook and will be modified/designed during this session.

Solution Guidelines

Page 11

PROCESS STAGES

This process consists of a formalized six stage process:
Stage 1 - Origination is complete when a customer, either internal or external identifies an area requiring an Change and completes a Summary Sheet describing the details of the change.
Stage 2 - The Management Business Analysis (MBA) Team is called together to consider upcoming Changes. The team considers business needs, future forecasted changes, as well as customer and marketing inputs. They will approve or reject Changes and may also choose to bundle or separate changes for a smooth introduction.
Stage 3 - Engineering Change Notice (Change) meeting. The Change meeting allows for rapid exchange of information about the change and allows for feedback for questions and problems quickly. The Change coordinator notifies a designer if he is required to attend the Change meeting to further explain his change.
Stage 4 - Implementation Analysis Phase. Purchasing and/or the Change coordinator determine the implementation date of the Change. The Change coordinator enters the changes on PMS with implementation date and distributes the "Pending Change" report daily.
Stage 5 - Implementation. The change is implemented on the product.
Stage 6 - Distribution of documents for the change. The vault photocopies and distributes the Change package when it is complete according to a distribution list showing the requirements of each department.

Page 12

POST PSR Change PROCESS

Originator completes Change Summary including date 1 on Change summary sheet   <STAGE 1>

Originator or MBA rep presents Summary Sheet to MBA   <STAGE 2>

MBA signs Summary Sheet and fills in date 2 on Change Summary Sheet

Tech Change Coordinator fill in Change # and documents affected on Change Summary Sheet

Change Coordinator releases Summary Sheet to vault

Vault Coordinator makes copies of Summary Sheet

Tech or Change Coordinator presents change to Change committee and enters date 3 on Change Summary Sheet   <STAGE 3>

Change Committee analyses details of change implementation

Change Coordinator establishes implementation date and enters date 4 on Change Summary Sheet   <STAGE 4>

Anyone who needs an implementation date change contacts Change coordinator who manages implementation date

Change implemented and Change coordinator fills in date 5 on Change Summary Sheet   <STAGE 5>

Changed design documents are copied and distributed per distribution list   <STAGE 6>

Page 13

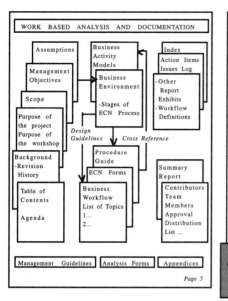

WORK BASED ANALYSIS AND DOCUMENTATION

- Assumptions
- Business Activity Models
- Index
  - Action Items
  - Issues Log
  - -Other Report Exhibits
  - -Workflow Definitions
- Management Objectives
- Business Environment
  - -Stages of ECN Process
- Scope
- Purpose of the project
- Purpose of the workshop
- Background
  - -Revision History
- Table of Contents
- Agenda

Design Guidelines   *Cross Reference*

- Procedure Guide
  - ECN Forms
- Business Workflow
  - List of Topics
  - 1...
  - 2...
- Summary Report
  - Contributors
  - Team Members
  - Approval
  - Distribution List ...

| Management Guidelines | Analysis Forms | Appendices |

Page 5

BACKGROUND - REVISION HISTORY

Issue 1 - Major revisions to reflect changes to Summary Sheet and adjustments to the process.

Issue 2 - More detail on the responsibility for the Change Guide. Addition of a statement on the scope of the Change Guide. Update Stage 2 and Front Sheet to include the ALE (Approved Liaison Engineer) approval required for foreign Products. New definition for Stage 4 to agree with actual procedure.

Issue 3 - Major changes to broaden the scope of the guide and make changes to the process:
- Include standardization and TMI sections
- Changes to Product Structure
- Swedish process

Totally new process for Stage 1.

List of Abbreviations:
CRF - Change Request
CHANGE - Engineering Change Notice
MBA - Management Business Analysis Team
PMS - Production Management System
Responsibility for the Guide - The Technology Change Coordinator is responsible for updating the Post PSR Process Guide. Proposed changes or improvements to the process are welcome from anyone involved with the process. They are to be submitted to MBA through the MBA representative on the Change Process Change Request Form (See appendices) If the proposal is accepted the Change Team is asked for its input. The change usually has a trial period. If the trial proves successful, the change will be implemented as part of the process.

Background

Page 6

Business Activity Model Originating Phase

======== **ORIGINATING PHASE** =========

A. WORK ENVIRONMENT
- Originating Sources
- Common Change Request Form Information
- Change Summary Form Information
- Form Control Numbers
- -Common Request Form
- -Engineering Change Notification (MDA)
- Approval Levels
- Change Process Status Code

Page 14

B. RECEIVED WORK .... **Originating Sources**
Page 21 .... **1.1 Common Request Form**
- -Categorize Problem
- -Prioritize Problem

C. INITIAL PROCESSING .. CRF Information Management
- Date Stamp
- Assign CRF Number

D. MONITOR AND ASSIGN .... **Technology Coordinator**
- Log / Review CRF
- Assign CRF for Evaluation / Recommendations

E. WORK IN PROGRESS .... **Technology Engineer**
- 1.2 Technical Evaluation
  - -Verify Problem/Diagnosis
  - -Determine Alternate Solutions
  - -Select/Document Solution
  - -Assess Technical Risk
- 1.3 Need for Change
  - -Verify change/prototype
  - -Assess cost of change

Page 22 .... -**Create Change Summary Sheet**

F. RECORDING RESULTS ... CRF Information Management
- Update CRF Information
- Log / Modify CRF Status
- File Documentation

........................**Change Information Management**
- Assign Change Control
- Update Change Information
- Log / Modify Change Status
- File Documentation

Page 15

Business Activity Model Analysis Phase

== **BUSINESS AND TECHNICAL ANALYSIS PHASE** ==

D. MONITOR AND ASSIGN .... **Technology Coordinator**
- Sort/List Pending/Recycle CRF/Change Documents
- Review CRF/Change Summary Information
- Prepare Agenda for MBA Meeting
- Call MBA Meeting as Required

E. WORK IN PROGRESS .. Mgmt Business Analysis Meeting
- 1.4 Review Change Documents
  - -Target Implementation Date
  - -Assess Financial Risk
  - -Set Priority / Class of Change
  - -Re-evaluate Recycled Change
  - -Approve / Reject Change - Signature

D. MONITOR AND ASSIGN .... **Technology Coordinator**
- Distribute Change Summary to Change Committee
- Call Technician Analysis Meeting
- Log/Update Change Status

Page 16

E. WORK IN PROGRESS .... **Technical Analysis Meeting**
- 1.5 Technical Analysis
  - -Demonstrate Prototype / Sample Change
  - -Identify Documentation Requirements
  - -Itemize Coordinated Activities
  - -Recycle/Hold Change for Clarification

D. MONITOR AND ASSIGN .... **Change Coordinator**
- Review Change Information
- Coordinate Implementation Analysis Activities

E. WORK IN PROGRESS .... **Materials**
- 2.1 Implementation Analysis
  - -Price Old/New Parts
  - -Determine Approximate Delivery Dates
  - -Identify Stock on Hand
  - -Obtain Drawings for Incoming Inspection
  - -Identify Tooling Changes

E. WORK IN PROGRESS .... **Methods**
- 3.1 Implementation Analysis
  - -Determine Shop Aid Date
  - -Determine Assembly Fixture Availability/Cost
  - -Identify Rework
  - -Identify Capital Expenditures

E. WORK IN PROGRESS .... **Test**
- 4.1 Implementation Analysis
  - -Determine Test Fixture Availability/Cost
  - -Determine Test Program Changes/Dates

F. RECORDING RESULTS .... Change Summary Info. Mgmt.
- File Documentation Package

Page 23 .... **Log/Activity/Process Status Code**

Page 17

Business Activity Model Implementation Phase

==== **IMPLEMENTATION ANALYSIS PHASE** ====

D. MONITOR AND ASSIGN .... **Change Coordinator**
- Review Change Implementation Information
- Prepare Implementation Analysis Meeting Agenda
- Call Implementation Analysis Meeting as Required

E. WORK IN PROGRESS...Implementation Analysis Meeting
- 1.6 Implementation Analysis
  - -Estimate Implementation Date
  - -Determine Junking Requirement/Business Risk
  - -Present Material Handling Plan
  - -Recycle/Hold Change for Clarification
  - -Approve Implementation Plan - Signature

Page 18

D. MONITOR AND ASSIGN .... **Change Coordinator**
- Distribute Change Summary to Implementing Depts.
- Coordinate Implementing Department Activities

E. WORK IN PROGRESS .... **Technology**
- 1.7 Engineering Design Capture
  - -Complete Documentation
  - -Device Programming
  - -Loaded Device
- Ensure Complete Documentation Package

E. WORK IN PROGRESS .... **Materials**
- 2.2 Update PMS
  - -Update Database
  - -Notify Change Coordinator
- 2.3 Vendor Order Placement
- 2.4 Vendor Deliverables
  - -Items Received In-house
- 2.5 Incoming Inspection
  - -Verify to Specifications/Drawings
  - -Accept/Reject Vendor Deliverables

E. WORK IN PROGRESS .... **Methods**
- 3.2 Develop Shop Aid
  - -Determine if Work Order Required
  - -No Work Order
    - -Send Shop Aid to Shop Managers
    - -Layout Operator Generates Labels
  - -Work Order Required

Page 19

- -Match Work Order to Production
  - -PC Generates Labels
  - -Coordinate Shop Aid Release
- 3.3 Distribute Shop Aid to Production

E. WORK IN PROGRESS .... **Test**
- 4.2 Test Implementation
  - -Pull Related Documentation from Vault
  - -Obtain Photo Tools / Drill Data
  - -Order / Change Fixtures
  - -Change Test Programs / Fixtures
- 4.3 Determine if Loaded Device Used
  - -Release Loaded Device Changes to Shop Floor
    - -Golden EPROM/Master Disk/Loaded Device Spec.
- 4.4 Prove in Fixtures/Programs

E. WORK IN PROGRESS .... **Manufacturing**
- 3.4 Implement Change

E. WORK IN PROGRESS .... **Quality**
- 5.1 Pull appropriate Documents/Shop Aids/VCR
- 5.2 Audit/Evaluate Product
- 5.3 Identify if Corrective Action Required

F. RECORDING RESULTS.............. Change Information Mgt.
- Log Activity/Process Status Code
- File Documentation Package

D. MONITOR AND ASSIGN .... **Change Coordinator**
- Review Implementation Activities
- Ensure Implementation Date is Met

H. MANAGEMENT REPORTS
Page 24 ... **Operational Statistics**
- Change Intervals and Costs

Page 20

Change PROCESS / GOLDEN STANDARD FORMS CHANGE REQUEST FORM

Originator: _____   Change Request #:_____

Requested Change:_____
_____
_____
_____

Advantages of Change: _____
_____
_____

Disadvantages of Change: _____
_____
_____

Recommended trial period from _____ to _____

Trial Results: _____
_____
_____

Change Approval: _____ ____ _____ ____
Planning Tech Manuf. Eng. Tech

Design Scenario

Page 21

ENGINEERING CHANGE NOTICE (Change)

Originator:		MDA:	Change Number:
STD/Base/CHG	Unit Cost	VOL/YR	Implementation Cost

Requested Implementation Date:	Co-ordinated Activities/ Programmable Chip Information:	Change Class	E

Product Description	Old Rel	New Rel	Eng Code	CPC	Dates
					Orig. Mgt.

Change Class

A	Customer Sites/ Finished Goods
AR	Finished Goods/ Work in Progress
B	Standard Change Work in Progress
ES	Implement When Parts Arrive
D	Implement Pre-PSR
E	Implement on Material Useup
ER	Implement on Units Failing Test

Reason for Change | CI

CI	Cost Reduc/Improv
DC	Design Correction
DI	Design Improvem't
DO	Doc'tation Change
NF	New Feature
NR	New Release
PA	Prod. Agreement
TT	Technical Trial Rel.
FT	Field Trial Release
PP	Pre-Prod. Build
PS	Prod Sample
TM	Temporary

Basic Reason for Change:

Change/Reason for Changes:

Design:	Manuf:	Mtls:	Prod Mgt.

Page 22

DELTA

ENG CODE: .   CPC CODE: .
DIFFERENCES BETWEEN SL: .   AND SL: .

ITEM	QUANTITY		CPC	ENG	DESCRIPTION	NEW	UNIQ	DESIGNATION		CURRENT UNIT COST
	OLD	NEW						OLD	NEW	

DATASET CHANGES: List all drawings/documents/electronic files (Assembly Drawings, Circuit Schematics, Neutral Files, Phototools, Test Specs, etc.) except stocklists and release controls that are being added or changed.

DATASET NAME	Str/Iss	Promise Date	DATASET NAME	Str/Iss	Promise Date	ISO DOC'TS	Str/Iss	Promise Date

Page 23

Change MONTHLY METRICS

1990	JAN	FEB	MAR	APR	MAY	JUN	SEPT	OCT	NOV	DEC
POST PSR ECN'S										
NO. OF POST PSR ECN'S	8	29	24	19	20	17	42			
TIME TO MBA	1	1	1	1	2	3	1.5			
TIME TO EST. IMPLEMT'N	4	1			1.5	0.5	1			
IMPLEMT'N OF CHANGE	25	18.5	15	8	17	20.8	9.45			
TIME TO VAULT	11	14	14	25	19	24	43			
QUALITY (%ERROR/CHANGE	12%	10%	15%	15%	12%		7%	7%		
CALGARY PRE PSR ECN'S										
NO.OF CHANGES COMPLETE	4	4	2		7	9	10			
TIME TO DT'S COMMITTEE	1	1.5	2	4	4.5	2	1			
TIME FROM DT TO TECH	2.5	2	4.25	1		2.5	1			
TIME TO IMPLEMT'N		3	5	6.9	8.5	10	11.5	1.5		

Page 24

(GOA) GLOSSARY OF ACRONYMS

AD - Assembly Drawing
AS - Assembly Specifications
CF - Common Features
CL - Conductive Layers
CS - Circuit Schematic
CX - Commercial Specifications
DA - Development Authorization
DF - Design File
DD - Drill Data
DK - Diskette
DL - Difference List
DN - Design Notes
DP - Development Plan
DR - Pre Gate 2 Design Review
DS - Product Specification
DT - Drill Tape
FD - Functional Description
FT - Phototool
G1 - PSA Document (Signoff Sheet)
G2 - Gate 2 Signoff document
HB - Handbook
  HL - Hole and Land data
  IS - Intraconnect Schematic
  LD - Loaded Device spec
  MH - Manufacturing Handbook

Appendices

Page 30

Index

WORKBOOK 15

Communications interface to network retail systems

REQUIREMENTS ANALYSIS

JULY 18-20,1989

MEETING WORKBOOK

Page 1

WORKSHOP AGENDA FOR BUSINESS ANALYSIS

* Executive Sponsor Opening Remarks

* Introductions and Administration

* Background Materials
  - Data Interfaces

* Workshop Process

* Management Guidelines
  - Contributing Management
  - Purpose
  - Scope
  - Management Objectives & Expectations
  - Business Assumptions

* Solution Guidelines
  - Concept Overview
  - In Store Data Manager (ISDM)

* Business Requirements Analysis
  - Analysis Forms

* Action Items / Issues Log

* Summary and Closing Remarks

Page 3

WORKSHOP ATTENDEES

BUSINESS CONTRIBUTORS

NAME	COMPANY
Gordie G	ABC Stores Inc.
Chris P	Retail Division
Gerry H	Retail Division
Tim B	Back Office Applications
Paul S	Retail Division
Jay K	Retail Division
Ray N	Assoc. Wholesale Grocery
Paul M	Assoc. Wholesale Grocery
Fotis M	Retail Management Systems
Jim R	Retail Management Systems
Jenny B	ABC Stores Inc.

WORKSHOP FACILITATOR

Tony Crawford   Crawford & Associates

Page 4

CONTRIBUTING MANAGEMENT

PROJECT TITLE : Project
DATE : May 26, 1989

EXECUTIVE SPONSOR

NAME: H.S.S
TITLE: Vice-President, Information Services

The Executive Sponsor makes no proprietary claim to the output from this workshop. The material generated by the session is granted to the Food Distribution Retail Systems Group.

MANAGEMENT SUPPORT

NAME: Ray A
TITLE: Director of Retail Sales, Sales Department

NAME: Gordie G
TITLE: Senior Project Manager

Management Guidelines

Page 7

PURPOSE OF THE PROJECT:

Simplify the exchange of data between service providers and point of sale equipment manufacturers and value added software developers. Specifically the focus of this workshop will be on the requirements for the data interchange between the source and the target application.

PURPOSE OF THIS WORKSHOP:

Involve representatives from service providers, point of sale equipment and value added software manufacturers in a structured meeting to discuss the development of the interpretive layer of the Standard Language Interface Platform.

The level of detail will be :
  - Description of scope and business objectives
  - List function and business purpose
  - Describe the language syntax to support business purpose
  - List the interpretive process rules for the function
  - Describe changes to current documentation

A document will be produced from this workshop to provide direction for further analysis and system development activities in a workshop setting on July 18 - 20, 1989

The final workshop document will be used by the software developers for each company represented to implement their own technical design.

Page 8

SCOPE OF THE PROJECT

INTERFACE LOCATION
Any application supported by a value added software vendor and point of sale equipment manufacturer or service provider.

DATA GROUP
In store file in a retail grocery store
- Product
- Other files defined to the dictionary at a later date

BUSINESS FUNCTION INTERFACE REQUIREMENTS
- Header dictionary initialization
- Item dictionary initialization
- Create view detail
- Insert header
- Insert detail
- Update
- Select
- Delete
- Add replace
- Other

INCLUDING
- Error and conflict resolution

EXCLUDING
- Security
- Method of communication
- Back up recovery
- Application code
- Administration responsibility

Page 9

IN STORE DATA MANAGER (ISDM)

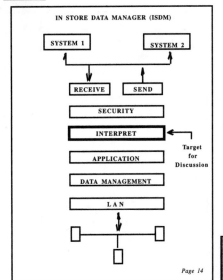

Page 14

INTERPRETIVE FUNCTIONS

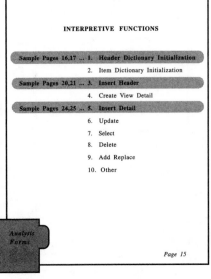

Sample Pages 16,17 ... 1. Header Dictionary Initialization

2. Item Dictionary Initialization

Sample Pages 20,21 ... 3. Insert Header

4. Create View Detail

Sample Pages 24,25 ... 5. Insert Detail

6. Update

7. Select

8. Delete

9. Add Replace

10. Other

Analysis Forms

Page 15

BUSINESS ENVIRONMENT   **FORM A**

FUNCTION: HEADER DICTIONARY INITIALIZATION

Guidelines : Describe the above function in terms of a business purpose and define the language syntax to accomplish the desired result.

BUSINESS PURPOSE

Establish the formats and sizes of information for header record change.

CONCEPT NOTE:

This is a provided paper dictionary that uses a predefined format for the first 14 fields, plus 3 user-defined fields. This is implicit to the interpreter and uses a create table statement equivalent to the following:

LANGUAGE SYNTAX

CREATE   TABLE   HEADER_DCT
(H01 CHAR (2),   H02 CHAR (6),   H03 CHAR (12),
H04 CHAR (6),   H05 CHAR (8),   H06 CHAR (8),
H07 CHAR (50),   H08 DATE (5),   H09 TIME (4),
H10 DATE (5),   H11 TIME (4),   H12 DATE (5),
H13 NUMBER (6),   H14 CHAR (6),   H15 CHAR (30),
H16 CHAR (30),   H17 CHAR (30));

This is built in and not actually transmitted.

Page 16

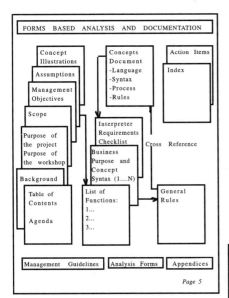

FORMS BASED ANALYSIS AND DOCUMENTATION

DATA INTERFACE

Background - The Food Distribution Retail Systems Group has been addressing issues surrounding support of POS equipment in a multi-vendor environment for several years. A Dynamic Record Concept was introduced at the November, 1987, meeting and centers around using a common language to describe a data element's location, size, and form within a data record. This allows data transfer between software products without using a fixed record format. Two committees were established at that time to investigate its potential.

The first "Database" committee reviewed the data elements needed to support POS systems and established a list of fields. This committee worked with POS equipment manufacturers and value added software vendors to produce a list of common data elements for POS and DSD store systems. This list includes field identifications for space management, label printing, price verification, and inventory management.

The second "Language" committee investigated the development of the Dynamic Record Translation Concept and has developed a subset of the ANSI Structured Query Language (SQL). It is presently working on identifying and documenting the Functional Requirements for software that must be written to support the concept. This software will construct and decode data exchanged using the standard language interchange platform.

Action plan - involve marketing representatives in a structured workshop to further define their business requirements.

Background

Page 6

MANAGEMENT OBJECTIVES AND EXPECTATIONS

- Provide guideline for an industry standard

- A change made in a local environment should not affect the universe

- Respond to a constantly changing environment

- Improve cost effectiveness of providing multi-vendor support

- Remove dependency from external technical constraints

- Protect value of future software investment

- Provide portability across a variety of technical platforms

- Improve service for system users

- Improve efficiency, availability and timing of information

- Simplify data interfaces

- Support variety of hardware and software

- Common approach for information interchange

Page 10

ASSUMPTIONS ABOUT THE PROJECT

BUSINESS ASSUMPTIONS:

- Multi-vendor relationship environment will continue to exist
- More demand for ad-hoc information from store data systems
- This approach will become the defacto standard for the group involved
- The environment will be dynamic enough to accommodate other applications to target

TECHNICAL ASSUMPTIONS:

- Based on SQL language as defined and modified for this application
- Dependent on interpretive layer
- Interface will work through a data dictionary
- Data dictionary will be maintained using same concepts and methods used for application file
- This environment should be viewed as batch as opposed to interactive
- The language describes the format of the data to be enhanced

NOTE:

- Use of transaction file versus direct processing to target file to be defined - refer to pros and cons chart on next page (and in Action Items in Appendices).

Page 11

CONCEPT OVERVIEW

WHOLESALER

```
          HOST 1
          Primary
                              POS
Retail    ISDM      T & A     HOST 2
          Product
ACG       DSD       Hand
                    Held
          HOST
          Third
          Party
```

Concept allows for application of the interpreter process to interchange date to any application.

LANGUAGE OVERVIEW - Header contains pre-action, control and ownership information. Transaction data provides detail information in the form of data values.

Solution Guidelines

Page 13

PROCESS REQUIREMENT CHECKLIST   FORM B

FUNCTION: HEADER DICTIONARY INITIALIZATION
Guidelines: Consider the business purpose described in form A and results obtained from the language. Use the checklist to describe your analysis.

ANALYSIS CHECKLIST	PROCESS RULE
☐ Syntax	☑ Standardize Header_DCT as Header Table name
☐ Data	
☐ Expression	☑ Basic system requirement eg. Built in
☐ Justification	
☐ Key	☐
☑ SIL Revision - Describe item table using similar syntax as header	☐
☑ Define H13/Action Types (6 Characters eg. Add)	☐
☑ Define Dictionary (8 Characters_DCT eg.Item_DCT,Header_DCT)	☐
☑ Other - Future potential to extend definitions for H13	☐

Page 17

BUSINESS ENVIRONMENT   FORM A

FUNCTION: INSERT HEADER
Guidelines: Describe the above function in terms of a business purpose and define the language syntax to accomplish the desired result.

BUSINESS PURPOSE

Provide data values to identify the transmitted batch such as the date to apply, the source, the destination etc.

CONCEPT NOTE:

This is the vehicle to provide control information to the application. Applies to all detail data that follows and is effective until another INSERT INTO HEADER_DCT or end of transmission is encountered.

EXAMPLE

INSERT INTO HEADER_DCT VALUES ('HM','010101','HOST01','000001','AUDIT',,,89075,1630 89082,1700,89090,10,'CHANGE','PRICE   CHANGES',,,);

Page 20

PROCESS REQUIREMENT CHECKLIST   FORM B

FUNCTION: INSERT HEADER
Guidelines: Consider the business purpose described in form A and results obtained from the language. Use the checklist to describe your analysis.

ANALYSIS CHECKLIST	PROCESS RULE
☑ Syntax - Following is not a reserved word	☑ Must be the first record in a batch.
☑ Data - Optional and mandatory field to be defined. Modify the 14th field to be 50 byte field	☑ Add commas to support multiple rows as general language rule for insert.
☐ Expression	
☐ Justification	☑ Error check for only one row for insert header.
☐ Key	
☑ SIL Revision - Refer to error handling	☐
☑ Define syntax example and include headers	☐
☑ Redefine to group with parens. and commas.	☐
☑ Other - error handling must recognize inconsistencies and mandatory fields.	

Page 21

BUSINESS ENVIRONMENT   **FORM A**

FUNCTION: INSERT DETAIL

Guidelines: Describe the above function in terms of a business purpose and define the language syntax to accomplish the desired result.

BUSINESS PURPOSE

Add, change, delete and replace a detail record in the transaction file.

CONCEPT NOTE:

The instructions for the type of maintenance are provided in the INSERT INTO HEADER_DCT in H13.
Insert detail is row and column sensitive.

EXAMPLE 1

INSERT INTO ITEM_DEL VALUES
(4634),(4635),(4636),(4638),(4639),(4640);

EXAMPLE 2

INSERT INTO ITEM_DEL VALUES
(4144600723,2.62),5154600028,7.98),(7135301114,123);

NOTE: Decimal place is required or it will be implied as placed after last digit. eg. 2.62 = $2.62 and 123 = $123.00

Page 24

PROCESS REQUIREMENT CHECKLIST   **FORM B**

FUNCTION: INSERT DETAIL

Guidelines: Consider the business purpose described in form A and results obtained from the language. Use the checklist to describe your analysis.

ANALYSIS CHECKLIST   **PROCESS RULE**

☐ Syntax   ☑ Requires the named CREATE VIEW or TABLE to have been previously created.

☐ Data

☐ Expression - Decimal place is implied after last digit   ☑ Validate H13 in HEADER_DCT

☐ Justification   ☐

☐ Key   ☐

☑ SIL Revision - Include decimal place in all SIL examples   ☐

☑ Remove statement regarding decimal in transmission   ☐

                             ☑ NOTE: Similar syntax to INSERT HEADER
☐ Other

Page 25

ACTION ITEMS	DATE	NAME
Edit SIL Document		G H
Complete workshop document		TC, SV
Define error scenarios		T B
Define Format of data to host		T B
Define relationship between interpreter and application		PS, CP
Prepare agenda and results presentation for 1 day meeting in July		G G
Review Transaction File - Pros & Cons		Team

Appendices

Page 37

TRANSACTION PROCESSING

Use of transaction file versus direct processing to target file. Pro's and Con's analysis based on workshop findings, steering committee review and approval by Food Distribution Retail Systems Group.

PROS AND CONS CHART

Pros - USING A TRANSACTION FILE - Cons	
1-Shorten expression and communication time using SQL standard	1-Requires more development effort
2-Treats a transaction explicitly as a transaction	2-Requires specific SIL naming convention

Pros - NOT USING TRANSACTION FILE - Cons	
1-Operates directly on the target table	1-Requires additional SIL verbs

Page 38

Index

WORKBOOK 16

Record transfer system shares data between
divisions and head office and third party

RECORD TRANSFER SYSTEM

Page 1

WORKSHOP AGENDA FOR BUSINESS ANALYSIS

* Executive Sponsor Opening Remarks

* Introductions and Administration

* Workshop Process

* Management Guidelines
  - Purpose
  - Scope
  - Management Objectives & Expectations
  - Business Assumptions

* Solution Guidelines
  - Systems Overview
  - A to H Model

* Business Requirements Analysis
  - Screen and Report Exhibits

* Action Items/Implementation Activities

* Summary and Closing Remarks

Page 3

WORKSHOP TEAM MEMBERS

SPONSORS
Doug C   Director OPS Planning
Ray H   Director Special Projects

CO-ORDINATORS
John G   Mgr. CUIST Access Project
John D   Mgr. COE Prov. Methods

BUSINESS CONTRIBUTORS
XYZ -   Divisional Billing Managers
           Headquarters Accts. Receivable & Marketing
ABC -   Ontario and Quebec

TECHNICAL CONTRIBUTORS
XYZ Corporate Tax
Divisional Business Systems
HQ Business Systems

WORKSHOP FACILITATOR
Tony Crawford   C

DOCUMENTATION
Peter T

Page 4

PURPOSE OF THE PROJECT
Implement an electronic transmission of the billing statement
and pricing details from divisions to head office and third party.

ANALYSIS GUIDELINES
Implement Business representatives in a structured workshop to
discuss the billing statement and price/detail environment and
define requirements for an electronic transfer mechanism.

The level of detail will be:
     -Define purpose and scope
     -Define objectives and assumptions
     -Identification of data and record format
     -Schedule and operation procedures
     -Data security, accuracy and retention
     -Opportunity for process improvement
     -Outline of development and implementation activities
(Including pilot function and testing for general acceptance)

The workshop documented product will be used as input to
development activities for system implementation which will
include pilot function and testing for general acceptance.

Sponsoring Executives	Title
Doug C	Director OPS Planning
Ray H	Director Special Projects

Management Guidelines

Page 5

Page 9

SCOPE OF THE PROJECT

LOCATIONS
     -All Central Office Divisions
     -Accounts Receivable
     -HQ Marketing
     -Provisioning
     -Controllers
     -Purchasing

TRANSFER RECORD
-Billing Statement
-Price Details
-Excluding Order Acknowledgments

BUSINESS FUNCTIONS
-Gathering and consolidation of Division Data
-Validation and release of divisional data
-Consolidation and editing of transfer data
-Scheduling of electronic transfer
-Operational and error notification reports
-internal system data transfers

Page 10

MGMT. OBJECTIVES/EXPECTATIONS

-Reduce interval;

-Improve customer service;

-Avoid courier lead time and cost;

-Avoid duplicate data entry effort

-Simplify forms operational procedures;

-Reduce clerical and paper content;

-Improve management reporting;

-Secure and accurate data;

-Timely release of transfer data;

-Standards for billing and pricing information;

-Basis for improved internal processes including auditability
-Growth capability;

-Transfer confirmation and error notifications;

-Avoid costs of error detection and correction;

-Provision for local print.

Page 11

5.0 Divisional Operations

Sample Page 20   5.1   Release Schedule Sheet
Sample Page 21   5.2.1   Divisional (IBM)
Sample Page 22   5.2.2   Availability Matrix
                 5.3.1   Divisional (IBM)
                 5.3.2   Divisional (HP)
                 5.3.3   Availability Matrix
                 5.4   Data Sources and Error Corrections
                 5.5   Transfer Record Summary

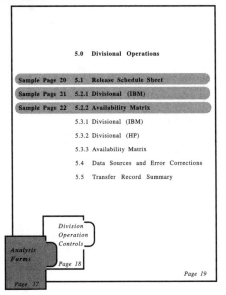

Division Operation Controls

Page 18

Analysis Forms

Page 17

Page 19

5.1 RELEASE SCHEDULE

RELEASE SCHEDULE MEMORANDUM

Billing Statement Due Date

HQ and dates for division schedules

Release Schedule Memorandum - A printed memorandum
providing schedule dates for divisions and headquarter
operations will be provided and used as a guideline for record
transfer deadlines (similar to current process).

Operationally divisions can transfer records at any time within
the transfer schedule and monitor the status of batches as they
are sent and received in the system.

Page 20

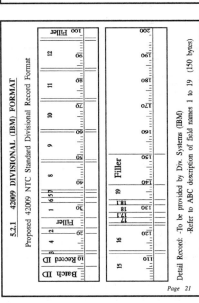

Page 21

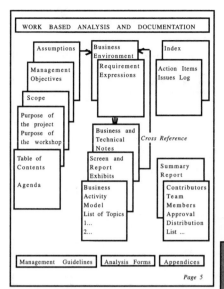

WORK BASED ANALYSIS AND DOCUMENTATION

Assumptions — Business Environment — Index

Management Objectives — Requirement Expressions — Action Items Issues Log

Scope

Purpose of the project
Purpose of the workshop

Business and Technical Notes — *Cross Reference*

Table of Contents

Screen and Report Exhibits — Summary Report

Agenda

Business Activity Model
List of Topics
1...
2...

Contributors Team Members Approval Distribution List ...

| Management Guidelines | Analysis Forms | Appendices |

Page 5

PURPOSE OF DOCUMENT

This document contains the user defined external design for the Billing and Price Detail record transfer system. It outlines the functionality described by in a joint meeting. The external design and issues documented herein provides the basis for further detail design and development at Headquarters and Divisions.

SYSTEM BACKGROUND

The record transfer system works on the principle of providing an information path for fixed record formats from the division systems to the HQ systems via a consolidation point at HQ systems. This document describes the operating environment and system functions in three sections; Division Operations, HQ Operations and Third Party Operations. The sections are illustrated in the system schematic and the business model listing key activities and system functions.

These system functions will be developed and presented in a summary report. (See Action Items / Implementation Plan)

Background Materials

Page 6

Page 7

A. **WORK ENVIRONMENT...Division Operational Controls**
    Divisional Record Formats (IBM/HP)
    Page 20 . . . Release Schedule Sheet
    Page 21,22 Standard Record Format
      -Billing Record
      -Pricing Details
      Transfer JCL
B. **RECEIVED WORK ....Division Operations**
    (Data Entry Using Operational Systems)
    Link to HQ System
      -Establish Transfer Capability
      -Inquire Transfer Status
    HQ Originated Error
    Reject Condition Report
      -Correct Data at Source System
C. **INITIAL PROCESSING ....On-Line Support**
    Format Data to Standard Record Layout
    Create Control Record (Div. HASH Totals)
      -Trailers
      -Identify Batch/HASH and Area Totals
    Attach Transfer JCL
A. **WORK ENVIRONMENT..........HQ Operating Controls**
    Release Schedule Sheet
    Data Record Format
    Page 31 . . . Edits / Tables / Completeness Rules
    Error Condition Codes
C. **INITIAL PROCESSING ....Edit Utility**
    Extract / Edit Inbound Records
    Identify Source / Final Batch
    Balance Record HASH Totals / Area Totals
    Identify Error Status / Append Error Code
    Reject Inbound Batch
    Log Transfer Activity
    Print Accounts Receivable Report
C. **INITIAL PROCESSING ....Consolidate / Format Utility**
    Update Transfer Record
    Electronic Receipt Acknowledgments
D. **MONITOR AND ASSIGN ....HQ Operations**
    Transfer Record Status Summary
E. **WORK IN PROGRESS............Operations**
    Link to System
    Advise Final Status
    Page 34 . . . Release / Rerelease Transfer Records
    Page 36 . . . Determine Transfer Status
    Page 36 . . . Determine Problem Source
F. **RECORDING RESULTS ....Release Utility**
    Validate Link
    Strip Division Trailers
    Create Control Record (HASH Totals)
      -Trailers
    Page 34 — - Identify Source / HASH and Area Totals
    Transfer Records
    Log Transfer Status
A. **WORK ENVIRONMENT..........HQ Operational Controls**
    Transfer Schedule
    Page 31 . . . Edits / Tables / Completeness Rules
C. **INITIAL PROCESSING ....Edit Utility**
    Edit Inbound Records / Files
    Balance HASH / Area Totals
    Identify Error Status / Append Error Code
    Send Acknowledgment / Notifications

Page 15, 16

BUSINESS ASSUMPTIONS

Month end deadlines for electronic transfers;

Confidential information will be protected;

Utilizes divisional systems which produce billing statements on a common form

Manual processes still exist in some divisions;

Provision of data in incremental phases towards complete data transfer;

All divisions will use a standard record format;

All divisions will utilize electronic transfer and eliminate all existing and supporting paper documents sent in due course;

New divisions will be integrated into record transfer system;

Separate files for and price detail.

TECHNICAL ASSUMPTIONS

Transmission vehicle will be 56 KB line

Implement current system security methods.

Page 12

SYSTEM DIAGRAM

Divisions

Data Flow — Sources — Operational Systems

Edit Reformat Utility — Error Report

Error Reports — Several Sources — Status Inquiry

Outbound

Headquarters

Inbound Data — Edit Validate Consolidate Utility — Batch / File Summary

Accounting Detail Report

Release Utility — Release

Outbound — Error Rejects Acknowledge

Inbound Data — **Headquarters**

Edit Utility

Solution Guidelines

Page 13

Page 14

5.2.2 DATA AVAILABILITY MATRIX

Proposed 42009 statement format for electronic transmission

Field	Data Element	3SD	TND	NAD	PWR	DSD
	Batch ID					
	Record ID					
1	Statement Due Date	Y	Y	Y	Y	Y
2	Area	Y	Y	Y	Y	Y
3	Division	Y	Y	Y	Y	Y
4	Number	Y	Y	Y	Y	Y
5	Category	Y	Y	Y	Y	Y
6	No. of Charges	Y	Y	Y	Y	Y
7	Final Flag	Y	Y	Y	Y	Y
8	Previous Billing	Y	Y	Y	Y	Y
9	This Months Bill	Y	Y	Y	Y	Y
10	Provincial Sales Tax	Y	Y	Y	Y	Y
11	Total	Y	Y	Y	Y	Y
12	Amount Federal Taxable	Y	Y	Y	Y	Y
15	Incidental Amount TPP	N	N	N	N*	Y
16	Incidental TPP - PST	N	N	N	N*	Y
17	PST Code/ Province	Y	Y	Y	Y	Y
17.1	PST Rate Charge at Inst.	N*	N*	N*	N*	N*
18	FST Code	N	N	N	N	N
18.1	FST Rate	N	N	N	N	N
19	Estimate	Y	Y	Y	Y	Y

Y - Provide now and will provide in Phase 1
N - Do not provide now and will not provide in Phase 1
N* - Provided manually. But will provide in Phase 1

Page 22

6.0 HQ Operations

6.1 Release Schedule Sheet

6.2.1 Billing Record Format

6.2.2 Price Detail Format

Sample Page 31... 6.3 Edits and Completeness Rules

6.4 Error Condition Codes Table

6.5 Edit Tables

Sample Page 34... 6.6 HQ System Functionality

6.7 Accounts Receivable Report

Sample Page 36... 6.8 Transfer Summary

6.3 EDIT / COMPLETENESS RULES

EDIT / COMPLETENESS RULES

Billing	Price Detail
Area Code	Area Code
Division	
Category	
$ = Numbers	
PST Codes	
FST Codes	

Edit / Completeness Rules - Data at the divisional level will be edited and formatted to the standards defined by users for the final destination (Headquarters) record content. This means that the same edit and completeness rules will be used at all points of record transfer. These include the use of tables and edit formulas shown above.

Additional Edits and Logic Tests

-Order# not edited during transfer process
-Quantity can be zero
-Item #, Sub item will be defined as 3 digits each
-No edit / validate on extended price
-Extended Price can be zero

HQ Operations

Page 27

Page 31

6.6 HQ SYSTEM FUNCTIONALITY

EDIT / VALIDATION FUNCTION

-The utility edits each record for correct data using tables and logic routines defined in the previous section.
-Errors due to imbalanced HASH totals are identified and the batch is rejected.
-Error code(s) displayed in sorted list by batch and record ID.
-In addition to error detection, system acknowledges valid batches.
-Using the source code and the batch ID the status of the batch is listed with status codes which provide a user dialogue.

FORMAT / RELEASE UTILITY

-Using the trigger to release the batches the system removes the headers and the trailer detail for a larger set of records.
-In addition, system creates HASH totals for the $ amounts in a batch and for the billing record the $ amounts by area code. A record ID number is appended to each record and a trailer record is created for each batch with the following information:

        Trailer
        Billing / Pricing Detail
        Batch ID
        Record Count
        HASH Total(All records)
        Area Totals (Billing only)
        Date / Time

Page 34

6.8 BATCH TRANSFER SUMMARY

```
        BATCH   TRANSFER   SUMMARY
                                        DATE
Division  Batch   Records  Status  Date  Time  Final
          ID                       Sent  Sent  Trans
_____  _____  _____  _____  ____  ____  ____
_____  _____  _____  _____  ____  ____  ____
_____  _____  _____  _____  ____  ____  ____
_____  _____  _____  _____  ____  ____  ____

Schedule Transfer Date: _____
1 Release
```

Operator Feedback Information

The system operator uses the batch transfer summary screen to be aware of scheduled transfer dates and the status of files as they are extracted from divisional systems and prepared for transfer to HQ.

The system prints an error list at the source printer ID with information from one or more error conditions to take appropriate action at the source system.

Page 36.....

6.8 BATCH TRANSFER SUMMARY Cont'd

Using the status screen the operator can send valid files to the headquarters system by pressing the RELEASE function key. The system logs and displays the date and time of a successful files transfer. In addition it identifies the FINAL record status.

The following status codes are used to provide a dialogue for the user:

CODE	DESCRIPTION
VALID	* A batch has been received with no errors
INVALID	* A batch has been received with one or more errors
XMIT	* A valid batch has been consolidated and transmitted to

Page 36 Cont'd

ACTION ITEMS

ISSUES   LOG
1. Follow up NSD requirements for integration into record transfer system.
2. Phase 1 includes all division and data. Define Phase 2.
3. Assess security methods to meet audit requirement.
4. Define operational tables for FST / PST Code / Rate Category / Area.
5. Define use of FST / PST rate at time of billing / delivery/.
6. Ensure same table values / updates between all locations.
7. Verify need to identify FST amount per item.
8. Determine edit rules for codes plus qualifier.
9. Resolve HP vs IBM format requirements and support new data defined.
10. Define batch to format.
11.Use existing JCL/utility to link HQ: initiate transfer.
12. Define system features key benefits.
13. Put dialogue in status codes incl. final flag by division.
14. Develop and present summary report outlining System Functions

Appendices

Page 39

Page 40

IMPLEMENTATION PLAN - KEY STEPS

TASK	TARGET
Assign / Resolve issues	2 / 14
Develop external design documentation	2 / 14
Design Network	3 / 1
Identify common function	3 / 14
Proposed shared activity	3 / 14
Review specification / divisional agreement	3 / 14
Division estimate their own effort requirement	3 / 14
Define conversion for divisional interface (for input logic)	6 / 1
Code programs	6 / 1
Acceptance test	6 / 1
Start pilot site (3SD)	6 / 1
Start parallel test site	
Further define System Functions and present in a summary report.	

Page 41

SYSTEM DESCRIPTION SUMMARY REPORT

Division - A schedule for transferring information is provided on a memo listing transmission deadlines and operating time frame. Standard record formats are defined and used throughout the system. Records are batched and control information generated in detail Trailer records for transfer validation. In addition a Batch ID and a Record ID is generated in each record to trace error conditions. The system can identify a final status and record information to indicate the final transmission from the division for the given time period. A batch job with the appropriate JCL code is used to transfer the batch of records to HQ system.

HQ System - The HQ system receives incoming records and validates the transmission integrity using the Trailer information. It edits the data and errors are detected through the application of validation logic and table value comparisons. In addition errors are detected using validation logic to test transmission totals and values in the Trailer system. The system provides the operator with timely reports and an inquiry screen for feedback and dialogue in the use of status codes. These identify error conditions and transmission information. A detailed error list is printed to trace errors and inform division personnel to correct errors at source. An accounts receivable report is generated from the consolidated records as the valid batches are available from several sources. The system uses the same monitoring and status screen to identify errors and release records to the destination system.

Page 42

Index

Page 45

‖‖ Acknowledgments

Since 1978 interactive workshops for business planning and design has been my life and the time of my life. I have met a greater number of interesting people and been involved in more exciting situations than I ever imagined possible. My first acknowledgment for direction must go to Chuck Morris of IBM Corporation. We discussed similar ideas during working visits to customers near to neat places like Banff Springs and other great Canadian golf courses. It's too bad I can't hit a ball that isn't moving, but I have fond memories and might learn yet. Chuck, I hope you are as proud of this representation of our original work as I am of the opportunity to experience our companionship in thoughts, attitudes, and experiences.

I doubt this book would have been written for publication if it were not for a recommendation from Capers Jones who knew me in the early days of JAD. He said to a publishing agent, "If you want a JAD book you should talk to Tony Crawford, but get him to be more authoritative on the subject." Another source of encouragement came from Ed Yourdon who has reviewed and recognized my work and provided helpful hints and a "Come on Tony, your fans are waiting."

Many people have influenced my methods of working to achieve the best environment for good business analysis. For me the first hints that things could be different came from attending a James Martin Seminar. I literally broke my foot to get there and hobbled away somewhat inspired with two volumes of class notes and a walking stick signed, "Just the Support IBM needs - James Martin." I reminded him of this trophy on my office wall when we met again to video tape a JAD *"Questions and Answers"* forum. Actual support to develop the JAD concepts in 1979 came from IBM Canada through my managers Doug Croth and Brian Turnaway. They knew we were on to tricky things and gave me every assistance to test and promote the idea. I become consumed and enthusiastic about the subject, and JAD became my work baby. My own talking baby was heard to say Daddy Jaddy which christened me Mr. JAD and led to Chuck being known around the office as Grandpa JAD.

As IBM published results, people attended our education programs and participated in workshop assignments. Over the years for continuous improvement I have benefited from discussions with many people, including direction from John Gorham, Sue Hoben, Clark Hussey, Jason Liner, Paul Oster, Jan Peterson, Gil Smith, Linda Speckman, John Tullet and Maryl Wesolowski. Ideas for JAD workshops and documentation guidelines were discussed with Gary Rush and Dorine Andrews. I am very grateful to Gretchen Imlay, Carolyn Goodlander, Marsha Millar and Randy Raynor for pointers about business language for the technique. International thanks to Earl Hickok and work in the Arctic Circle, my IBM colleagues in Hong Kong, Japan and Singapore, John McFadden with an Australian outlook, Jim Reber in Belgium and Tony Allwright in Holland. At the time of documenting JAD results, I received the most encouraging support from Ray Ahlgren on the longest phone call in praise of this approach. Another source of much appreciated material came from Mary Craven and Pete Hobbs in their contributions describing project results. My special thanks go to Barbara DuBrule for her insightful commentaries on early drafts and to Mary Rottino and Paul Becker for their editorial assistance to publish this manuscript.

In creating a consulting practice it has been my pleasure to coach and work with outstanding facilitators who have contributed much to the maturity of *Classic*JAD and our support systems. Caroline Thornton, Bruce Bowman and Colette Wasson have implemented these concepts for many satisfied customers. Earl Brochu became an associate at the time of this writing and provided many noteworthy hints and developed new training materials. The working knowledge of another associate, Roman Soltys has provided invaluable input to the development of this book and the ABCWorkbook(™) system for workshop documentation.

Inspiration to explain the details behind these techniques has also resulted from my involvement with professional groups and consulting organizations. In this, I have appreciated the advice from Bill Perry of the Quality Assurance Institute about system quality issues, and Tom Flecher, Greg Fouquet and Marc Moresky of Ernst and Whinney for plans to integrate these techniques with project management consulting. I thank Paul Bassett of Netron for sharing his knowledge of CASE technologies and also Gopal Kapur's Center for Project Management project management considerations. More recently, I have been fortunate to have worked on several interesting assignments for Larry Shick and Ted Keys of Price Waterhouse Canada. Their enthusiastic use and endorsement of the approach led to a training program to transfer the required skills for Price Waterhouse consultants to use the Book Building Process(™) and workshop techniques during client engagements for business engineering. Sponsored by Len Rutman in the Ottawa office and managed by Howard Cohen the experience from practical use of these guidelines has been presented at several conferences and documented here in the examples of workshop results.

Sampling is a technique known in the music industry whereby new material is created from the blending of known work. There is much to learn from others. At the time I needed to explain the JAD document life cycle, I found useful illustrations in the "Testing in Software Development" book published by British Computer Society. Along the way people have always asked "What is JAD?" It is much easier to explain in sampling popular language from "Re-engineering the Corporation" by Mike Hammer. It makes for topical discussion and in conversation with Steve Ralphs and Alec Dorling we described the synergy with the *Classic*JAD approach. With this background, our own corporate re-engineering created the Process Improvement Institute-PII(™) and coined several "PI" acronyms to carry our basic principles into relabelled workshop processes. Revisions start in chapter five in cross-references to Process Improvement Expectations PIE(™) for business plans and Process Improvement Models PIM(™) for business design specifications.

All these and many other contributions have resulted in these developments. The work continues in sharing the experience with like-minded people working on similar initiatives. For me, the most exciting among these is working on distinctly Canadian contributions to the development of international Software Process Assessment Standards compatible with ISO9000-3 for the SPICE (Software Process Improvement Capability dEtermination) project. I also look forward to continuing to promote and refine these workshop techniques and invite your comments and assistance.

Anthony Crawford
Director, Program Products
Process Improvement Institute

December 1993
Fax 1-800-4NEWJAD
(In Canada (905) 849–0252)

Index

Process Improvement Institute

A division of Anthony Crawford and Associates Phone (905)845 3844   Fax 849 0252

This book is presented as classroom material in a one day education program. It is also used to assist team participation in business re-engingineering assignments. For more information about skill transfer programs, consulting services and workshop documentation support systems, please call:
(905) 845-3844 or Fax (905) 849-0252. In Canada and U.S.A. 1-800-4NEWJAD
Or write: 461 Lakeshore Road West, Oakville, Ontario, Canada. L6K 1G4